THE REBIR
OF EDUCATI

THE REBIRTH OF EDUCATION

SCHOOLING AIN'T LEARNING

LANT PRITCHETT

Center for Global Development
Washington, D.C.

The Rebirth of Education: Schooling Ain't Learning may be ordered from:
BROOKINGS INSTITUTION PRESS
c/o HFS, P.O. Box 50370
Baltimore, MD 21211-4370
Tel.: 800/537-5487; 410/516-6956
Fax: 410/516-6998
Internet: www.brookings.edu

Library of Congress Cataloging-in-Publication data is available.

ISBN 978-1-933286-77-8

9 8 7 6 5 4 3 2 1

Printed on acid-free paper

Composition by Circle Graphics
Columbia, Maryland

Contents

Acknowledgments

I have incurred enormous intellectual and personal debts over the eight years since 2004 that I have worked on the current volume. I give thanks to six groups of people.

First, I have to thank the many coauthors of papers I have written in that time. Deon Filmer is the person with whom I really started writing about education and from whom I have learned the most over the years. In addition I have written papers on education with Amanda Beatty, on overambitious curricula and on learning progress over time; Amer Hasan, on educational goals; Rinku Murgai, on teacher compensation in India; Varad Pande, on local government and schooling in India; and Martina Viarengo, on high performers and "superstar" economics and on inequality in performance across schools in the public and private sector. In addition, I count as coauthors the team that produced the World Development Report 2004, "Making Services Work for the Poor": Junaid Ahmad, Shanta Devarajan, Jeffrey Hammer, Deon Filmer, Ritva Reinikka, Shekhar Shah, Agnes Soucat, Nazmul Chaudhury, and Steven Commins.

Second, many people have directly helped in the production of this book. Duriya Farooqi helped me complete an earlier book. Amanda Beatty read and edited nearly every chapter of the current book. Emily Hurst, my daughter-in-law, provided the illustrations that begin each chapter. Laura Carter worked as a researcher in India and managed the ASER (Annual Status of Education) data. Isaac Pritchett, my son, helped with the references. Bruce Ross-Larson, editor and writing counselor extraordinaire, raised his subtle eyebrows sufficiently to convince me that my "almost there" manuscript was not so. I thank John Osterman, who handles publications at the Center for Global Development, for steering the book toward production, and the Brookings Institution Press publications staff for their professional support in getting the book into print and out into the world.

Third, this book stands on the shoulders of giants of research into education. Of course, thanking them does not imply that they would agree with me or even that I agree with them, just that reading these writers' original research has taught me something: Tahir Andrabi, Paul Atherton, Abhijit Banerjee, Rukmini Banerji, Michael Clemens, Jishnu Das, Sonalde Desai, Esther Duflo, Paul Glewwe, Eric Hanushek, Asim Khwaja, Geeta Kingdon, Michael Kremer, Marlene Lockheed, Karthik Muralidharan, Ritva Reinikka, Justin Sandefeur, V. Sundararaman, and Ludger Woessmann.

This book contains new data. The task of creating new data is thankless so I want to thank those that perform this difficult but essential role. The data produced by Pratham-ASER in India represent a huge leap in scale and conceptualization of assessing performance, and Madhav Chavan, Rukmini Banerji, and Wilima Wadhwa deserve kudos for pioneering this new approach, which has spread. In addition, the company Educational Initiatives and its managing director, Sridhar Rajagopalan, have also pioneered in the development and application of testing learning and capabilities in India.

Fourth, I thank Nancy Birdsall at CGD for her support of this book and of my earlier work. She has been enormously supportive of my work on education and has provided incisive commentary and nudges to finish this book.

Fifth, I thank my own life teachers. Choosing just one at each level of my education I would like to thank Mr. Martin (grade six); Ms. McCabe (grade eight); Gail Young (grade eleven); James MacDonald, at Brigham Young University; Jerry Hausman, at MIT; Larry Summers, postgraduate work; and Keith Warner, my tennis teacher. Perhaps none of them meant to teach me what I learned from them, but the unexpected insight is the beauty of education.

Last, my family. Grandpa Hayward's favorite excuse for getting out and getting away with doing just about anything was that he "had to see a man about a horse." My own version of Grandpa's excuse is "I am working on my book." Since I worked some at home I am sure if my children were to imitate "working on a book," they would stare blankly into space or pace around in pajamas or mutter to themselves "yes, that's it" at inopportune moments. I have tried, unsuccessfully, to convince them all that taking a break from working on a book is working on a book.

My wife, Diane, has a doctorate in political science, has taught choral music in American and international schools, has been a school administrator, and is a teacher in the truest and noblest sense of the calling. I would not be the same without her and our thirty happy years of marriage—and neither would the book.

Preface

The Millennium Development Goal of achieving universal primary education by 2015 will be met in nearly all countries. This book, however, documents a deeply disturbing reality behind that fact: for hundreds of millions of children in the developing world, schooling is not producing "education" in any real sense. As the book subtitle says: schooling ain't learning.

It is "education," of course, not sitting in school, that is included in the United Nations Declaration of Human Rights, and that is viewed universally as both an end of the development process and one of the most powerful means for achieving development. Since the early days of the Center for Global Development in late 2001, we have been concerned with education, and in particular how the actions of the rich and powerful countries can most effectively and quickly support developing countries in making education a reality for all of their citizens—from our contribution to the education MDG prepared for the Millennium Development Project a decade ago, to efforts in the last several years to promote and study the effects of Cash on Delivery Aid pilot projects in improving education outcomes for children in low-income countries, to evaluation of the impact of particular interventions on the performance of schooling systems, to the recent report *Schooling Is Not Education! Using Assessment to Change the Politics of Non-Learning*, which relies heavily on the evidence presented in this book.

Much of my own work, before the Center opened its doors, was focused on education and its consequences for individual income, women's labor-force participation, and countries' long-run growth and distribution of income—indeed for development itself broadly conceived. That work also included a study of the link between the quality of schools children attend and the number of years they complete.

Despite all of that personal and institutional history, this book by CGD senior fellow Lant Pritchett surprises and worries me. Indeed it stuns me on two counts: first, the almost numbing but thoroughly convincing completeness of evidence on the learning problem in so much of the developing world; and second, Pritchett's adamant refusal to set out any single better (spider) "model" for school systems to produce learning. He instead promotes fostering the conditions for new, undiscovered, context-specific (starfish) approaches.

The evidence, from recent assessments, that something needs to be done to improve education is overwhelming. Here is just a sampling:

— In India less than half of children surveyed in grade 5 could read a story for second graders (and over 1 in 4 could not read a simple sentence), and only slightly more than half could do subtraction. Results over several years were getting worse, not better.

— In Tanzania over 65 percent of students who sat the 2012 examination for secondary school (Form IV) completers failed, with the worst possible results. In re-scored results using an earlier, more lax standard, more than 40 percent failed.

— In Indonesia, Jordan, Malaysia, Oman, Thailand, and Tunisia, scores on an internationally comparable mathematics and science test in 2011 declined overall compared to earlier years. (Chile's and Korea's scores were up and Iran's were roughly constant.)

Pritchett's idea for a "rebirth" of education has little to do with organizational systems and much to do with breaking schools free of their century-old roots in an entirely different and far less interconnected and interdependent global economy. That will be difficult. The success of the last several decades in getting to near-universal primary school enrollment has built in patterns of thought, advocacy, and action that are hard to alter—even when it is clear that "more of the same" won't do.

Like Pritchett's earlier CGD book on migration, *Let Their People Come*, this one presents a challenge of the first order. Easy answers, he argues, even if they will do some good, will not be enough. It is a bold and controversial challenge, but one that we at CGD are committed to promoting.

Nancy Birdsall
President
Center for Global Development

Introduction: From Universal Schooling to Universal Learning

Every book has to have a story, a simple story that tells why the author wrote the book, why people should read it, and what the book says. Here is my book's story. In 2006 I was living in New Delhi, working for the World Bank. I had occasion to take an overnight train to eastern Uttar Pradesh to visit an education project that was being run by Pratham, an Indian NGO that works on improving learning of the basics; the program was undergoing a rigorous evaluation by researchers from MIT. The Pratham team would visit a village and do very simple tests of the children's mastery of literacy and numeracy. After a few days of testing, public meetings would be organized to reveal and discuss the results. The locally elected village leader, all the parents of the village, and the government school principal were invited to these meetings.

I arrived at the village meeting just after the results had been presented. They were bad—really awful (though, as we shall see in the next chapter, not atypical). Most fifth-graders could not read a simple story (many could not even recognize the letters of the alphabet), and few could do simple division. Since the testing had been done by Pratham workers and local volunteers in the children's homes and neighborhoods, by the time of the meeting most parents knew the results for their child. For many parents this was the first time they had had any feedback on what their child was actually learning—or not learning.

At the meeting, a man of about fifty stood up, looked straight at the principal of the local government school, and said, "You have betrayed us. I have worked like a brute my whole life because, without school, I had no skills other than those of a donkey. But you told us that if I sent my son to school, his life would be different from mine. For five years I have kept him from the fields and work and sent him to your school. Only now I find out that he is thirteen years old and doesn't know anything. His life won't be different. He will labor like a brute, just like me."[1]

The man was right. In Uttar Pradesh and the rest of India, and in many other countries around the world, the promise of schooling—getting children into seats in a building called a school—has not translated into the reality of educating children. Getting children into schools was the easy part. Schooling has seen a massive expansion such that today, nearly every child in the world starts school, and nearly all complete primary school (as their country defines it). This expansion of schooling is a necessary first step to education, but only a step.

Education is the preparation of children to assume their adult roles in society as loving parents, as engaged citizens, as contributors to society and their communities, and as productive workers. The premise is that schooling and education are linked: a child who spends more years in school is thereby expected to acquire more education—more skills, more capabilities, more competencies. Yet, tragically, it has been demonstrated again and again that this is not always the case. Schoolin' ain't learnin'.

Division is an arithmetic competency that children are expected to learn. In India, the data from the simple assessments done by ASER in 2009 show that of eight children who enter fourth grade not knowing how to do a simple division problem, *only one* will learn in the fourth grade—which means that seven of eight children will not. The same data show that of five children who enter fourth grade not able to read a simple story, *only one* will learn to do so in fourth grade. This means that four out of five who cannot read when they start fourth grade will not be able to read after they finish fourth grade. The results pertaining

---

1. The speaker's words were translated for me.

to year-to-year progress are even worse when conceptual understandings that go beyond rote learning are measured. A nationwide assessment of sixth-graders in India done by Educational Initiatives (2010) found that half could multiply a three-digit number times a two-digit number when the question was posed in the standard way they had been taught it. Yet when children were presented with an arithmetically much simpler question that probed whether they understood conceptually that multiplication was repeated addition, the proportion correct on a multiple-choice test was *worse* than random guessing. An Indian child who finished school at age fifteen in 2012 and who works to age sixty-five will be in the labor force in the year 2062. These children are emerging from primary schooling or even junior secondary or secondary schooling with so few skills that they are unprepared for today's economy, much less for the economy of 2030 or 2062. Their lack of basic education is a burden they will bear for decades.

The problem of inadequate education cannot be solved with more of the same. With so little learning per year, just increasing the number of years children stay in school adds very little learning. Even if Ghana manages to achieve a goal of having every child complete grade nine, if it retains its 2007 learning per year, only 20 percent of children will complete grade nine having more than a minimally acceptable threshold of learning.

More problematic still is that if additional inputs are used as badly as existing inputs are, they will barely budge learning outcomes. Pushing in more of the same standard inputs won't lead to improvements. If your bicycle tire has a hole, pumping in more air won't do much good. This isn't because you don't need air in the tire; it is because you have to fix the hole first, and then add the air. Pumping more books, more teachers, or more training into existing systems is just a palliative measure.

My story then got even more interesting. After the villagers had expressed their poignant disappointment about the consequences for their children of their lack of learning in school, the school principal was asked to respond. He said, "It is not our fault. We do what we can with your children. But you [are] right, you are brutes and donkeys. The children of donkeys are also donkeys. We cannot be expected to teach your children. They come from your homes to school stupid and you cannot expect that they will come home from school anything other than stupid."

In the hullabaloo that followed this insulting speech, it became clear that the principal had no concern for what his students or their parents thought. He had all the power in the relationship, he knew it, and he was not shy about displaying it.

It is frightening that this headmaster's response is typical of the insouciance and brutality of power in top-down modes of government schooling in Uttar Pradesh, and in India more generally, with, of course, variations from state to state. As a leading issue, teachers often just don't show up, or if they do, they don't bother to engage in teaching. Less than half of teachers are both present and engaged in teaching on any given school day (Chaudhury et al. 2006), a pattern of teacher behavior that has persisted despite being repeatedly documented, beginning with the *Public Report on Basic Education in India* (UNDP 1998), better known as the PROBE report. Second, a household survey in India (not just Uttar Pradesh) found that about one out of five children reported being "beaten or pinched" in school—just in the previous month (Desai et al. 2008). More shocking still, the same study found that a child from a poor household was twice as likely to be beaten in a government school as was a child from a rich household. Third, a recent study (Bhattacharjea, Wadhwa, and Banerji 2011) did close observation of classrooms in five states of India (not including Uttar Pradesh) looking for any of six "child-friendly" pedagogical practices—simple things such as "students ask the teacher questions" or "teacher smiles/laughs/jokes with students." In observing 1,700 classrooms around the country the researchers found *no child-friendly practices at all* in almost 40 percent of schools—not a smile, not a question, nothing that could be construed as child-friendly engagement. Fourth, another recent study in Uttar Pradesh (Atherton and Kingdon 2010) compared the learning outcomes of children who had regular civil service teachers and those who had "contract teachers," who were on one-year renewable contracts and were not part of the civil service. The children with a contract teacher learned twice as much a year as children with a regular teacher, even though the civil service teachers were paid three to five times more than contract teachers.

I find that this story leaves everyone outraged, but in two very different ways. One group is outraged by my *telling* the story. If this is you, this book is not for you. The other group is outraged by the story itself and the facts about learning (which I will show in the next chapters are hardly unique to India) and the slow progress. How has the beautiful and hopeful promise of universal schooling led to these tragic results and poor learning outcomes? How can these awful circumstances persist in publicly controlled schools—even in a full-fledged democracy like India? What can we as local, national, and global citizens do to realize the promise of quality education for every child—and not just schooling? This book is for you.

Two key concepts about schooling systems allow the persistence of these terrible outcomes, both of which I introduce with metaphors from the animal kingdom.

Spiders versus Starfish

School systems have become spider organizations. Ori Brafman and Rod Beckstrom in their 2006 work, *The Starfish and the Spider: The Unstoppable Power of Leaderless Organizations*, contrast "spider" organizations, which are centralized, with "starfish" organizations, which are decentralized. They propose nine criteria to distinguish centralized from decentralized modes of organization:

> Is there someone in charge?
> Is there a headquarters?
> If you thump it on the head, does it die?
> Is there a clear division of roles?
> If you take out a unit, is the whole harmed?
> Are knowledge and power concentrated?
> Is the organization rigid?
> Are units funded by the organization?
> Can you count the participants?
> Do groups communicate through intermediaries?

They adopt the metaphor of a spider because a spider uses its web to expand its reach, but all information created by the vibrations of the web must be processed, decisions made, and actions taken by one spider brain at the center of the web.

The starfish, in contrast, is a very different kind of organism. Many species of starfish actually have no brain. The starfish is a radically decentralized organism with only a loosely connected nervous system. The starfish moves not because the brain processes information and decides to move but because the local actions of its loosely connected parts add up to movement.

In many countries, the legacy system of schooling is a large government-owned spider. These systems are top-down bureaucracies that attempt to control the entire system from a central location at the national or state/provincial level, deciding which schools get built to which teacher gets assigned to what school to what subjects are taught. When spider systems work, they are terrific at logistical tasks. The expansion of schooling is amenable to spiders. If you want to build

100,000 primary schools quickly and at low cost, a top-down program that cranks out standardized schools following a five-year plan is a great way to do it.

There is, however, increasing recognition that lots of problems, perhaps especially those having to do with educating children, are not just exercises in logistics. Spider systems that attempt to force round-peg tasks that require local judgment and control, such as teaching a child, into square-hole bureaucratic organizations can fail, and when they fail, their lack of robustness means they fail completely.

The fundamental difference between spider and starfish systems is not the usual battleground of "markets" versus "government," as critiques of spider systems come from the ideological left and right. James Scott's powerful *Seeing Like a State: How Certain Schemes to Improve the Human Condition Have Failed* (1998) distinguishes the "high modernism" of top-down spider bureaucracies from the kind of horizontal, traditional practical knowledge manifested in the skills of local craftsmen. Scott, a Marxist political scientist, argues that governments have often failed when they have imposed spiders where starfish were needed. William Easterly (2006), an economist who is very far from a Marxist, has prominently critiqued foreign aid by contrasting "planners" with "searchers," terms that capture many of the same distinctions between spider and starfish approaches. Elinor Ostrom (2008), an eclectic political scientist who won the Nobel Prize in Economics in 2009, attended to "polycentric" systems in which hierarchical power (spiders) does not prevent the emergence of self-organizing systems (starfish).

The Uses of Camouflage

A second metaphor from the animal kingdom important to my thesis has to do with camouflage. Camouflage is a deception that is often key to survival in the animal world. Predators' camouflage allows them to more easily sneak up on prey. Prey use camouflage to avoid and hide from predators. Some animals gain a survival edge through mimicry, sporting camouflage that makes them look like other animals. Some species of flies have evolved to look like bees. The eastern coral snake, which has distinctive black, red, and yellow bands, is highly venomous and best avoided. The scarlet king snake can't be bothered with all that poison and venom, but with its black, red, and yellow bands it looks a lot like the eastern coral snake and scares off predators by mimicking its visual cousin. With mimicry, the form provides survival value without the function.

In the 1980s the organizational theorists Paul J. DiMaggio and Walter W. Powell (see DiMaggio and Powell 1983; Powell and DiMaggio 1991) considered how organizations might use camouflage to enhance their chance of survival. Organizations need legitimacy. When organizations have a difficult time establishing legitimacy, they may resort to simply looking like other, successful organizations. The danger is that if the ecosystem endows both actual performers and their mimics with the same survival value, then systems can lock in to long-term stagnation because the process of ecological learning, whereby performers displace mimics in the population, is blocked.

The particular danger of isomorphic mimicry is that the mimics might look just as good as, or better than, actual performers when both groups are assessed only on inputs and process. In fact, in many schooling systems today, things seem to be getting better, but only because there is so little measurement of actual learning. In India the recent Right to Education Act declared that each child had a right to education—even clarified that the right included a "quality" education—but then defined the "quality" of schools strictly on inputs and process, without any reference at all to actual learning.

The Rise of Spider Schooling Systems

One might argue that spider systems' uniform domination of schooling is in and of itself a compelling argument that spider systems have some powerful performance advantage. If the fittest survive, the survivors are the fittest. Indeed, spider systems do have advantages, but not in promoting learning. Spider systems facilitate the control of socialization, which is in fact their principal rationale. Modern schooling systems were not built as spiders. Rather, historically in the now developed countries schooling arose as a starfish system, with many overlapping and competing national, subnational, local, and private types of schools. Spider systems arose by swallowing the starfish systems. This consolidation had little to do with improved learning and everything to do with the rise of centralizing ideologies and nationalisms.

As I stood in the meeting in the village in eastern Uttar Pradesh, a witness to the principal's brutal indifference and indeed outright hostility to the parents and students he was entrusted to teach, a school bus from a private school drove by the public school, returning children to their homes. I say "school bus," but in fact it was one of the improvised vehicles that India is famous for, painted a bright blue and adorned with other colors.

Uttar Pradesh is still one of the poorest places on earth. According to official statistics, 42 percent of rural Uttar Pradesh fell below India's national poverty line in 2004–2005. Yet there is a rapid rise of private schooling in rural Uttar Pradesh. According to an ASER 2011 survey (see Data Sources for a description of the survey), about 45 percent of all children in rural Uttar Pradesh were in private school. Even though government schools are free—and many benefits, such as a free midday meal, are available only to those enrolled in them—their quality is so low that even very poor parents will turn down a government school in favor of paying the full cost of a private school. Some may view a dynamic private sector as a panacea, a cure for all ills. Unfortunately, education is more complicated than that.

In 1981 Chile radically reformed its system of free basic education in two ways. First, it "municipalized" schools, so that rather than schools being controlled by the national government, each local government controlled its own schools. Second, it instituted a policy that money followed the student, so that private schools that chose to receive public monies (which came with some conditions) could receive more public resources, the more students they enrolled. This privatization led to a sustained rise in the number of students in private schools, so that by 2006 over half of all students in basic education were in private schooling.

In 1999, some eighteen years after the reform, Chile participated in a TIMSS (Trends in International Mathematics and Science Study) assessment of the mathematics abilities of eighth-graders. Chile's average score of 387 (on an Organization for Economic Cooperation and Development norm of 500) was not only well below that of a developing-country star like Malaysia but also below that of Turkey (429) and even much poorer Indonesia (403). Moreover, the tests in Chile that tracked performance found that the scores of fourth-graders at all types of schools were completely stagnant between 1996 and 2002. Twenty years after the massive move to private schools, there was no evidence that the reform had had the kind of dynamic positive impact on the system that many had hoped the increased competition in a private system would provoke.

When a government's spider systems break down, parents cope with the failure by moving to private alternatives, which constitute a parallel starfish system that is both effectively uncontrolled and unorganized and mostly consists of mom-and-pop low-cost schools. There is compelling evidence that when public systems are dysfunctional, the gains to parents of moving to these low-cost alternatives can be massive. But coping alone is not an alternative to failed systems.

Table I-1. Six features of systems of schooling in a progressive educational ecosystem.

Feature	How a starfish system works	Spider systems are the opposite
Open	Many different types of schools provide education, with distinct approaches allowed and encouraged.	Only schools under the spider's control are supported.
Locally operated	Actors are allowed the autonomy to operate, explore, and discover their own ways of operating.	Attempts are made to exercise control over not just the goals and broad parameters but the actual operation, down to the school level.
Performance pressured	A combination of common standards and measurement for "thin" accountability on outcomes from above and "thick" accountability inside schools and inside school communities from below guides development.	Systems are bureaucratically managed, with "thin" accountability on inputs and process, zero performance pressure on learning, and isolation from local control.
Professionally networked	Teachers, the key to any system, are embedded in their school but are also networked horizontally in communities of professional practice.	Teachers are hierarchically organized, both by top-down management and by top-down associations.
Technically supported	The system gives support to schools and teachers to provide them with the capabilities to succeed.	The system provides supervision of compliance, not support or empowerment for innovation.
Flexibly financed	Finance follows students and performance, with local control of allocations.	Finance flows internally, mainly directly to teachers, independent of performance.

Source: Extended from work by Brafman and Beckstrom (2006).

Just being a "starfish" ecosystem is not enough. What are the characteristics of an *effective* starfish ecosystem of schooling? As I argue in chapter 6, there are six key characteristics of an effective ecosystem for schools that produce learning. Such ecosystems are open, locally operated, performance pressured, professionally networked, technically supported, and financially supported. The salient differences between starfish systems and spider systems on these dimensions are summarized in table I-1.

Unleash the Power of Evolution to Change Education

This may seem, and is, a very odd book about education. Unlike nearly all in its genre, this is not a how-to book on education. Attention to the "how to" often misses the point of the "why to" of the agents in the system. The main value an economist like me—and I am emphatically not an expert in pedagogy or curriculum or classroom management—brings to a discussion of education is through asking two questions: "Why isn't it done this way already?" and "Why will it be done that way in the future?"

That is, when people argue that technique X is a better way to teach, I ask, "Why aren't teachers using X already?" Moreover, if X is a better way to teach and teachers are not now teaching that way, "Why will they do so in the future?" Spider system thinking assumes that the behavior of the entire system is determined at the top and hence changing the spider's mind about the how of teaching will change what actually happens. This leads lots of academics, including many economists, to devote their time to the nuts and bolts of the how without focusing on the why.

Evolution works the opposite way. The how is derived in a variety of ways from a single why. Lots of animals swim—fish, ducks, mammals, penguins, jellyfish, protozoa. The ways an animal can swim are limited only by the properties of water, and so there are lots of ways animals can swim. But they all swim to survive.

Suppose we wanted to increase the average speed of things that swim in a given ecosystem. One might set about to genetically engineer the perfect swimmer. Alternatively, one might just get more sharks in the water. This ups the ante: "Why swim fast?" Those that can't swim fast get eaten and those that don't get eaten reproduce. This produces ecological learning, where overall performance improves. "Planners"—and here I reference again William Easterly's work—want to design the perfect robot swimmer and, once having achieved their designed labor of love, are very reluctant to expose their precious design to any real test of performance. "Searchers" think not just about how to swim but about how to create ecosystems in which better swimming is an emergent property of the millions of choices of individuals in the system: lots of swimmers doing different things, an instructional system in the form of swimming lessons, and just enough sharks in the water to create a clear pressure.

Discovering Principles of Design, Not Blueprints of a Specific House

What would an ecosystem for basic schooling with the six key characteristics introduced above—namely, an open, performance-pressured, professionally networked, financially supported starfish system—look like? That question can be answered by posing an analogous one: What would a well-designed house look like? What a house looks like is limited only by the imagination of its designers (and some physical constraints). Even if well-adapted houses result from similar principles of design, the concrete expression of the design will be different. Similarly, there are many forms a school can take in a starfish ecosystem:

— *Community-controlled schools.* Groups of parents affiliated with the most local level of government may open their own schools (subject to some requirements) and attract students to the school.
— *Private providers.* For-profit and nonprofit private entities provide schooling, with some formula for how public sector resources are to follow the student.
— *Schools under small governmental jurisdictions.* Control is allocated, resulting in a level of autonomy that is close to the level of the school.
— *Charter schools.* Entry to operating such schools is strictly regulated, but once chartered, schools (even if they are still government schools) are allowed much greater autonomy than regular government schools.

The Rebirth of Education

If a modern Rip Van Winkle had gone to sleep in 1912 and woken up in 2012, he would have been bewildered and disoriented by the vast technological, economic, and social changes in the world. Overwhelmed and ill at ease, where could our 1912 Rip go in 2012 and feel right at home? He could visit a school. He would recognize the buildings, he would recognize the classrooms, he would recognize the content taught. He would recognize the organization inside the classroom, the pattern of the school day, the internal organizational structure of the school itself (a principal and teachers). More deeply, almost anywhere in the world he woke after his long sleep he would recognize the system of government-owned and government-operated schools.

The legacy systems of large-scale government production of basic schooling that span the globe, as central as they were to the social, political, and economic developments of the twentieth century, are now obsolete. Government-owned spider systems of schooling arose more than a century ago to prepare children for the "modern." Or, as Margaret Mead put it presciently in 1943, their purpose was to "turn the child of a peasant into a clerk." Spider systems of schooling arose to prepare children economically for the "new" world of Henry Ford's River Rouge factory, organizationally for the "new" world of the Prussian army and the British railroads, politically for the "new" world of the expansion of the voting franchise via the British Reform Act of 1918, and socially for the "new" world of the consolidation of ethnicities into nationalisms and nation-states. However, this new world for which the modern school was designed is now a very old—and obsolete—world.

The mismatch between the education that children need for the world they will face and what legacy systems of schooling can provide is growing. Open, locally autonomous, performance-pressured, professionally networked, technically supported, and flexibly financed starfish systems of education build on the legacy systems that successfully provided access to schooling, to give children the education they need for the century they will live in.

But everything comes at a price. The price of starfish systems is not financial—again and again, disruptive innovation in starfish systems provides ways to produce more learning with less money. The price of better education is allowing freedom, giving choices, and hence ceding power. This is a price that must be paid by the powerful, not known for their largesse. The purpose of the large, centrally controlled spider schooling system was to limit choices: of teachers about how they would teach, of students and parents about what they would learn.

Starfish systems must be open and locally autonomous, and that opens the way for choices, by parents and students, by headmasters and teachers. Choice means freedom and freedom means power. Schooling systems cannot prepare children for a future of freedom, diversity, and creativity in the absence of freedom, diversity, and creativity in the way education is provided.

CHAPTER 1

Schooling Goals versus Education Goals

Everyone has the right to education. Education shall be free, at least in the elementary and fundamental stages. Elementary education shall be compulsory. Technical and professional education shall be made generally available and higher education shall be equally accessible to all on the basis of merit.

UNIVERSAL DECLARATION OF HUMAN RIGHTS, ARTICLE 26

The goal of education is to equip children to flourish as adults—as parents and caregivers to the next generation of youth, as participants in their communities and societies, as active citizens in their polity, and as productive workers in their economy. The challenge of formal education is to supplement what parents can provide and, in a few formative years, build the foundation for a long and successful lifetime. The fundamental measure of success of any system of basic education is whether each successive cohort of children emerges from childhood equipped with the skills and capabilities for the world it will face.

We all know that each child needs schooling in this complex and rapidly changing world. We've seen massive expansions in schooling in nearly every country in the world. Eight Millennium Development Goals for all nations have been identified by the United Nations. One of them is that children "complet[e] a full course of primary schooling" by the target date of 2015. Each new cohort of youths enters adulthood having spent more and more time in a building called a school, so the

Millennium Development Goal concerning children's *schooling* is getting close to being met. But no one has ever really had only a schooling goal. We have *education* goals for our own and others' children. Schooling is the means to the goal of education. Are children around the world today emerging from the schooling they get with the education they need? No.

The accumulated body of research on performance in learning—from internationally comparable tests to assessments of curricular mastery to academic studies to civil-society-designed and -implemented tests—shows tragic results among schooled children. In recent studies in rural Andhra Pradesh, India (Muralidharan and Sundararaman 2010b), only around one in twenty fifth-graders could solve this arithmetic problem: $200 + 85 + 400 = 600 + \_\_\_$. Less than 10 percent of fifth-graders understood that one-fourth of a chocolate bar was less than one-third of a chocolate bar. In a different countrywide assessment in India, 60 percent of the children who had made it all the way to grade eight couldn't use a ruler to measure a pencil (Educational Initiatives 2010). Similar findings of very low levels of conceptual mastery emerge from Pakistan, Tanzania, South Africa, Indonesia, and other countries around the globe. Even in many middle-income countries such as Brazil, internationally comparable assessments reveal that more than three quarters of youths are reaching the age of fifteen without adequate learning achievement and are ill-equipped to participate in their economy and society (Filmer, Hasan, and Pritchett 2006). In educationally advanced countries, educators are rightly worried about twenty-first-century skills. Meanwhile, hundreds of millions of children finish schooling lacking even the basic literacy and numeracy skills of the nineteenth century.

The problem is that the *learning achievement profile,* the relationship between the number of years children attend school and what they actually learn, is too darn flat. Children learn too little each year, fall behind, and leave school unprepared. In most developing countries schooling goals are not fulfilling even the most modest education goals. Schoolin' just ain't learnin'.

Schooling: The Success of the Half Century

Some dreams do come true. On December 10, 1948, when the United Nations General Assembly adopted the Universal Declaration of Human Rights, universal free elementary education was a lofty ambition with little chance of fulfillment in the foreseeable future. Soon, international conferences declared not just the goal of universal education but specific

Figure 1-1. The years of schooling completed by the average adult in the developing world more than tripled from 1950 to 2010.

Years of schooling, population age 15 to 64

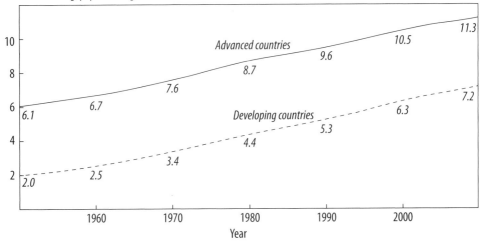

Source: Data from Barro and Lee (2011, table 3).

target years for the goal to be accomplished. In the early 1960s, conferences declared a target date of 1980. In 1990 the World Conference on Education for All in Jomtien, Thailand, declared 2000 to be the target year for "universal primary education and completion."[1] In 2000, the UN's Millennium Development Goals Report set a target and a date: "Ensure that, by 2015, children everywhere, boys and girls alike, will be able to complete a full course of primary schooling."[2] It did not happen in 1960 or 1980 or 2000, but in 2013 it really is about to happen. The vast majority of countries will meet the Millennium Development Goal target for universal primary school completion, and very few countries will miss it by much.

This expansion of schooling has been a global transformation, especially in the developing world. The population of labor force age in the developing world has now completed three times more years of schooling than in 1950, when 60 percent of the labor-force-age population had no schooling at all. Figure 1-1 shows that the average completed schooling of adults went from 2.0 years to 7.2 years in just the sixty years from

1. Clemens (2004) shows that meeting the time-bound enrollment targets nearly always implied expanding schooling systems in the most lagging countries far in excess of what any country had ever achieved.
2. See www.un.org/millenniumgoals/education.shtml.

Figure 1-2. Schooling in poor countries has expanded so rapidly that the average Haitian or Bangladeshi had more years of schooling in 2010 than the average Frenchman or Italian had in 1960.

Average years of schooling, age 15+

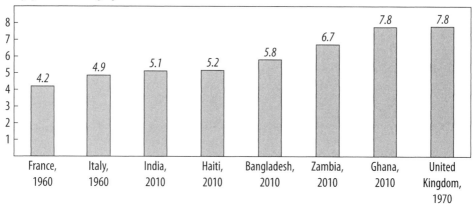

Source: Data from Barro and Lee (2011, table 3).

1950 to 2010. Just think of it! The cumulative schooling in 1950 represented the schooling achievement since the dawn of human civilization, and in the developing world, 6,000 years of recorded human history had led to societies with an average of only 2.0 years of schooling (which implies that most people had none at all). In just sixty years the average schooling of the population increased by 5.2 years. Progress in expanding schooling has been 100 times faster from 1950 to today than from 387 B.C., when Plato's Academy was founded, to 1950.

The astounding fact is that the average developing-country adult in 2010 had more years of schooling, 7.2, than the average adult in an advanced country in 1960, 6.8. As figure 1-2 shows, levels of grade completion in even very poor countries are higher today than levels in rich countries were even as late as 1960 or 1970. Ghana's 7.8 average years of schooling in 2010 was not attained by the UK until 1970. Countries known as educational laggards, such as Bangladesh and India, have high attainment compared to many European countries in 1960. Even countries often deemed educational basket cases, such as Haiti, have more-schooled populations than France and Italy had in 1960.

It is striking that all types of countries—rich and poor, economically growing and stagnating, democratic and nondemocratic, corrupt and clean—have expanded schooling. While progress on some goals, such as poverty reduction, economic growth, or eliminating corruption, has been

Figure 1-3. Schooling increased massively in nearly all countries, including corrupt, nondemocratic, repressive, and slowly growing countries.

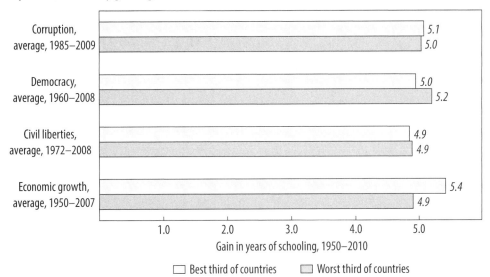

Gain in years of schooling, 1950–2010

☐ Best third of countries   ▨ Worst third of countries

Source: Author's calculations based on Barro and Lee (2011) data on schooling, ICRG data on corruption, POLITY 4 data on democracy, and Penn World Tables data on economic growth.

spotty, advancing the "human development" part of the UN's Human Development Index has been nearly universal. The Human Development Report 2010, prepared by the UN Development Program, showed massive schooling progress in nearly every country since 1970.[3] According to the standard sources,[4] the 2010 gross enrollment rate (GER) in primary school in peaceful, democratic, and prosperous Costa Rica was, not surprisingly, 110 percent. In neighboring Guatemala it was 113 percent. How can Guatemala—conflict-ridden, massively unequal, socially stratified, less than fully democratic, and poor—achieve the same enrollment as its much lauded neighbor? Enrollments are high nearly everywhere. Cambodia? 127 percent. In infamously corrupt Nigeria the GER reached 103 percent in 2006 (though it has since fallen). In the borderline "failed" state of Pakistan the GER in 2010 was 95 percent.

Good governments do schooling, but nearly all bad governments do it too. Figure 1-3 shows the gain in adult years of schooling from 1950 to

3. United Nations Development Program (2010).
4. Data from the World Bank reports: http://databank.worldbank.org/data/views/reports/tableview.aspx.

2010 for countries demonstrating a range of growth and governance performance. The best third of countries in controlling corruption saw their average schooling increase by 5.1 years and the worst third by 5.0 years. The most democratic third of countries saw schooling go up by 5.0 years and the least democratic third by 5.2 years. The freest third of countries saw schooling increase by 4.9 years and the least free third by 4.9 years. Economic growth generally increases resources available to families and governments, and facilitates expanding schooling. The top third in terms of economic growth saw schooling years increase by 5.4 years and the worst third by 4.9 years. The worst third on average had economic growth at zero percent, and began from a level of schooling of only 1.5 years, but schooling of the population more than tripled, even while their economies stagnated.

The success in expanding schooling was not the result of prosperous economies and democratic and capable regimes. Success happened because the goal of schooling was defined, and redefined, such that it could be consistent with the politics, state capability, and economic resources of every country. For the goal of universal schooling to be reached, the definition of schooling had to be made compatible with universal capabilities.

But there is a big problem with using schooling as the vehicle for achieving education goals. That problem is hidden in plain sight, right in the Millennium Development Goal. The Millennium Development Goal, like the original 1948 goal, is "universal primary *education,*" but the achievement of this goal is defined as universal completion of primary *school.* Even malign and autocratic governments wanted to expand schooling, and even weak and corruptible states could handle the logistics of schooling. Focusing solely on measures of schooling assumes that achieving schooling meets the goal of education, yet every person who can spell knows what happens when you assume.

Did reaching the goal of schooling keep faith with the goal of education?

Grade Learning Profiles: The Link between Schooling and Education Goals

Education prepares the young to be adults. The goal of basic education is to equip children with the skills, abilities, knowledge, cultural understandings, and values they will need to adequately participate in their society, their polity, and their economy. The true goals of parents, communities, and societies have always been education goals, and hence a multiplicity of learning goals. Schooling is just one of the many instruments in achieving an education.

An example of one possible education goal is all of a cohort of children at some age having a specified mastery of certain capabilities. This can be broken down into specific learning goals for children to attain by a specific age in a specific domain, such as reading fluently in their mother tongue by age ten, or being able to solve practical problems using arithmetic by age twelve, or having specific critical reasoning skills by age fifteen. An overall education goal would be a collection of learning goals such that a cohort emerges from youth equipped with all the skills, values, competencies, abilities, and dispositions desired by society. Early and intermediate learning goals, and goals in specified domains such as literacy or numeracy or science or history, are part of overall education goals.

The old saying that what gets measured gets done is not quite right, as not everything that gets measured gets done. The converse is more true: what does not get measured does not get done. Today, national governments and development agencies can provide data on myriad aspects of schooling: enrollments, expenditures, grade progression, completion, class sizes, budgets, and so forth. But on the education of a cohort there are next to no data. How many fifteen-year-olds today are ready for their future? No one knows.

Schooling and education goals are unified by the *cohort learning profile*. It has two elements, a grade attainment profile and a grade learning profile. The latter links years of school and capability. Figure 1-4 shows the learning trajectories of four hypothetical students, indicating their mastery (displayed on the vertical axis) as they persist, or do not persist, through schooling (demarcated on the horizontal axis). A schooling goal is measured as movement along the horizontal axis—another year in school moves the child along no matter what learning progress she has made—whereas dropping out stops schooling progress. A learning goal is measured along the vertical axis.

Schooling goals meet or exceed education goals based not only on whether students stay in school but also on whether the learning trajectory during schooling is steep enough. Suppose that the goal for school completion was a "basic" cycle of nine years. In figure 1-4, Bill drops out in grade four and meets neither an early learning goal, such as "reads fluently in grade three," nor a final learning goal, nor even a schooling goal. Jack reaches exactly grade nine, and thus meets a schooling goal, but his learning per year was too little to meet either an early or a final

Figure 1-4. The learning trajectories of individual students as they move through school provide the essential link between schooling goals and education goals.

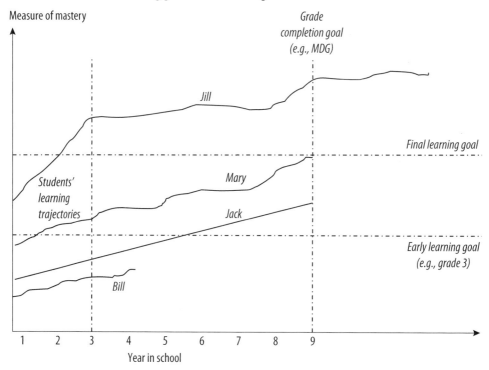

Source: Author's entirely hypothetical trajectories of four students.

education goal. Mary drops out in grade nine and Jill persists past grade ten, and both meet schooling and education goals.

A key empirical construct used throughout this book is the grade learning profile, or the distribution of student capability of children enrolled in each grade. This is the aggregate of the individual student learning trajectories for the students enrolled in each grade.[5] This distribution of mastery across students can be summarized in variety of ways. The proportion of students who are above a threshold—say, they can

5. The learning profile of those enrolled is a descriptive technique, not an assertion of causality. If only the children with the highest scores in grade three are allowed to progress to grade four, then the average child can know more in grade four than the average child in grade three, even if no child learns anything in grade three. The difference across grades in the learning profile does not imply children "learned" that much in a given grade, as the composition of students might change.

read a text fluently—is one summary of the learning profile. The average score on a common instrument that assesses capability in a domain across grades is another summary of the learning profile.

All legitimate schooling goals are reverse-engineered from education goals on the basis of assumptions about learning profiles. How long should the training of a doctor take? Well, start from the capabilities a doctor should have and make assumptions about how long it will take medical students to master those capabilities; this gives the length of medical school training. The training of an orthopedic surgeon takes a long time because the profession and the public rightly expect some level of competence before saw is placed to bone.

How long does it take to train a pilot? Churchill famously remarked, during the Battle of Britain, "Never in the field of human conflict was so much owed by so many to so few." Why were there so few Royal Air Force pilots? Not for lack of volunteers—those were many—but because it took time to train a pilot before you could put him in the air against the Luftwaffe with any hope of his survival. The Battle of Britain was a race of casualties of existing pilots against the learning curve for pilots. The Japanese practice of kamikaze lowered the training time by cutting out mastery of landing a plane, but at an obvious cost to the pilot.

Schooling goals are based on assumptions about length of schooling and educational attainment, but you cannot fool a learning profile by making assumptions. The RAF might have cut pilot training time and asserted that the shorter training would be enough—except that the Luftwaffe was the final exam, and shorter training meant that exam would be fatally final for too many pilots. You cannot just assume any old learning trajectory and make it true. Conversely, if the learning trajectories of students are flatter than it was assumed they would be, then kids come out of school knowing less than expected, and a schooling goal no longer meets an education goal. Whether learning goals are met hinges on the steepness of the learning trajectories of individual students.

Learning Profiles Are Too Flat: Three Illustrations from India

In this section, I use data from three different studies from India that use grade learning profiles to illustrate troublingly low levels of learning. Why India? First, having lived there for three years, I know the situation well and have confidence in the data. Second, there have been three recent pioneering efforts to measure student learning performance in India, each providing not just the usual reporting of mastery at a single grade but also learning profiles tracking performance across grades: the Annual Status of Education Report (ASER), the Andhra Pradesh Randomized Evaluation Studies, and the Educational Initiatives study. Individually these studies have advantages and disadvantages in coverage and technique, but together they paint a clear and coherent picture of incredibly shallow learning profiles, with at best weak mastery of the fundamentals, and even poorer progress in conceptual understanding. Third, in addition to these three assessments, two Indian states have recently participated in the Program for International Student Assessment (PISA), which is coordinated by the Organization for Economic Cooperation and Development (OECD), so we now have detailed studies showing the learning profile, with internationally comparable figures. Fourth, India is huge, continental in scope, so itself can be used to show variations in learning profiles across states. Fifth, although the data are drawn from Indian samples, I am really using India to illustrate the conceptual points that are applicable to other nations around the world.

Andhra Pradesh Randomized Evaluation Studies: Flat Grade Learning Profiles in the Basics

The researchers Karthik Muralidharan and Venkatesh Sundararaman, working with the Indian state of Andhra Pradesh, the Azim Premji Foundation, and the World Bank, are carrying out one of the most impressive studies of schooling and education ever, the Andhra Pradesh Randomized Evaluation Studies (APRESt). It is striking in several respects. First, it has been carried out on a massive scale with hundreds of schools across different districts in Andhra Pradesh. Second, it has examined not just one possible intervention to raise quality but a whole variety of interventions, from performance pay to increased school grants. Third, the research model uses randomization—assigning schools randomly to the various "treatments," and then comparing the results with those from a set of "control" schools—so that its findings have powerful claims to have identified the actual causal impacts of the treatments on learning. Fourth, the study developed (together with the organization Educational Initiatives, on which more in the next section) and used a sophisticated test that is able to assess both students' rote learning and their deeper conceptual understanding. Fifth, by testing students in multiple grades and tracking students over time, the study produced a series of both cross-sectional learning profiles (averages of skill mastery across grades) and actual student learning trajectories (tracking individual students over time). Given the richness of this research, I frequently draw on its

Figure 1-5. The learning profiles for children in grades 2–5 in Andhra Pradesh, India, show strikingly little progress in the fraction of children who can answer even simple arithmetic questions, and almost no progress at all for a hard question.

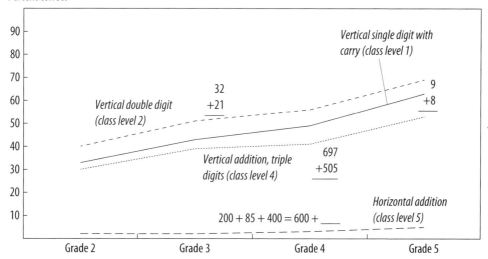

Percent correct

Source: APRESt study (Muralidharan and Sundararaman 2010a).

findings; but even before talking about the causal impact of the tested policy alternatives, one important set of findings is just what the learning profiles look like (see Muralidharan and Sundararaman 2010a).

To delve into the material on the learning profiles, we can start with the simple arithmetic problem of adding two single-digit numbers, say, 9 and 8. The best, though not so good, news is that 35 percent of children in grade two can answer this "grade one" question (the Indian curriculum stipulates that by grade one, students should be able to add two one-digit numbers). The bad news is that 65 percent cannot. The really bad news is that of the 65 percent that did not learn this simple arithmetic operation by second grade, only half learned it in the next three years of schooling. By the time these students finish the five grades of primary school, only 61 percent can do the simplest single-digit addition problems. Figure 1-5 shows grade learning profiles for a variety of learning benchmark questions. Slightly more children can do two-digit addition with no carrying over of digits, and somewhat fewer can do three-digit addition.

Performance on three-digit addition illustrates the stark flatness of the learning profile. The fraction who answered correctly increased very little in three full years of instruction, from just 30 percent in grade two to slightly over 50 percent in grade five, meaning that in three years, only one in five children learned to add three-digit numbers. Somehow roughly four out of five children who could not add in grade two were passed all the way to grade five without gaining this fundamental skill.

This lack of mastery of a rote skill is almost certainly an indication of weaknesses in deeper conceptual issues, such as not grasping the concept of place in a three-digit number. Even the dismal results on addition, unfortunately, exaggerate how many children understand arithmetic operations conceptually, as opposed to having simply memorized responses and a few procedures. When presented with a nonstandard form of addition, such as numbers in horizontal rows rather than columns—say, $200 + 85 + 400 = 600 + ?$—which requires some manipulation, there had essentially been no learning at all: only 10 percent of fifth-graders could answer that question. It might look harder in the horizontal arrangement than it actually is, since $200 + 400 = 600$, so the arithmetic is easy for a child that can understand the problem.

Mathematics is about concepts and their application, not about doing arithmetic for its own sake. Students gain very little from year to year in fundamental concepts such as weight, definitions, or fractions. In grade two, 30 percent of students could read the weights on two boxes and figure out which was the heaviest, but this percentage had increased to just 50 percent by grade five (table 1-1). So half the students in fifth grade still didn't get this fundamental concept about what numbers represent. As shown in the last column of table 1-1, "Percent who learned," only 12 percent of students (one in eight) who did not understand the concept one year got it right the next.

Nineteen percent of second-graders could recognize which geometric figure met the definition of a triangle, and by the fifth grade this had risen to only 35 percent. (Granted, this question is more conceptual that it might appear. First, the triangle in the question pointed downward, whereas in most of the examples, children would have seen triangles that pointed upward. So the child had to realize that rotating a figure does not change its classification as a triangle. Second, the test showed figures that are triangular, such as the cone, but not a triangle per se. This required the child to understand that in the context of geometry, "triangle" has a formal definition that does not always correspond to familiar notions of "triangular.") The total learning gain in three years was only 16 percent of the students. Of the 80 percent of children who could not answer this question in second grade, only 4 percent of those gained the ability in

Table 1-1. Students gain little conceptual mastery: only about 12 percent of children (1 in 8) make progress each year in answering even moderately conceptual (nonroutine) questions.

Question	Grade	Percent correct	Increase in percent correct	Percent who learned[a]
Which of the following is lightest box below?	2	30		
12. అన్నింటికన్న అతి తేలికయిన డబ్బా ఏది? దానిని టిక్ (✓) చేయుము.	3	39	9	13
700 గ్రా. 450 గ్రా. 325 గ్రా. 275 గ్రా.	4	41	2	3
ఎ. బి. సి. డి.	5	52	11	19
	Average gain, grade 2 to 5		7	12
Tick all the triangles below	2	19		
13 క్రింది వానిలో అన్ని త్రిభుజములను టిక్ (✓) చేయుము.	3	22	3	4
	4	25	3	4
ఎ. బి. సి. డి.	5	35	10	13
	Average gain, grade 2 to 5		5	7
How much of the figure is shaded?	2	21		
	3	27	6	8
	4	30	3	4
	5	48	18	26
	Average gain, grade 2 to 5		9	12

Source: APRESt (2010).

a. "Percent who learned" is the increase in the fraction correct divided by the fraction incorrect in the previous grade (e.g., 39 percent in grade 3 less 30 percent in grade 2, for a net gain of 9 percent of all students, divided by 70 percent who did not know in grade 2 = 13 percent). I assume no retrogress, that is, all of the net gain is due to learning, but since APRESt, the source of the data, does not have individual learning trajectories, I am unsure of the actual gain dynamics.

third grade. The progress in the conceptual skill of recognizing formal definitions is painfully slow.

The ASER Survey: Assessing Flat Learning Profiles in the Basics throughout India

Every year since 2005 the ASER assessment has been carried out by the New Delhi–based NGO Pratham and its partners and, now, the ASER

Centre, and it is planned to continue at least until 2016. (ASER is the name of the organization that administers tests and produces results, the name of the test, and the shorthand name of its report presenting test results. In addition, *aser* is Hindi for "impact." The assessment is described in the section "Data Sources.")

ASER uses a simple instrument to assess basic reading and arithmetic skills on a massive scale. The ASER exercise has several advantages. It surveys a sample of in- and out-of-school children. For a variety of reasons, nearly all assessments of learning are done only on in-school children, which gives an overly optimistic picture of an age group's learning achievement, as out-of-school (or behind-grade-for-age) children are not tested. Even if the system is designed so that a child of age fifteen should be in grade ten, in India, about half of the children that age have either dropped out or are in a lower grade. ASER results can be used to generate both grade learning profiles and cohort learning profiles, the latter combining the grade attainment profile and grade learning profile, which in India are very different.

Furthermore, the ASER exercise is massive and repeated regularly, and the raw data are available. More than 600,000 children are tested annually. The sample is drawn from almost every district (an administrative unit with an average population of around 1.5 million) in rural India, using population proportional sampling for the village sample, with thirty villages per district and twenty households per village. (Sampling and surveying in urban areas is much more complex and was done only once, in 2007.) The annual repetition of the exercise allows one to cross-check the reliability and validity of the estimates. Summaries of the data are readily available in the yearly reports; the raw data are available, with a lag, as well.

The ASER instrument is simple—and it takes an enormous amount of intellectual sophistication for a test to be this simple and still be useful. The reading test instrument is one page, with different competency benchmarks: letters, simple words, simple sentences, and a reading passage expected to be understood by grade two students. In the assessment, the child is shown words and progresses to his highest level of competency. (Owing to the great diversity in local languages in India, the test instrument is available in all of them, and children may choose the language.) The numeracy instrument is similarly simple. Children are asked whether they can recognize two-digit numbers, and can progress to the highest level tested, three digits divided by a single digit (say, 824 divided by 6).

Table 1-2. Cohort assessment of skill mastery in India: nearly three-quarters of 10- to 11-year-olds do not master four basic cognitive and practical skills, nor do more than a third of 15- to 16-year-olds.

State	Ages 10 and 11 (percent)			Ages 15 and 16 (percent)		
	Reading level 2 AND division	Tell time AND handle money	Do all four	Reading level 2 AND division	Tell time AND handle money	Do all four
All India	**31.7**	**54.8**	**26.9**	**67.5**	**85.7**	**64.5**
Low-performing states						
Karnataka	14.1	48.6	12.4	45.9	82.8	43.8
Uttar Pradesh	20.3	41.9	17.3	55.4	78.2	52.2
West Bengal	24.4	42.5	18.6	59.7	81.2	55.7
Middle-performing states						
Gujarat	24.8	55.4	21.5	62.4	85.9	59.8
Orissa	36.2	65.4	32.2	64.3	85.1	62.3
Andhra Pradesh	35.7	46.7	25.3	69.5	84.3	65.2
Rajasthan	33.1	55.6	28.4	74.5	87.8	70.6
High-performing states						
Kerala	46.9	85.7	44.6	86.2	95.8	83.7
Himachal Pradesh	58.7	68.0	49.7	88.6	94.2	87.3

Source: Author's calculations, based on ASER 2008 survey data.

I once traveled with the ASER test administrators in Uttar Pradesh, the largest state of India. It was emotionally devastating to see children eleven years old, supposedly in class three, who were unable to read simple words. I watched as one boy around ten years old who reported having been in school for three years turned the literacy test card this way and that, not even sure which way was up.

In 2008, ASER covered two other practical skills beside literacy and numeracy: telling time and handling money. For telling time, children were asked to state the time from pictures of two clocks. With money, children were asked questions such as "If this hand has two five-rupee coins and the other two has ten-rupee notes, which hand has more money?"

The cohort results show that less than two-thirds (64.5 percent) of children ages fifteen to sixteen had mastered all four of these skills. Table 1-2 shows three bottom-performing, three middle-performing,

Figure 1-6. Learning achievement profiles by grade attainment in Uttar Pradesh show shockingly low learning levels, even for grade 2–level skills.

Percent of students who have mastered skill

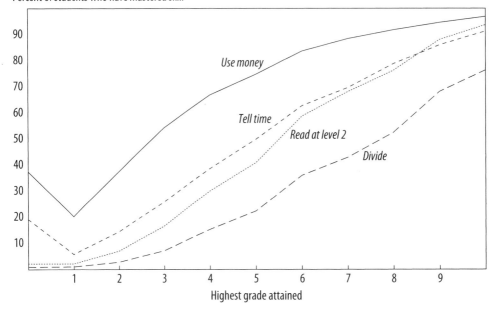

Highest grade attained

Source: Author's calculations based on ASER 2008 survey data.

and two top-performing states, along with the all-India (rural) average. In the low-achieving states, only about half the youths are competent in all four skills. In the highest-achieving states, these skills are practically universal. (Interestingly, children perform better on the practical skills, which they may have acquired out of school.)

ASER data for 2008 reveal strikingly flat grade learning profiles. In Uttar Pradesh (see figure 1-6), only 30 percent of children in grade four could read a simple passage. This is shocking, for nearly everything about the organization of the schools, method of teaching, and curriculum assumes that children in grade four can read. By grade five, 41 percent could read. This implies that 10 percent of children—only one in ten—learned to read a simple story in an entire year of schooling.

Table 1-3 shows reading levels for children enrolled in grades four and five in 2008 in Uttar Pradesh. The table may be thought of as a transition matrix (although the data track cohorts, not individual children) in which attending school increases the level of performance from one grade to the next. Nearly 21 percent of fourth-graders could recognize letters but not

Table 1-3. Children in Uttar Pradesh show little progress from grade 4 to grade 5 in reading.

Level of reading mastery	Grade 4		Grade 5	
	Percent at level	Cumulative	Percent at level	Cumulative
Nothing (does not recognize letters)	7.6		4.6	
Recognizes letters but cannot read words	20.8	28.3	14.5	19.2
Reads words but cannot read a paragraph	17.9	46.3	14.5	33.7
Reads simple sentences but not a story	23.1	69.4	22.6	56.3
Can read a short, grade 2–level story	30.6	100.0	43.7	100.0

Source: Author's calculations, based on ASER 2008 survey data.

read words, and if dropping out and repeating the grade are set aside, by grade five nearly 15 percent could still only recognize letters. The combined category of inability to read words or recognize letters fell from 28.3 percent in grade four to 19.2 percent in grade five, so there is some progress, but amazingly little. The result of this cumulative slow progress is that one in five children enrolled in grade five in Uttar Pradesh cannot even read simple words. This lack of any functional literacy means that everything else that is happening in school for these children is unlikely to make sense, as nearly all schoolwork in grade five involves some reading.

Educational Initiatives: Studying Flat Learning Profiles in Concepts

The problem of low learning levels is even worse than the ASER numbers reveal, for ASER assesses mastery of extremely basic skills in reading and arithmetic. A recent study by the Indian think tank Educational Initiatives (EI) probed not only "mechanical" learning but also conceptual mastery (Educational Initiatives 2010). EI's sample was 101,643 schoolchildren in grades four, six, and eight in 2,399 government schools in forty-eight districts and eighteen states in India, representing about 74 percent of the Indian population, urban and rural.

The EI study paired mechanical questions, asked in exactly the way the textbooks children would have been exposed to would, with conceptual questions covering the same material. Table 1-4 shows an example of this pairing. Multiplying a two-digit number times a three-digit number is computationally complex, but even without multiple choices, 48 percent of grade six students could calculate this multiplication. However, a conceptual understanding that multiplication is repeated addition is rare. Questions probing this understanding produced fewer correct answers by

Table 1-4. Performance on conceptual questions is often *worse* than random guessing, even when students do better on mechanical questions measuring the same skill.

Rote-based/mechanical questions	Percent correct	Understanding/conceptual questions	Percent correct
Write the answer.	47.9	25×18 is more than 24×18. How much more?	21.3
713		a. 1	
$\times 24$		b. 18	
		c. 24	
		d. 25	
What is the perimeter of this shape?	47.9	A thin wire 20 cm long is formed into a rectangle. If the width of this rectangle is 4 cm, what is its length?	16.7
15 8		a. 5 cm	
20		b. 6 cm	
		c. 12 cm	
_____cm.		d. 16 cm	

Source: Educational Initiatives (2010, p. 30).

grade six students on a multiple-choice question than random guessing would have produced.

Similarly, when presented with a triangle showing measurements of each side, almost half could calculate the perimeter. However, when presented with a problem in which students had to understand the concept of perimeter (for example, in a rectangle, perimeter is twice length plus twice width, so that if perimeter = 20 and width = 4, then length = 6), students again got this question right *much less* than random guessing would have yielded.

A second example from EI is related to simple concepts of length and measurement. Nearly all Indian textbooks teach measurement using an example in which an object, such as a pencil, is laid next to a ruler with the base of the object at zero (figure 1-7). However, if students are presented with the object displaced one centimeter from zero, they are thrown off. Typically, measuring length is taught in third grade. But most students appear to learn that "length is the number associated with the tip of the object" rather than actually learning the concept of length and measurement. Even as late as grade eight the most common answer to the question in figure 1-7 about the pencil length is "six centimeters"; only

Figure 1-7. The majority of students in India do not grasp the concept of measurement with a ruler, even by grade 8—more say the pencil is 6 cm long than the correct answer.

The length of the line in the figure above is 4 cm.
How long is the pencil shown in the picture?
(Use the ruler shown in the picture.)

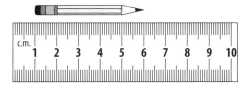

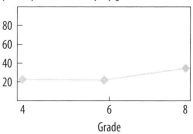

Percent of students answering
pencil question correctly, by grade

Source: Educational Initiatives (2010).

34.7 percent of eighth-graders get the right answer, and 38.8 percent continue to answer that the pencil is six centimeters long (the rest of the students, 26.5 percent, answer incorrectly, but something other than six centimeters). When children fail to acquire conceptual understanding early, low capability can persist.

Overall, these three assessments—ASER, APRESt, and EI—consistently show that the learning progress of Indian students is very slow, as shown in table 1-5. In the EI assessment, the average rate of increase of "percent correct" was only 4.9 percent per year of schooling, meaning fewer than one in twelve students gained the ability to answer a given question in a given year. In the APRESt study, this figure was 6.1 percent per year. One reason these rates are so low is that the EI and APRESt evaluations combined mechanical and conceptual questions, which demonstrated different rates of progress. The ASER results show that progress on even simple basic mechanical skills, such as reading a paragraph or dividing, was still slow. Four out of five students who entered a grade of basic education (grades two to eight) in India unable to read still were unable to do so even after another full year of instruction (see table 1-5).

The LEAPS Study: Following Students across Grades in Punjab, Pakistan

I want to illustrate one feature of learning profiles using data that track individual students over time on the same questions. Such data are

Table 1-5. Grade learning profiles show little progress in mechanical literacy and numeracy mastery from year to year, and even less progress in conceptual mastery.

Skill/competency by instrument	Average percentage point increase in fraction correct per year of schooling	Of students who didn't know skill, percent who learned in the next grade
Education Initiatives, all items asked across grades (4 and 6, 6 and 8, or 4, 6, and 8) in reading and mathematics, 18 states	4.9	8.5
APRESt, 11 common questions in mathematics (mechanical and conceptual), grades 2 to 5, four districts of AP	6.1	9.4
ASER 2011, division (3 digit by 1 digit, mechanical only), grades 2 to 8, all rural India	9.0	12.6
ASER 2011, reading grade 2–level story (mechanical only), grades 2 to 8, all rural India	11.8	21.8

Source: Pritchett and Beatty (2012, table 1).

available from a study conducted in Punjab, Pakistan. The three learning profiles presented so far are "synthetic": they track the performance of children in grades but do not track the same children. The Learning and Educational Achievement in Pakistan Schools (LEAPS) study is longitudinal, tracking around 6,000 Pakistani children from grades two to six, so researchers have each child's individual learning trajectory and can build up direct cohort (not grade) learning profiles.

These cohort learning profiles show results similar to those from India. On very simple skills that can be learned by rote, performance is high, but on skills that require even a modest degree of comprehension only about half of students master the skill at age- and grade-appropriate levels, and progress is very slow: only one child in five masters simple multiplication and one in seven masters simple division per year (table 1-6).

One feature that arises when tracking individual students and their answers to specific questions is that there appears to be some amount of learning and forgetting. The LEAPS questions are not multiple choice, so the odds a student gets it right by pure chance or guessing are low. Nevertheless, the increase in the averages from year to year across all students masks considerable "churning" in the individual learning trajectories, as

Table 1-6. Actual cohort learning profiles from tracking the same students over time in Pakistan show the same slow pace of learning as grade profiles.

Year tracked in the LEAPS study	Percent able to do two-digit addition, no carry: 36 + 61	Percent who learn in a year	Percent able to do three-digit addition, with carry: 678 + 923	Percent who learn in a year	Percent able to do multi-plication: 32 × 4	Percent who learn in a year	Percent able to do division: 384/6	Percent who learn in a year
1 (in grade 3)	85.5		56.1		52.2		19.3	
2 (mostly grade 4)	87.8	15.9	59.5	7.7	56.9	9.8	24.5	6.5
3 (mostly grade 5)	92.2	36.0	71.1	28.8	70.3	31.1	45.6	27.9
4 (mostly grade 6)	93.0	10.2	74.4	11.4	75.6	17.9	54.1	15.5
Average who learn per year		**20.7**		**16.0**		**19.6**		**16.6**

Source: Data from LEAPS 2007 study; calculations provided to author by LEAPS study authors.

some students get the question right in grade four but miss it when asked in grades five and six.

The Consequence of Flat Learning Profiles: Schooled but Uneducated

The grade learning profile can be thought of as a ramp to the door of opportunity, in civil society, in the polity, and in the economy. If the ramp isn't sufficiently steep, even walking it leaves you unable to get a foot in the door. In the first part of this chapter I focused on how shallow the ramp is: children progress little in conceptual mastery and capability as they move through school. Now I turn to the height most children in developing countries reach on the ramp, their cumulative learning at or near the end of schooling, which for most of them is at around age fifteen, or grade eight. Where does school leave children standing relative to opportunity? In Himachal Pradesh, India, 58 percent of students were assessed at level 0 on an international standardized science test, PISA, whose scale of levels runs from 1 to 6. That's right: most could not answer enough questions even to be placed on the scale. Tragically, as seen in results on internationally comparable exams, in this respect India is not so different from many other countries.

International Comparisons of Capabilities

There are many technical, even esoteric, details that go into constructing valid and reliable assessments, which are explained exceptionally well by Koretz (2008). A very small handful of people in the world are expert in assessment, and I am not one of them, nor would I expect most of my readers to be. But a few simple characteristics of assessments are central to understanding reports from two main international comparative assessments, PISA, which is coordinated by the OECD, and the Third International Math and Science Study (TIMSS), a project of the National Center for Education Statistics and the U.S. Department of Education (see Gonzales et al. 2004; OECD 2009):

— First, what is the skill set domain that assessments are trying to measure the mastery of?
— Second, how well do those assessments capture that?
— Third, how are those measures scaled?

Both PISA and TIMSS assess overall performance in large domains. PISA covers language, mathematics, and science and is intended to capture the students' ability to apply learning from these domains to real-world contexts. TIMSS measures students' conceptual mastery of the typical mathematics and science curriculum.

I work on the premise that these two assessments provide reliable and valid measures of mastery of the learning domains they cover.

The remaining issue is the scaling of these measures. Any assessment contains questions, gets answers, assigns points to answers for each question, assigns an importance to each question, and comes up with a number. The choice of number is arbitrary (a test in school can be scaled as "percent correct" from 0 to 100; the SAT is scaled from 200 to 800; the ACT test is scaled from 1 to 36). Both TIMSS and PISA have chosen to norm their results so that the average score of students from OECD countries is 500 and the student standard deviation is 100. PISA also classifies students by their "level" of performance on the basis of their score, where each of six levels is described in competencies within each of the three subject areas. A description of the tasks students at the lowest levels should be able to perform is provided in table 1-7.

In 2009, two states in India, Himachal Pradesh and Tamil Nadu, participated in PISA. For the first time in decades there was an internationally

Table 1-7. PISA results for two Indian states and OECD comparison figures: half or more of Indian students were in the lowest categories in reading, mathematics, and science.

Domain	Region/state	Percent below level 1 (or below level 1a for reading)	Description of level 1 (or level 1a) capability in the domain	Percent below level 2
Reading	Himachal Pradesh	60.1	Tasks at this level require the reader: to locate one or more independent pieces of explicitly stated information; to recognize the main theme or author's purpose in a text about a familiar topic; or to make a simple connection between information in the text and common, everyday knowledge. Typically the required information in the text is prominent and there is little, if any, competing information. The reader is explicitly directed to consider relevant factors in the task and in the text.	89.2
	Tamil Nadu	49.6		82.7
	OECD	5.7		18.8
Mathematics	Himachal Pradesh	61.8	At level 1, students can answer questions involving familiar contexts where all relevant information is present and the questions are clearly defined. They are able to identify information and to carry out routine procedures according to direct instructions in explicit situations. They can perform actions that are obvious and follow immediately from the given stimuli.	88.1
	Tamil Nadu	55.6		84.8
	OECD	8.0		22.0
Science	Himachal Pradesh	57.9	At level 1, students have such a limited scientific knowledge that it can only be applied to a few, familiar situations. They can present scientific explanations that are obvious and follow explicitly from given evidence.	88.8
	Tamil Nadu	43.6		84.5
	OECD	5.0		18.0

Source: Compiled from PISA (OECD 2010, tables B.2.2, B.3.2, B.3.4).

comparable benchmark of how an in-school cohort of Indian children performs in language, mathematics, and science.[6] The results are consistent with flat learning profiles: fifteen-year-olds, even those still in school, mostly lack even the most basic education (see table 1-7). In Himachal Pradesh, about 60 percent of children were *below* the bottom category, that is, they did not even reach level 1a in reading or level 1 in math.

The PISA data allow us to compare the distribution of student capability from low to high across countries. Figure 1-8 shows the distribution of student results in mathematics for Tamil Nadu and Denmark, a country with typical OECD results. The huge difference in the average score—351 in Tamil Nadu versus Denmark's 503—also implies that many more students are in the bottom category (55.6 percent in Tamil Nadu versus 4.9 percent in Denmark) and fewer in the top category. In Denmark, 11.6 percent of students are in the highest two categories (levels 5 and 6) of PISA capabilities. In Tamil Nadu, the estimate for these same categories is zero percent, since there were too few students in the categories to measure accurately.

Linking Grade Learning Profiles to Assessment Results

Assessments of cumulative learning at a given age or grade and learning profiles represent the same reality in different ways. A flat learning profile results in low capabilities, and low capabilities means the learning profile was flat. This is because the distribution of scores of any population, such as students in grade eight in Himachal Pradesh or Tamil Nadu, is the result of the starting point plus the cumulative learning profile of the tested population.

This basic, if not definitional, link between learning profiles, end-of-basic-education student outcomes, and, with grade attainment profiles, cohort learning attainment is a core issue of this book. Figure 1-9 shows a pair of three-dimensional figures that link the distribution of results across students with learning trajectories. A grade learning profile—such as progress in an average score or in the percentage of students above a threshold—summarizes the evolution of testing distribution

---

6. Himachal Pradesh and Tamil Nadu are considered among the educationally more progressive states, having achieved high levels of enrollment and grade completion. One drawback of the PISA, though, is that it assesses only fifteen-year-olds in school, not a whole cohort of fifteen-year-olds, so the results are overly optimistic. A footnote warns that PISA could not verify that the sampling in Tamil Nadu and Himachal Pradesh met quality standards as they could not be confident the sampling frames of fifteen-year-olds were complete. No one knows what bias this might have induced (OECD 2009).

Figure 1-8. A comparison of student 2009 PISA mathematics score distributions in Denmark and in Tamil Nadu, India, shows distinct differences in achievement.

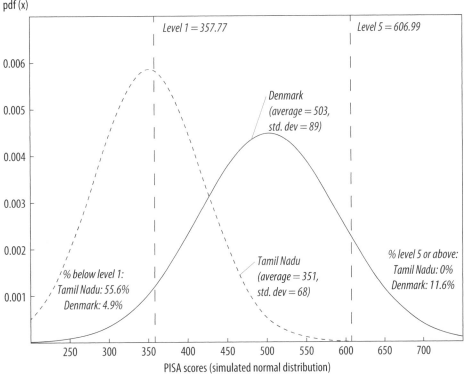

Source: Author's simulations using PISA data (OECD 2009).

summary statistics. Conversely, each distribution of results is the cumulative result of learning trajectories.

Figure 1-9 combines the three elements of a measure of capability in some domain (the y-axis), the progression through school (the x-axis), and the distribution of students (the z-axis). Three-dimensional diagrams can be hard to understand, but they show the whole picture most effectively. Figure 1-9 shows that in each year of schooling, there is a distribution of student capability in any subject. For example, we can start at the beginning of grade three in mathematics. During the school year, some children learn more than others, some learn more in some years than in other years, some have good teachers and learn a lot, others have bad teachers and learn little. There is also forgetting and "depreciation" of learning over time. The net learning of each child across a school year,

Figure 1-9. The (average) grade learning profile tracks the gains in the mean of distribution of student capability.

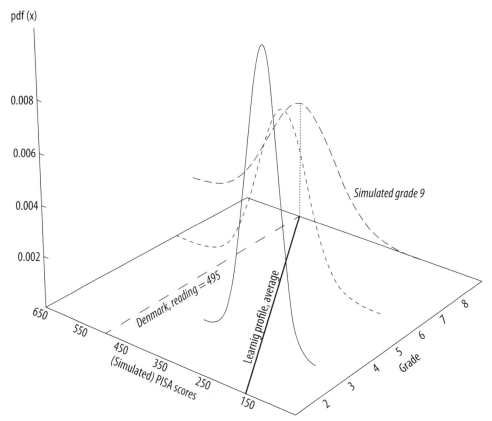

Source: Author's simulations using PISA data (OECD 2009).

plus some dynamics of grade progression, results in a new distribution of capability in mathematics of students enrolled in grade four. This process repeats in subsequent grades. If children are tested at age fifteen, in grade nine (82 percent of Danish fifteen-year-olds were in grade nine), the resulting distribution of capability is a result of the cumulative learning trajectories from conception to age fifteen.

In figure 1-9, I assume the average child in both Denmark and Himachal Pradesh begins at 160 "PISA score equivalents" in grade one.[7] We

7. Actually, controlling for other factors in a multilevel model, the estimated average gain per year in the PISA reading score across OECD countries is 40 (OECD 2009, table A1.2), which implies that if the grade nine score was 500 after eight years of constant gain, the initial grade one value would have been 160.

know that Danish children at age fifteen, most of them in grade nine, have an average PISA score of 503. This means the learning profile must have taken them from their initial point (whatever we assume it to be, in this case 160) to that score of 503 at age fifteen in grade nine over the course of their schooling (and out-of-school) learning experiences. Assessments of a cohort are inextricably linked to grade learning profiles, though not necessarily as simply as the graph suggests. The three-dimensional graph illustrates that the grade learning profiles in two dimensions (grade and capability) summarize the distributions across students into a single number (say, the percentage of students who answer a question correctly, or an average score across an index of items, or, as we shall see later, the percentage of students below some threshold). I show three full distributions across students along this trajectory for grades three, six, and nine.

Comparing capabilities across a sample of students of either a certain age or grade in part means comparing learning profiles. For instance, suppose that children in Denmark and Himachal Pradesh begin at 160 "PISA score equivalents" in reading.[8] The average score in reading in Denmark for those fifteen years old is 495 (like the math score of 503, very typical of an OECD country), whereas in Himachal Pradesh it is 317. The grade learning profiles must have led to these different distributions. But the main point, illustrated in figure 1-10, is that the initial capability plus the grade-to-grade learning (and forgetting) dynamics over time add up to cumulative acquired capability. If we are concerned that children are leaving school inadequately prepared for adulthood, we must focus on the *entire* learning profile, both out-of-school learning (including even any relevant preconception issues) and the in-school grade learning profile.

International Performance Comparisons: Developing Countries versus OECD Countries

The 2006 PISA report states, "PISA assesses how far students near the end of compulsory education have acquired some of the knowledge and skills that are essential for full participation in society. In all cycles, the domains of reading, mathematical and scientific literacy are covered not

---

8. Of course, it is much more complex than this, as children in Himachal Pradesh may have suffered from in vitro malnutrition, diseases, or other early disadvantages, and hence may have been much less reading-ready upon entering grade one than Danish children. Moreover, grade progression is much more irregular in India than in Denmark, so the average score for fifteen-year-olds represents children in many different grades in Himachal Pradesh, which means the actual PISA score is an enrollment-weighted average across the grades.

Figure 1-10. Comparison of assessed reading capability in grade 9 in Himachal Pradesh and in Denmark in grade 9 illustrating the link between lower capability and a flatter learning profile.

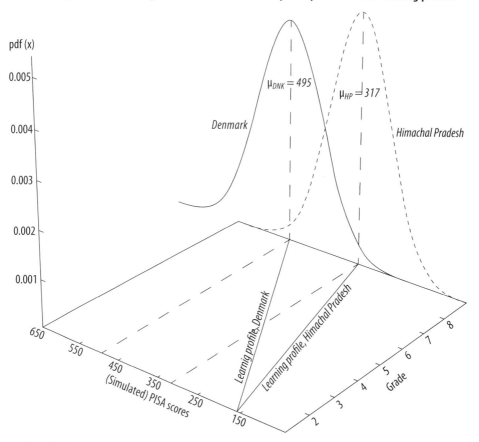

Source: Author's simulations, based on PISA 2009(+) (OECD 2009) averages and distributions.

merely in terms of mastery of the school curriculum, but in terms of important knowledge and skills needed in adult life." In other words, PISA's aim is not only to capture the simple decoding skills of reading or procedural skills of arithmetic but to assess how these skills prepare children for adulthood. PISA's target population for assessment is "15-year-old students attending educational institutions located within the country, in grades 7 or higher." The sampling is therefore explicitly student-based, not cohort-based (OECD 2009).

Table 1-8 compares only selected countries evaluated in the PISA program. Except for using Denmark as a benchmark, as a development

Table 1-8. PISA results show that 15-year-old students in developing countries are massively behind the typical OECD country students in mathematics capability.

Country/Region	Year (PISA round)	Average	Percent at level 1 or below (<420)	Percent at level 5 or above (>607)	Country student standard deviations behind Denmark[a]	Average student from country X in Denmark's distribution[b] (percentile)
Denmark	2009	503	13.6	13.7		
OECD	2009	496	22	12.7		
Developing countries						
Average		391	64.2	0.9	1.4	11.2
Himachal Pradesh	2009+	338	88.1	0	2.3	3.2
Tamil Nadu	2009+	351	84.8	0	2.2	4.4
Panama	2009	360	78.8	0.4	1.8	5.4
Tunisia	2006	365	72.5	0.5	1.5	6.1
Peru	2009	365	73.5	0.6	1.6	6.1
Qatar	2009	368	73.8	1.8	1.4	6.5
Brazil	2006	370	72.5	1	1.4	6.8
Colombia	2006	370	71.9	0.4	1.5	6.8
Indonesia	2009	371	76.6	0.1	1.9	6.9
Tunisia	2009	371	73.6	0.2	1.7	6.9
Argentina	2006	381	64.1	1	1.2	8.5
Colombia	2009	381	70.4	0.1	1.6	8.5
Brazil	2009	386	69.1	0.8	1.4	9.4
Jordan	2009	387	65.3	0.3	1.4	9.6
Argentina	2009	388	63.6	0.9	1.2	9.8
Indonesia	2006	391	65.7	0.4	1.4	10.4
Miranda, Venezuela	2009+	397	59.5	0.3	1.3	11.7
Malaysia	2009+	404	59.3	0.4	1.4	13.3
Mexico	2006	406	56.5	0.9	1.1	13.8
Costa Rica	2009+	409	56.7	0.3	1.3	14.5
Chile	2006	411	55.1	1.4	1.1	15.1
Trinidad and Tobago	2009	414	53.2	2.4	0.9	15.9

(continued)

Table 1-8. PISA results show that 15-year-old students in developing countries are massively behind the typical OECD country students in mathematics capability. (*continued*)

Country/Region	Year	Average	Percent at level 1 or below (<420)	Percent at level 5 or above (>607)	Country student standard deviations behind Denmark[a]	Average student from country X in Denmark's distribution[b] (percentile)
Thailand	2006	417	53	1.3	1.1	16.7
Mexico	2009	419	50.8	0.7	1.1	17.3
Thailand	2009	419	52.5	1.3	1.1	17.3
Mauritius	2009+	420	50.1	1.6	1.0	17.6
Chile	2009	421	51.1	1.3	1.0	17.8
United Arab Emirates	2009+	421	51.3	2.9	0.9	17.8
Uruguay	2009+	427	47.5	2.4	0.8	19.7

Sources: For columns 1–4, PISA (OECD 2010, tables B.3.1 and B.3.2). For columns 5–6, author's calculations, based on PISA (OECD 2006, 2010) data and means and standard deviations for Denmark.

a. Estimating the standard deviation from 5th and 95th percentiles under assumption of normal distribution.

b. Assuming a normal distribution for Denmark.

expert I focus on the participating developing countries. Even for the mostly middle-income developing countries participating in PISA, it is striking how low the learning levels are relative to Denmark's. One way to illustrate this low learning is to ask where the average student in a developing country would rank if that person were taking the test in Denmark. Brazil is a large middle-income developing country. The average in Brazil was 370, so the typical Brazilian student would be below the seventh percentile (6.8) in the Danish distribution.

TIMSS's approach is slightly different from PISA's in that TIMSS attempts to assess mastery of the mathematics curriculum in grade eight. Nevertheless, the results for developing countries are similar to PISA's in respect to fifteen-year-olds' capability and application. In table 1-9 I again compare the developing countries to an OECD country—in this case Australia, chosen because I love kangaroos.

First, the average developing country is at only 386 (on a similar OECD student norm of 500 average, with 100 as the OECD student standard

Table 1-9. Results from TIMSS show developing countries are far behind in mathematics capabilities.

Country	Average score	Percent below low benchmark (400)	Percent above high benchmark (550)	Country student standard deviations behind Australia[a]	Average student from country X in Australia's distribution[b] (percentile)
Australia (as a typical OECD country)	499	11	24	0	50
Developing countries					
Average	386	56	4	1.4	10.5
Qatar	307	84	0	2.1	0.8
Ghana	309	83	0	2.1	0.8
Saudi Arabia	329	82	0	2.2	1.6
El Salvador	340	80	0	2.2	2.2
Kuwait	354	71	0	1.8	3.3
Botswana	364	68	1	1.8	4.4
Oman	372	59	2	1.3	5.4
Colombia	380	61	2	1.5	6.6
Morocco	381	59	1	1.5	6.8
Algeria	387	59	0	1.9	7.8
Egypt	391	53	5	1.1	8.6
Syria	395	53	3	1.3	9.4
Indonesia	397	52	4	1.2	9.8
Bahrain	398	51	3	1.2	10.1
Iran	403	49	5	1.1	11.2
Tunisia	420	39	3	1.2	15.9
Jordan	427	39	11	0.7	18.1
Thailand	441	34	12	0.6	23.1
Lebanon	449	26	10	0.7	26.3
Malaysia	474	18	18	0.3	37.6

Source: TIMSS (2008, Exhibit 1.1, 2.2, D.2).
a. Estimating standard deviation from the 5th and 95th percentiles under the assumption of a normal distribution.
b. Assuming a normal distribution for Australia.

deviation). Australia is at 499, which is very near 500 and a full student standard deviation above 400.

Second, more than 50 percent of developing-country students are below the "low" international benchmark of 400, compared to only 11 percent for Australia. Conversely, on average, only 4 percent are above the "high" international benchmark, compared to 24 percent for Australia. Again, if one calculates how far behind the country is relative to its own distribution, we find that developing countries are typically one to two country full OECD student standard deviations behind Australia. Finally, similar to the PISA comparisons to Denmark, the typical developing-country student is only in the tenth percentile of the performance of Australian students.

Eric Hanushek and Ludger Woessmann (2009) have done the most complete compilation of all of the available international tests into a single comparable measure of learning. How far behind on their composite measure are students in lower secondary schools in developing countries? Figure 1-11 scales their overall country averages by the OECD student standard deviation and shows that nearly all developing countries are one or more international assessment student standard deviations below the OECD average.

The Best (and the Richest) Developing Countries' Performance

In a world of global competition, success, especially in some economic activities, may depend on more than the average skills of the typical worker but also on the number of superstars among the globally best (Pritchett and Viarengo 2009). But even in upper-middle-income countries such as Mexico or Brazil, low average performance on PISA and TIMSS tests, combined with often low variance across students, means that very small fractions of students are in the two top global distribution categories (see the column "Percent at level 5 or above (>607)" in table 1-8 and the column "Percent above high benchmark (550)" in table 1-9).

If we look just at the top category—roughly the global top 10 percent—things are even more dire. Pritchett and Viarengo (2009) calculated that even in Mexico, a country with more than 100 million people, all of the Mexican students who achieved the global top 10 percent yearly in mathematics could fit into one smallish auditorium—there are only around 3,000 to 6,000 total. Hanushek and Woessmann (2009) have also calculated the proportion of students tested who were in the global top 10 percent. As figure 1-12 shows, in most developing countries it is significantly less than 1 percent.

Figure 1-11. Students in most developing countries are at least an OECD student standard deviation behind the OECD level of learning.

OECD student standard deviations from 500

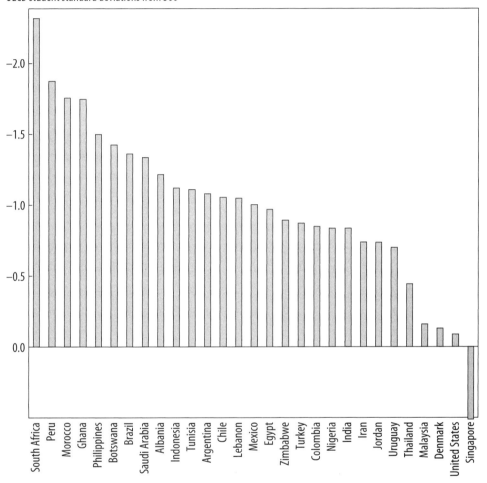

Source: Adapted from Hanushek and Woessmann (2009).

That there are very few students at the top levels of performance means that the problems with educational systems do not affect only poor children. Zero percent of students at PISA levels 5 and 6 means zero percent of students from poor families and also zero percent from rich families reach this level because zero is zero.

In figure 1-13, Filmer (2010) compares the scores of children from the bottom and top quintiles of the available countries by socioeconomic

Figure 1-12. Developing countries are producing very small proportions of students in the global top 10 percent.

Percent

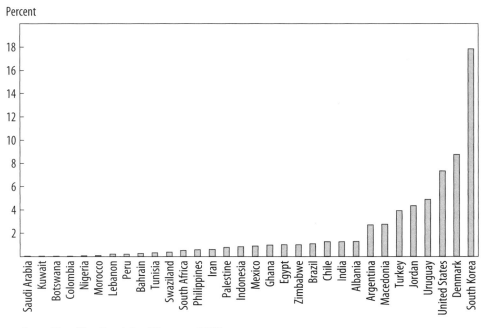

Source: Adapted from Hanushek and Woessmann (2009).

Figure 1-13. Inequalities in PISA 2006 reading test scores show that learning outcomes are the worst for the poorest in poor countries, but are pretty awful for the richest, too.

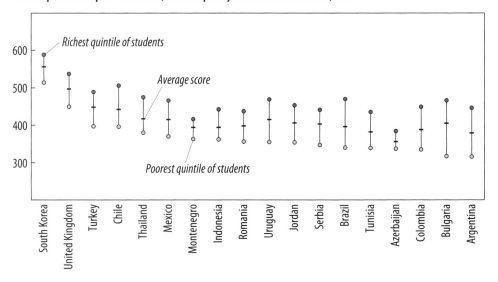

Source: Filmer calculations with PISA data, provided in private communication with the author.

status using data from PISA. Not surprisingly, massive gaps—roughly 100 points—separate the learning outcomes of richer and poorer students. Perhaps more surprising, even the rich in developing countries also lag. For example, in Indonesia, the richest quintile has scores around 450—less than the 500 for the *poorest* quintile in Korea or the same as the poorest quintile in the UK. So in poor countries, the richest are still getting a mediocre education, and the poor cannot be said to be getting any education at all.

Meeting a Learning Goal for All Children

So far nearly all the results we have used measure the capabilities of pupils in school. Since, with the exception of ASER, sampling and testing are nearly always school-based, we do not know much about the learning of out-of-school children. This means that the grade learning profiles, as depressing as they are, actually exaggerate the overall progress of a cohort of children, for the results do not account for students who drop out or fail to progress. A genuine learning goal should not be based solely on the learning of those currently enrolled but should reflect the skill set of the entire cohort, including those who never enrolled or who enrolled and later dropped out. How close are developing countries to a cohort-based learning goal: that every child should emerge from childhood into youth and adulthood educationally equipped for life?

The short answer is that no one knows. In the push for schooling, education got pushed aside. The world has reams of data on schooling but almost none on learning. Very few countries can track the learning achievements of its students over time. Very few have measures of learning achievement based on cohort rather than on enrolled students. Deon Filmer, Amer Hasan, and I (2006) attempted to estimate how many fifteen-year-olds in various countries were currently meeting a learning goal (the results of our study are presented in table 1-10). To arrive at these estimates we had to make several assumptions, because existing information was inadequate. We assumed PISA level 1 proficiency as an illustrative "low" learning goal. As a "high" learning goal, we calculated what proportion of fifteen-year-olds was above the OECD mean value of 500.

Second, we needed assumptions to estimate the learning levels of a complete cohort from only school-based tests. PISA tests fifteen-year-olds, who are in different grades, so we used the learning levels across the tested grades and did the simplest possible thing: we extrapolated linearly the distribution of achievement (by extrapolating the mean and keeping

Table 1-10. Even in middle-income countries with high average levels of schooling, and thus meeting the MDG schooling target, between one-third and two-thirds of 15-year-olds do not meet even a low learning goal.

Country	Percent of a cohort of 15-year-olds not meeting a low learning goal (PISA level 1 proficiency) in 2003				Average years of schooling, 2005	Cohort completion of grade 5 (percent)
	Mathematics	Reading	Science	Average		
Brazil	78	57	64	66	7.19	80.3
Turkey	67	50	57	58	6.44	90.4
Indonesia	68	45	39	51	5.58	94.4
Mexico	50	39	38	42	8.44	92.7
Uruguay	39	31	31	34	8.08	*
Thailand	34	19	26	26	6.82	97.6
Greece	17	8	7	11	9.9	*
USA	9	5	3	6	12.1	*
Japan	3	5	3	4	11.2	*
Korea	2	0	2	1	11.5	*

Source: Filmer, Hasan, and Pritchett (2006, tables 2, 3, and 4), Barro and Lee (2011) for average years, Filmer (2010) for cohort completion.

*Note available. Cohort completion data is from Filmer (2010), available only for countries with DHS surveys.

the coefficient of variation constant). Fortunately for us, the results are quite robust to the assumptions, and both the ASER and EI data from India suggest that linear extrapolations past the very early grades do not do too much violence to actual learning profiles by grade.

The results of our calculations, as presented in table 1-10, are sobering. Mexico provides a useful example. Mexico in many ways is on the verge of being a developed country (and is now a member of the OECD). Primary schooling is nearly universal, and the average level of education for those age fifteen and above is nearing nine years. But in 2003, according to our calculations, half of fifteen-year-olds were at proficiency level 1 or below for mathematics, 39 percent for reading, and 38 percent for science. In Korea those numbers for 2003 were 2 percent, zero percent, and 2 percent, respectively.

According to our calculations (which were based on the best data we could find and the most plausible assumptions we could make), things are worse in the middle-income countries of Brazil, Turkey, and Indonesia. Averaged across the three PISA subjects, over half of the recent cohort is below a potential learning goal. In mathematics, in each of these three countries two-thirds of fifteen-year-olds are below a standard that is essentially universal in Korea.

TIMSS tests children in grades four and eight, rather than an entire cohort, and includes a variety of developing countries. This means that to calculate a cohort learning goal deficit, one must make assumptions. The first part, the grade attainment of a cohort, is widely available from household surveys. To calculate achievement for each grade, Filmer, Hasan, and I (2006) did the simplest possible simulation: we took the mean score given for grade eight (grade nine for Rajasthan) and then extrapolated it backward and forward using a grade increment, calculated as the linear increment to get from a minimum of 100 on enrolling in school to the observed score. We assumed that the coefficient of variation of student scores was constant across grades. Then, using the assumption that scores follow a normal distribution, we calculated the fraction of students at each grade attainment level who would be above any given threshold. We chose a potential low learning goal in the TIMSS assessment of 420, for three reasons. This is roughly a typical country student standard deviation on the TIMSS (which is around 80) below the OECD normed score of 500. Second, this is near the threshold for proficiency level 1 in PISA (although the two instruments are not comparable). Third, the only country with both a learning goal calculation and a TIMSS 2003 score is Indonesia, and choosing 420 gives an estimate of 56 percent for Indonesia, which is modestly better than the 68 percent estimated from TIMSS, but not wildly off. To be sure, these calculations are weak, yet their very weakness supports my overall contention concerning the lack of information on learning as opposed to schooling. These calculations provide some information about the achievement of cohorts.

Poorer countries are more likely participate in TIMSS than in PISA, which probes mainly middle-income countries, and the TIMSS results are more striking (I report these results in greater depth in chapter 2). In Ghana, 98 percent of a cohort fails to achieve a learning goal of 420; in the Philippines, 67 percent, and in Rajasthan (bearing in mind the lack of TIMSS comparability), 75 percent. Even when schooling is completed the deficits in education are massive.

Despite the failures of schooling, the victory of schooling can now lead to the rebirth of education. Nearly all children in the world start school. Most of them progress. The goal of universal completion of primary schooling has been achieved in nearly all countries. Schooling goals were never based on the notion that the schooling was itself the goal; no one even thought the true and total objective was just coming to a building called a school for a certain length of time. Time served is how we characterize prison terms, not education. Rather, schooling goals were based on the belief that schooling would lead to education, that children who completed the required schooling would be equipped for life. We know now that this is untrue. At the low pace of learning common in the developing world, completion of just primary education provides almost no one with adequate skills, and even completion of a "basic" education of eight or nine years of schooling leaves half the students unprepared for the twenty-first century.

The question is, what is to be done?

CHAPTER 2

More Schooling Alone Won't Necessarily Give an Education

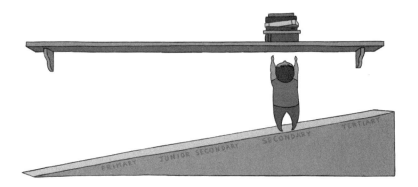

The easiest thing for any successful social movement to do is to ask for *more*, especially more of the same. More of the same provides more to existing interests without demanding anything new. As public schooling has been one of the most universally successful social movements in history, it is tempting to try to solve the problem of too little learning by asking for more schooling.

The beauty of a universal *schooling* target is that more *is* an answer. Once a school has just been built *here*, replicating it—its building, equipment, and staffing—over *there* is the obvious next step. And, as we saw in chapter 1, this works: schooling has more than tripled in just sixty years.

Much advocacy is still focused on more schooling. Certainly the remaining unschooled children deserve additional resources and attention. Children who never enroll in any school today are mostly the world's triply disadvantaged—born to poor parents, in remote regions of poor countries, and into a socially disadvantaged or marginalized group.[1] The drive to enroll the remaining poor and disadvantaged groups leads to targeted policy instruments, such as "conditional cash transfers"[2] or targeted scholarships or innovations intended to ameliorate specific issues that limit enrollment.[3] However, as we saw in the previous chapter, these instruments cannot be the organizing goal for the world's education systems, as currently those who never enroll in any school are only a tiny part of those who lack an adequate education. Advocates also focus on expanding the number of schooling years to be completed for the currently enrolled. With (near) universal primary school completion achieved, attainment goals expanded to universal elementary (lower primary plus upper primary grades) school completion or universal basic schooling (defined to include "junior secondary," up to eighth, ninth, or tenth grade), and even to universal secondary school completion, up to twelve years. To illustrate that there is no end to the logic (or political viability) of just asking for more, advocates in rich countries now argue for universal tertiary schooling.

A universal education target would be easy to meet if it could be achieved the same way as universal schooling was: more, more, more, and eventually we get there. If this were true, then the same coalition of parental demand, informed advocacy, altruism, and political self-interest that was the "access axis"—the social and political movement that achieved universal schooling—could work again. Grade-completion-based schooling goals (like the Millennium Development Goal) could seamlessly morph into learning achievement goals, with no need for innovation, systemic change, disruption, or creative destruction. In other words, nothing hard would need to be done.

More schooling alone will get more kids an education—but leave millions of children still without an adequate education. This chapter shows that the expansion of schooling alone, without any improvement in the pace of learning, the steepness of the grade learning profile, can result in only very limited progress toward educating developing-country youth.

---

1. Lewis and Lockheed (2007) discuss the "double disadvantage" of girls in poor countries, particularly from marginalized groups, who make up the bulk of out-of-school children.

2. These are transfers whose primary purpose is usually to transfer income to households, but making receipt of a cash transfer conditional on household behavior, such as the use of health services or child enrollment, has also been shown to have an impact on enrollment rates (Fiszbein and Schady 2009).

3. Oster and Thornton (2010), for instance, use a randomized experiment to evaluate the impact of menstruation control technologies on girls' school attendance in Nepal (and find no impact).

When little learning happens per grade, completing more and more grades just won't help that much in achieving universal capabilities. For instance, at the average pace of progress observed on the Educational Initiatives (EI) questions in India from grades four to six to eight, it would take sixteen years of schooling to get 90 percent of students producing correct responses on tests of rudimentary reading and arithmetic skills.

Flat learning profiles mean that expanding schooling is no guarantee of reaching, or even of making substantial progress toward, a learning goal. I estimate that in Ghana in 2007, only 9.7 percent of a cohort were above a minimal international threshold of mathematics capability (a TIMSS score of 420, which represents the global bottom 20 percent). Suppose that, at its current learning profile, Ghana achieved universal completion through grade nine. Only 19.7 percent would have been above that threshold. The accomplishment of universal basic education would have led to only one in ten more children meeting one reasonable learning goal. More generally, I show that at current learning profiles, even if the typical developing country achieved universal completion through grade nine, more than half of its students would not meet even a low international benchmark in learning. Unfortunately, while more schooling might be a necessary condition to achieving universal education, it is far from enough.

To disentangle the progress toward *cohort* learning goals—how many of a cohort of children leaving school age have adequate capabilities—from just learning achievement of those in school, we need to combine *grade learning profiles*, discussed in the previous chapter, with *grade attainment* profiles.

Grade Attainment Profiles

One way of summarizing the dynamics of schooling is to use information from household surveys about grade completion of a cohort to see, at least retrospectively, what fraction of an age-based cohort completed what grade (or higher). In a massive exercise, Deon Filmer at the World Bank compiles, on an ongoing basis, household survey data from over seventy countries (and for many countries, across multiple years). Using data on fifteen- to nineteen-year-olds, a cohort that is at (or near) basic education completion, Filmer calculates grade attainment profiles for these countries.[4]

---

4. See http://iresearch.worldbank.org/edattain/. I used the data from the 2010 database.

Figure 2-1. Grade completion profiles illustrate the difference between enrollment and retention as sources of schooling attainment deficits.

Percent completing given grade or
higher, cohort age 15–19

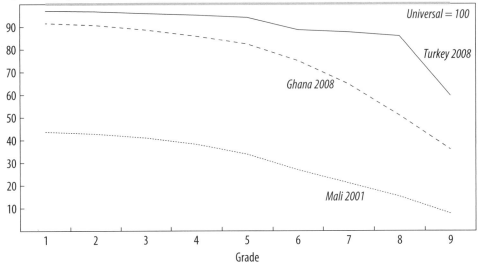

Source: Filmer (2010). Database at http://iresearch.worldbank.org/edattain/.

Grade attainment profiles have several advantages over enrollment rates. First, because they look at fifteen- to nineteen-year-olds, they give a picture of a cohort's attainment history—whether children enroll, how they progress across grades, and when they finish schooling. With grade attainment data, one can decompose the proximate contributions to lack of universal grade completion—for example, is it due to lack of enrollment or to attrition? In looking at Mali's fifteen- to nineteen-year-old cohort in 2001 in figure 2-1, for instance, it is clear that most of the deficit in universal completion can be attributed to those who never enrolled, as many did not complete even grade one, and these mostly never enrolled. This reveals an access problem.

Thankfully, as a result of efforts to expand schooling around the world, it is rare for children never to have enrolled in school. Ghana's cohort of fifteen- to nineteen-year-olds in 2008 shows the much more common pattern (see figure 2-1). Nearly all had participated in at least some formal schooling since 93 percent had completed at least grade one. But the combination of a low retention rate and a high dropout rate means that only 75 percent completed grade six, only half reached grade eight, and only 36 percent completed grade nine. Turkey's 2008 cohort is representative of a country with nearly universal completion through grade eight (as grade eight completion was made compulsory), followed by a sharp drop-off in the transition to grade nine: 86 percent made it through grade eight, whereas only 60 percent completed grade nine or higher. So even in an upper-middle-income country such as Turkey, many students complete their studies by grade eight or nine.

The second advantage of grade attainment profiles is that researchers can show grade completion differences by socioeconomic conditions. Grade attainment data are usually from household surveys, whereas enrollment data, which are usually from official sources, generally allow disaggregation only by gender or location.[5] In developing countries, grade attainment curves have shifted up as more children have enrolled and persisted through the system longer, primarily through enrollment of poorer families (using a Filmer and Pritchett [2001] wealth index as a proxy for households' socioeconomic condition). The changes in grade attainment profiles in Bangladesh illustrate the enrollment gains among the poorest. Figure 2-2 shows the grade completion profiles of cohorts in 1993–1994 versus 2007, thirteen years later, and compares the grade attainment profile of the richest 20 percent of households with that of the least wealthy 40 percent. Since the richer were already mostly in school, the bulk of the gains came from expanding the enrollment of the poorer parts of the population.

There is no question that continuing the momentum for universal primary education—to bring every child into school—is a necessary condition for learning. Moreover, it is inevitable that more and more countries will move to higher and higher levels of compulsory schooling, and hence join a widespread push for universal basic education of eight or ten years. However, the expansion of schooling in and of itself, without improvement in learning, will not adequately equip children for their future.

5. The Demographic and Health Surveys, funded by the United States Agency for International Development and implemented by ICF, and other surveys allow children to be linked to their households, and hence their enrollment can be linked not just to gender or rural/urban residence (which can be done with school-based data) but also to paternal and maternal education (Filmer 2000), household assets, and household wealth (Filmer and Pritchett 2001).

Figure 2-2. Expanding grade attainment has mainly been about including the poor (example of Bangladesh).

Percent completing given grade or
higher, cohort age 15–19

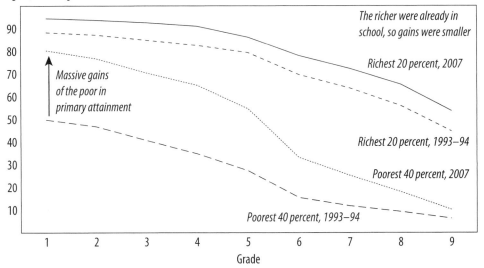

The richer were already in
school, so gains were smaller

Richest 20 percent, 2007

*Massive gains
of the poor in
primary attainment*

Richest 20 percent, 1993–94

Poorest 40 percent, 2007

Poorest 40 percent, 1993–94

Grade

Source: Filmer (2010). Database at http://iresearch.worldbank.org/edattain/.

Learning Progress as a Combination of Grade Achievement and Learning Profiles

As in the previous chapter, I start with examples of specific questions and then move on to population averages for broad domains such as reading or mathematics. Any overall education goal will have a number of learning goals that reflect the capabilities of the cohorts around the age they leave school. Tracking a learning goal requires a *cohort learning achievement profile*, which encapsulates children's mastery over desired educational competencies at any given age. A cohort learning achievement profile combines grade attainment and grade learning profiles.

Flat Learning Profiles Mean Reaching Proficiency Takes Too Long

The Education Initiatives learning assessment discussed in chapter 1 features common questions asked in different grades in language and

Table 2-1. Flat empirical learning profiles in India and Tanzania imply that even universal secondary school would not bring achievement in basic skills in reading and mathematics.

	Increment per year, in average percent correct	Total schooling years to reach	
		90 percent correct	100 percent correct
India: EI Language (median)	4.9	18.7	22
India: EI Math (median)	5.3	14.3	16.3
Tanzania: grade 2 proficiency across Kiswahili, English, and math, grades 4–7	8.7	13	14

Sources: For India, Educational Initiatives (2010). For Tanzania, Uwezo (2011).

Note: I use median for EI because in one set of language questions, the increment is 1.4 per year, which substantially lowers the mean.

mathematics.[6] This characteristic of the assessment tool allowed me to calculate changes in the percentage of students who are able to answer questions correctly per year of attendance, to derive a grade learning profile. As shown in table 2-1, the median pace per grade across different grade combinations is 5.7 percent, meaning that 5.7 percent of students who do not show mastery of the material on one year's testing are able to give correct answers after an *entire additional year* of instruction.

Taking the learning pace calculations a step further, I used the empirically observed profiles to ask the hypothetical question (supposing these learning profiles represented actual causal learning relationships): how many years would a cohort need to be in school before mastery became even near universal, such as 90 percent correct, or universal, 100 percent? If I make hard (and dubious) assumptions, the calculation is easy. Take the questions on language asked in grades four and six. These questions are simple enough that over half of students could answer them in grade four. By grade six, on average 64 percent could answer these same questions. This means a gain of about 6.4 percentage points per year. How many years are needed to get this cohort to 90 percent correct? It would

6. In the math section there were twelve questions common to grades four and six, eleven questions common to grades six and eight, three questions common to grades four and eight, and three questions common to all three grades four, six, and eight. In language there were six questions common to grades four and six, fifteen common to grades six and eight, and four common to grades four, six, and eight.

take five additional years (rounded up to whole years of schooling), or eleven total years of schooling, to reach even 90 percent correct for basic language skills expected of fourth-graders.

Across all mathematics questions, the average is 14.3 years to reach 90 percent correct, or more years than is provided by universal primary, universal basic, or even the typical twelve years of secondary schooling. And keep in mind this is not to reach a target of sophisticated understanding and ability to do applications. It is just to reach very basic competencies in language, such as being able to complete sentences with a word, and in mathematics, such as doing simple arithmetic. In language overall (including questions asked beyond grade four), there is slower progress still: it would take 18.7 years of schooling to get 90 percent mastery of basic language capabilities.

As we saw in the previous chapter, India is not alone in slow learning progress. For Tanzania I estimated how long, given the existing learning profile, it would take to get universal proficiency. Here I used data from Uwezo Tanzania, an ASER-like basic skills test in Kiswahili, English, and mathematics. Uwezo reports the percentage of students meeting the low proficiency standard expected of grade two students (similar to ASER proficiency levels discussed in chapter 1) across all three subjects.[7] By the end of grade seven in Tanzania, only 41 percent of students are proficient in the three fundamental subject areas. At that pace it would take thirteen years of schooling to get 90 percent of the students performing at the grade two level. At the current shallow grade learning profile, achieving universal secondary *schooling* would not even produce universal grade two *education*.

Disappointingly, the results in table 2-1 are *optimistic*. These are empirical profiles of enrolled students in those grades and not causal learning profiles, that is, how much more the same set of children would learn if they stayed in school. To the extent that children who do poorly on tests are more likely to drop out than other children, then empirical profiles of cross sections of students by grade will overstate the actual learning of individual students. As a simple example, suppose we tested a class of students, and half answered the question correctly and half did not. Suppose that none of the students who answered incorrectly progressed to the next grade (they either dropped out or repeated the year) while all of those answering correctly progressed. Suppose, again

7. With the exception that the Uwezo standard for level 2 mathematics includes only multiplication, not division.

Figure 2-3. Looking only at an empirical learning profile, and not taking into account dropout rates and repeating a year, can overstate learning progress per year.

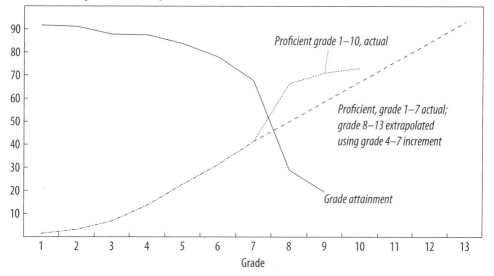

Percent of cohort (grade attainment) proficient

Sources: Uwezo Tanzania (2010, Appendix A, table 1, and author's extrapolations); Filmer (2010) for grade attainment.
Note: Actual and extrapolated figures are identical for grades one through seven.

hypothetically, no one learns anything at all over the year. Then the average percentage of students answering correctly goes from 50 percent to 100 percent from one grade to the next purely mechanically, owing to selective lack of progression. In this case the empirical profile—which goes from 50 percent to 100 percent—does not represent a causal learning profile, which was, by assumption, completely flat.

The differences between empirical and causal learning profiles can be illustrated with data from Uwezo Tanzania. Figure 2-3 combines the empirical learning profile, showing the fraction of students proficient in all three subjects by year of schooling compared with the 2010 grade attainment profile of a cohort aged fifteen to nineteen years. By the time students complete basic education in Tanzania (grade seven), only 41 percent are proficient in grade two basics. This figure jumps to 66.5 percent for those in the first year of secondary school (grade eight), which might lead one to think there are large learning gains between grades seven and eight. However, the grade attainment profile shows a significant dropout rate when students move from basic to secondary education. While

68 percent of the cohort complete grade seven, only 29 percent complete grade eight or higher, so nearly 40 percent of students drop out between grade seven and grade eight. If students with less proficiency drop out, the empirical learning profile will show a jump in proficiency across grades not because children learned but because those who knew less dropped out.

Cohort Learning Profiles: Combining Grade Completion and Learning Profiles

We are interested in more than the learning of those in school; we are interested in the education of all the children in a cohort. With the setup we have so far, we can mechanically decompose the empirical learning achievement of a cohort into (1) the *grade completion profile*, or the fraction of a cohort of a given age, arrayed by their highest level of schooling completed, and (2) the *empirical learning achievement profile*, or the level of competency or skill proficiency at each level of grade completion. These profiles are both featured in tables 2-2 and 2-3. By "mechanical" decomposition, I emphasize that no assertions are made about causality or about what could or could not be achieved with various policy instruments (that comes much later). Although there is a lot of arithmetic to this decomposition, it is just simple arithmetic.

Table 2-2 illustrates the combination of grade completion and learning profiles using the raw all India ASER data from 2008 on ability to do division (ASER 2009).[8] I compare the achievement of a fifteen- to sixteen-year-old cohort from a low-achieving (54 percent) Indian state, Uttar Pradesh, with that of a high-achieving (88 percent) state, Himachal Pradesh. How much of that gap is (mechanically) the result of their different grade attainment profiles and how much is (mechanically) an effect of the empirical learning profile?

Himachal Pradesh has higher grade attainment than Uttar Pradesh, with very few children in Himachal Pradesh completing only grade eight or below and 62 percent of fifteen- to sixteen-year-olds currently attaining grade ten or above. In Uttar Pradesh, in contrast, 56 percent of students attain less than ten years of schooling. The more striking difference between these two states is that at each level of grade attained, the ability to divide is strikingly higher in Himachal Pradesh. In grade ten in Himachal Pradesh, 94.6 percent of students can divide, whereas in Uttar

---

8. ASER uses one-digit into three-digit division as a benchmark that is supposed to be achieved by grade two, according to the Indian curriculum.

Table 2-2. Cohort learning profiles are the multiplicative product of grade attainment and learning achievement by grade, illustrated with two states in India.

	Uttar Pradesh			Himachal Pradesh		
Grade	Percent of children attaining up to specified grade (Grade completion profile) I	Percent of grade able to divide (Empirical learning profile) II	Percent of cohort with given grade attainment and able to divide III (= I × II)	Percent of children attaining up to specified grade (Grade completion profile) I	Percent of grade able to divide (Empirical learning profile) II	Percent of cohort with given grade attainment and able to divide III (= I × II)
0	4.0	1.9	0.1	0.4	0.0	0.0
1	0.5	31.5	0.2	0.1	100.0	0.1
2	0.9	9.6	0.1	0.2	66.7	0.2
3	1.3	5.7	0.1	0.2	0.0	0.0
4	1.8	13.5	0.2	0.2	0.0	0.0
5	7.2	12.6	0.9	1.7	36.4	0.6
6	3.5	25.3	0.9	1.4	44.4	0.6
7	5.3	37.5	2.0	2.8	67.6	1.9
8	14.6	43.1	6.3	12.0	73.1	8.8
9	17.3	63.0	10.9	19.3	87.9	16.9
10	32.1	72.0	23.1	40.3	94.6	38.1
11	6.5	80.7	5.3	17.2	96.5	16.6
12	4.9	83.7	4.1	4.4	100.0	4.4
Fraction of those aged 15–16 able to divide		**54.1**				**88.2**

Source: Author's calculations using ASER 2008 data (ASER 2009).

Pradesh, even of the children who manage to make it to grade ten, only 74 percent can divide.

The proportion of a cohort that can divide at each grade attainment level is shown in table 2.2, in the third column under each state. This figure was calculated by taking the proportion of the cohort with each level of grade attainment (including none at all) times the fraction of those of each cohort at that grade attainment who can divide. For instance, in Uttar Pradesh, 7.2 percent of the fifteen- to sixteen-year-olds completed only up to grade five. Of these, only 12.6 percent could divide. So the fraction of the cohort who could divide and attained at most grade five is $0.072 \times 0.126 = 0.009$, or .9 percent of the cohort.

The average *cohort* learning achievement is just the sum of the third column for each state—the fraction who can divide. Cohort learning achievement profiles are very rare because one needs to have tested the entire cohort, not just those in school. So a school-based examination in grade ten in Uttar Pradesh would reveal that 72 percent of those who took the exam could divide, but this is only 32 percent of the entire cohort aged fifteen to sixteen years. The true cohort average has to include those 4 percent who never enrolled, almost none of whom can divide, and the 7.2 percent that dropped out after grade five, of whom only 12.6 percent can divide, and so forth. So only 54 percent of the cohort aged fifteen to sixteen years can do simple division, much lower than the grade ten average of 72 percent.

With the grade completion and learning profiles for these two states, we can, in table 2-3, hypothesize about how Uttar Pradesh could increase the proportion of children able to do division. What if more children in Uttar Pradesh simply stayed in school longer? For example, what if Uttar Pradesh had Himachal Pradesh's level of grade attainment but at Uttar Pradesh's observed learning profile? That massive increase in schooling in Uttar Pradesh would improve the cohort mastery of division from 54 percent to only 66 percent (column IV of table 2-3).

Conversely, suppose that at exactly its same grade attainment, Uttar Pradesh were able to achieve the same empirical grade learning profile as Himachal Pradesh, so that children learned more per year. Then the cohort mastery of division would increase from 54 percent to 76 percent. This is almost double the gain in learning from increasing enrollments. Obviously, if Uttar Pradesh did both, then it could achieve the same cohort mastery (88 percent) as Himachal Pradesh. But Uttar Pradesh could be two-thirds of its way to Himachal Pradesh's *cohort* performance by improving the learning of those in school, while they get only one-third of the way there by expanding enrollment.

Expanding Enrollment Does Little to Meet Education Goals

As we move from a single concept (such as doing division) to a broader assessment of skills in a domain (such as mathematics, reading, science, or history), the analysis becomes more complicated, but the same arithmetic applies, and the findings are similar. The point is obvious, but worth stressing. If a country has a shallow learning profile, this means

Table 2-3. Expanding Uttar Pradesh's grade completion to that of Himachal Pradesh while keeping the same learning per grade increases cohort mastery only modestly.

	Uttar Pradesh: Actual			Uttar Pradesh: Hypothetical scenarios		
Grade	Percent of children attaining up to grade X (Grade completion profile) I	Percent of grade able to divide (Empirical learning profile) II	Percent of cohort with given grade attainment and able to divide III (= I × II)	Uttar Pradesh learning profile, Himachal Pradesh grade completion profile IV	Uttar Pradesh grade attainment, Himachal Pradesh learning profile V	Uttar Pradesh achieves both grade completion and learning profile of Himachal Pradesh VI
0	4.0	1.9	0.1	0.0	0.0	0.0
1	0.5	31.5	0.2	0.0	0.5	0.1
2	0.9	9.6	0.1	0.0	0.6	0.2
3	1.3	5.7	0.1	0.0	0.0	0.0
4	1.8	13.5	0.2	0.0	0.0	0.0
5	7.2	12.6	0.9	0.2	2.6	0.6
6	3.5	25.3	0.9	0.3	1.5	0.6
7	5.3	37.5	2.0	1.0	3.6	1.9
8	14.6	43.1	6.3	5.2	10.7	8.8
9	17.3	63.0	10.9	12.1	15.2	16.9
10	32.1	72.0	23.1	29.0	30.4	38.1
11	6.5	80.7	5.3	13.8	6.3	16.6
12	4.9	83.7	4.1	3.7	4.9	4.4
Fraction of those aged 15–16 able to divide		54.1		65.6	76.4	88.2

Source: Author's calculations, based on ASER 2008 data (ASER 2009).

students make little progress in learning per year of schooling, and hence expanding years of schooling does not move them very far toward meeting a learning goal. It can take a lifetime to climb a mountain if the slope is too gentle.

Analysis using broad assessments gets more complicated for two reasons, one easy and one hard. The easy part is that broad assessments of a learning domain produce an entire distribution of results across students, some scoring high, some low, rather than just one yes/no for each student. I addressed this issue by moving from a spectrum of performance across students to the equivalent of a simple yes/no by using a threshold score in the distribution of student performance. As I did with PISA and TIMSS data in chapter 1, I chose a level of mastery—say, a score of 400 on the PISA exam or 420 on the TIMSS—and examined what fraction of students were above that level.

The hard part is that almost no one tests cohorts; rather, *enrolled* students are tested. Most internationally comparable examinations set the age or grade of the assessment so that nearly all students in wealthy countries are still in school, and for wealthy countries, the discrepancy between enrolled and actual cohorts is negligible. But this is not true of poorer countries. To get from an estimate of the performance of enrolled students to an estimate of cohort performance, we need the distribution of the test results for the out-of-school children—but these children are not actually tested. This is a difficult problem because we need something we don't have. To fill in the missing data, I made some assumptions that allowed me to work from the data I do have to the information I wanted, and imputed how the distributions of performance by grade would evolve.

Learning Effects of Increasing Enrollment and Attainment versus Steepening Learning Profiles: Some International Comparisons

I started by using TIMSS data to calculate how much countries can gain from enrollment expansion. Using TIMSS data is the easiest because the TIMSS sampling frame is grade-based, and the assessment tests all children in grade eight. To impute the distributions in other grades, the assumption I made for TIMSS was that the learning profile is linear and takes students from an assumed minimum of 100 to their observed score in grade eight, in equal increments.[9] For instance, the 2003 TIMSS score for the Philippines is 378, so I assumed that the total progress was $378 - 100 = 278$ over seven years of schooling; thus the increment of learning per year is 39.7 (278/7). My second assumption was that the distribution of the scores is exactly Gaussian normal, and my third

---

9. As in the previous chapter, the assumption about grade one levels is not about what a first-grader would in reality score on the TIMSS—a first-grader likely couldn't even read the test, and mechanically, I don't think scores are even meant to go this low. The assumption is entirely hypothetical and simply illustrates how a first-grader would perform on TIMSS-like units. The assumption of 100 as a minimum obviously biases the steepness of the learning profile down (compared to zero), but the assumption that progress is all learning (as opposed to persistence of better students) biases it up.

Table 2-4. Progress in universal education requires both expanding schooling and raising the learning profile.

Country	TIMSS grade 8 Avg.	TIMSS grade 8 Std. Dev.	Percent of recent 15- to 19-year-old cohort completing grade 9 or higher	Percent of a cohort estimated to exceed a minimal learning threshold of 420 — Actual (Existing grade completion profile and estimated learning profile)	Hypothetical scenarios for improvement — Expansion to universal enrollment through grade 9	Hypothetical scenarios for improvement — Learning profile steeper by one country student standard deviation	Hypothetical scenarios for improvement — Both universal enrollment and more learning
Ghana (2007)	309	92	35.9	9.7	19.7	31.4	56.9
Philippines (2003)	378	87	55.5	32.8	46.8	61.8	80.5
Colombia (2007)	380	79	53.1	30.5	47.6	57.5	82.1
Egypt (2007)	391	100	61.4	38.3	52.1	63.4	78.9
Indonesia (2007)	397	87	67.9	42.3	55.6	68.8	84
Turkey (2007)	432	109	44.5	43.3	64.4	58.6	73.5

Source: Author's calculations described in the text, using data from TIMSS (2003 and 2007 surveys) and grade attainment data from Filmer (2010).

assumption was that the dispersion of the distribution of performance, measured by its coefficient of variation, stays constant across grades.

Using these three assumptions, data from TIMSS 2003 and 2006 (TIMSS 2003, 2007) and the grade attainment data from the Demographic and Health Survey (DHS) (Filmer 2010), I calculated what fraction of a cohort was above a threshold of 420 in mathematics, a potential learning goal in mathematics for TIMSS (for an explanation of why I chose 420, see chapter 1). In table 2-4 I show TIMSS means and student standard deviations, the percentage of a cohort attaining grade nine or higher, and the fraction of the cohort testing above 420, for six developing countries with recent TIMSS data.

I am comparing grade nine achievement for two reasons. First, grade nine is typically the highest grade proposed as part of "basic" education (primary plus junior secondary), while grades above nine are typically considered "secondary" schooling—although of course, in many countries grade seven or eight ends basic schooling and grade nine is already part of the secondary cycle. Second, on a more practical level, for technical reasons I can only get grade attainment profiles of cohorts only through grade nine,[10] so it is what it is.

What if these six countries were somehow to achieve universal completion of schooling through grade nine at exactly their existing learning profile? How many more students would reach a learning goal? This actually has an easy answer: it is just the fraction who would be above 420 at grade nine. In a country like Ghana, with a very shallow learning profile, reaching universal grade nine attainment does not increase learning by much. The fraction above 420 (as one possible illustrative learning goal) increases only from 9.7 to 19.7 percent of children. Even with universal completion of grade nine (basic schooling), 80 percent of children would not meet even a minimally defined learning goal in mathematics competency.

Naturally, countries with higher initial performance get more out of expanding grade nine attainment. But in many of these countries, there are not that many children not already making it to grade nine, so the potential gains from enrollment alone are limited. For example, in Colombia, by just expanding grade nine attainment to universal, the fraction of children meeting the 420 learning threshold rises from 30 percent to 48 percent, which is a substantial gain: almost one in five children move above the 420 threshold. But still, half of children are below a learning goal at grade nine. Egypt and Indonesia move toward a universal learning goal with expanded enrollment, but only to barely above half of students above the learning goal at universal grade completion. Only in already quite high-performance countries such as Turkey would enrollment expansion alone get the country significantly more than halfway to a learning goal.

10. The technical problem is censoring. If we observe a fifteen-year-old who has only completed grade nine, he or she may later complete grade ten or grade eleven, while a fifteen-year-old who completed grade six is likely out of school. So the trade-off for a given survey is that older cohorts (such as those aged twenty-five to twenty-nine) would give less censoring and hence could estimate better the higher levels of the grade attainment profile, but would be less topical as they would be about education events often complete ten years or more prior to the survey. Since in most poor countries grade attainment through grade nine is very low, the choice was made to use cohorts aged fifteen to nineteen years and only estimate the profile through grade nine, where censoring is a minor problem.

I also ask a different hypothetical question: what if these countries did nothing to expand enrollment but somehow managed to raise their learning achievement *by a full student standard deviation?* How to do that is a big question, one that will occupy the rest of the book. But suppose that countries were able to steepen their learning profiles. In every country (excepting Turkey), raising learning achievement in this thought experiment produces much bigger learning gains than achieving universal completion by expanding enrollments. The fraction meeting the TIMSS score of 420 learning goal in Ghana goes from 9.7 percent to 31 percent—twice the gain from enrollment expansion. In Colombia, the learning goal attainment goes from 30 percent to 57 percent, and in the Philippines from 32 to 61 percent.

Not surprisingly, the combination of higher grade attainment and raising the learning profile is most effective in helping students meet a learning goal.

The decomposition of the *cohort* achievement into cohort grade completion and a learning profile is easy to see graphically. That is, the graphs are necessarily complicated as they have to collapse three dimensions (grade, score, and distribution across students) into a two-dimensional diagram. But once you get used to the graph, the point about the relative contribution getting to a higher level by either walking farther out a flat ramp or walking the same distance up a steeper ramp is easy to see.

I use Ghana's TIMSS results from 2007 to illustrate the current reality and the two scenarios. Figure 2-4a shows the reality. The "normal" distribution[11] areas (which look like onions or Christmas ornaments) at each grade level show the distribution of competence in mathematics for students at that grade level. This is based on the TIMSS mean of 309 and standard deviation of 92 (shown in table 2-4) for the performance of grade eight students. The distributions for all other grades are extrapolated using the assumptions (discussed above) of (1) a linear learning profile from a minimum of 100 in grade one to the grade eight score of 309, (2) a constant coefficient of variation across grades, and (3) a normal distribution of scores in each grade.

The total size of the "normal" shape at each grade is the proportion of the fifteen- to sixteen-year-old cohort completing that grade level or higher. For instance, since 13.8 percent of the cohort has grade seven as

---

11. These are "normal"-shaped in that they follow the equations of a Gaussian probability distribution, but the graphs are two-sided rather than the usual distributions, for entirely aesthetic reasons.

Figure 2-4a. Only 9.7 percent of a Ghanaian cohort aged 15–19 years is above a minimum learning threshold in mathematics.

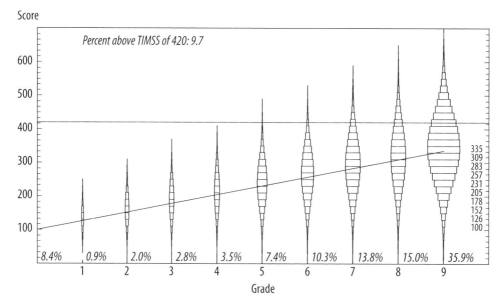

Source: Author's calculations, based on TIMSS 2007 survey data and Filmer (2010) data.
Note: The size of the distribution shape for each grade corresponds to the proportion of 15- to 19-year-olds completing the specified grade or higher. The proportion is also indicated numerically above each grade. Area of distribution shapes above 420 represents the total population above 420, which in this case is 9.7 percent.

the highest grade completed, the area of the onion shape at grade seven has 13.8 percent coverage of the total area in all of the figures.

The beauty of this graph (again, I realize it is not beautiful at first, but it will grow on you) is twofold. First, the percentage of students meeting a learning goal is just the fraction of the area of all the shapes *above* the hypothetical learning goal. In 2007, only 9.7 percent of the fifteen- to sixteen-year-old cohort was above 420—which is the cumulative area above the line at 420.

The second beauty of the graph is that it can easily illustrate two basic ways of increasing the number of students who meet a learning goal. The first way is by increasing grade attainment, which is visually pushing the area of the curves representing grade completion to the right along the same learning profile: more and more kids get to higher and higher grades, but their scores are increasing at the same learning profile pace. Figure 2-4b shows the limit of this—all students have completed grade nine, so all 100 percent of the onion-shaped "normal" area is in grade nine.

Figure 2-4b. Achieving universal grade completion in Ghana increases the proportion of students above a minimum mathematics learning threshold only from 9.7 percent to 19.7 percent.

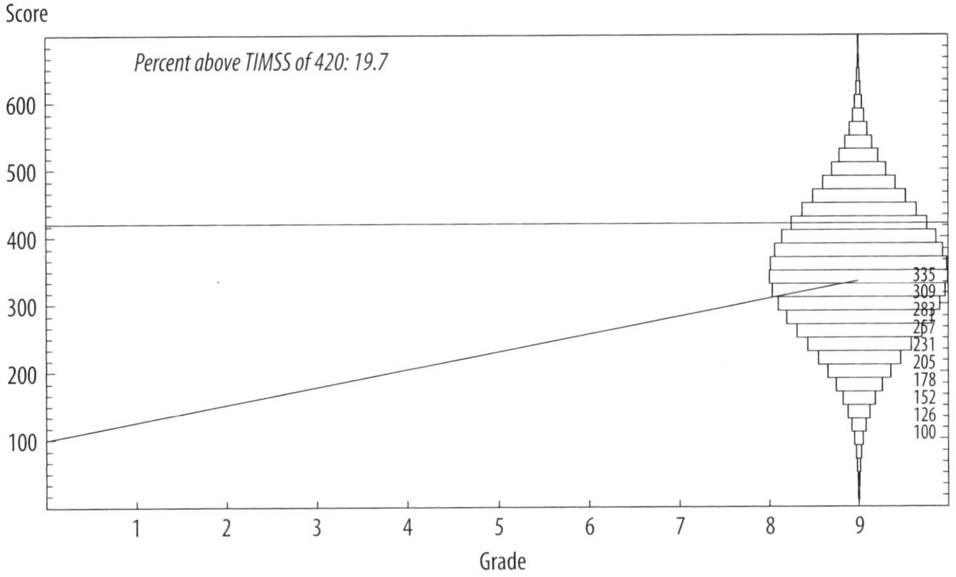

Score

Percent above TIMSS of 420: 19.7

Grade

Source: Author's calculations, based on TIMSS 2007 survey data and Filmer (2010) data.

In this case, the percentage meeting the learning goal is simple: it is just the proportion of the area of the grade nine achievement distribution above the stipulated learning goal. But since the average at grade nine is only 335, only 19.7 percent of a cohort is above 420 even with universal basic completion.

The second way of increasing the number of students who meet a learning goal is by increasing learning per grade, or steepening the profile, so that a child with the same attainment demonstrates higher achievement. Visually, this is raising how fast the onion bulbs shift up per year. What if Ghana found a way to steepen its learning profile by a student standard deviation (which, for Ghana, is 91 points)? The average child who made it to grade nine would have a score of 439 (near Turkey's current level). This means that now 31 percent of a cohort would be getting minimally adequate learning achievement. The other 69 percent still would not be above that level, but the gain from a steeper learning profile is twice as big as that achieved through reaching universal enrollment alone.

And what if Ghana managed to reach universal grade nine attainment *and* increased learning per grade? Then the fraction of children at age

Figure 2-4c. Steepening the learning profile in Ghana increases the proportion of students above a minimum mathematics learning threshold from 9.7 percent to 31.4 percent, double the increase in learning from universal grade 9 enrollment.

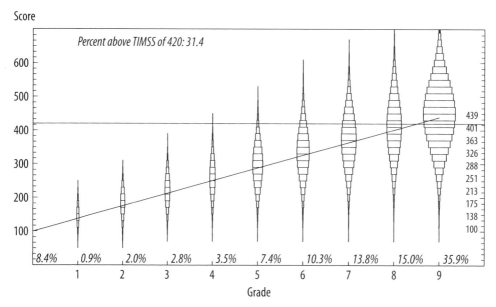

Score

Percent above TIMSS of 420: 31.4

Grade

Source: Author's calculations, based on TIMSS 2007 survey data and Filmer (2010) data.

fifteen with some modest command of mathematics (above 420) would increase from less than 10 percent to more than 50 percent.

Figure 2-5 shows four graphs together for the Philippines constructed using TIMSS 2007 survey data—base case, universal grade completion, a steeper learning profile, and both grade completion and a steeper learning profile. These show the gains from enrollment expansion and learning profile improvement separately and the gain from both. Enrollment alone gets to less than half, steepening the learning profile alone gets to around 60 percent, while with both, 80 percent are reaching the learning goal.

These illustrations using mathematics scores are just that—illustrations. The point is that reaching a high level of capability means walking very far if the walking path is nearly flat. This is true of any educational objective, from reading to creativity to tolerance to critical thinking.

These illustrations are not to be mistaken for a proposal to adopt "above 420 on TIMSS in mathematics" as a learning goal. Rather, I am making two simple points. First, the objective of school isn't school. Schooling has to be about goals measured in terms of achieved

Figure 2-5. Steepening the learning profile *and* increasing enrollment in the Philippines is the optimal strategy to maximize learning: it increases the proportion of students above a minimum mathematics learning threshold from 32.8 percent to 80.5 percent.

a. Philippines simulated cohort learning achievement profile, 2003

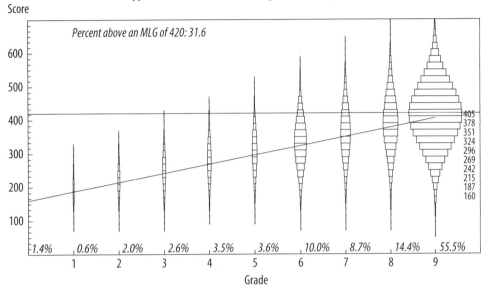

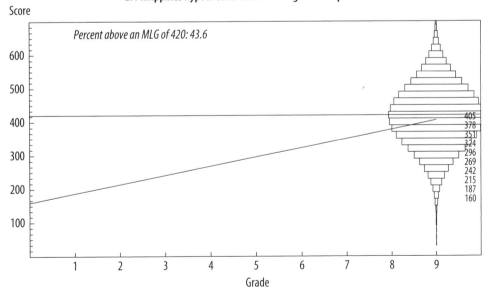
b. Philippines hypothetical at universal grade completion

Source: Author's calculations, based on TIMSS 2007 survey data and Filmer (2010) data.

(continued)

Figure 2-5. Steepening the learning profile *and* increasing enrollment in the Philippines is the optimal strategy to maximize learning: it increases the proportion of students above a minimum mathematics learning threshold from 32.8 percent to 80.5 percent. (*continued*)

c. Philippines same grade completion, profile steeper by a student standard deviation

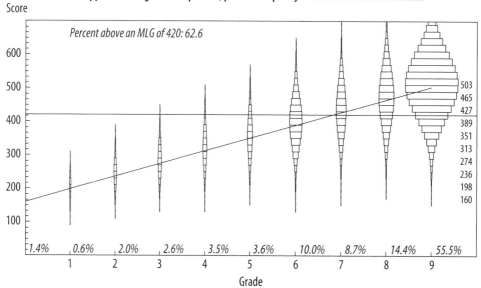

Percent above an MLG of 420: 62.6

−1.4%   0.6%   2.0%   2.6%   3.5%   3.6%   10.0%   8.7%   14.4%   55.5%

Grade

d. Philippines universal and profile steeper

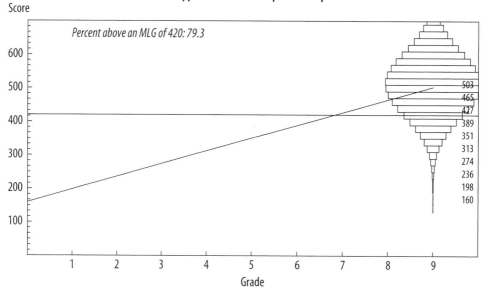

Percent above an MLG of 420: 79.3

Grade

Source: Author's calculations, based on TIMSS 2007 survey data and Filmer (2010) data.

capabilities. What exactly these desired capabilities are is up to the society (and parents and students) to decide, and there will be many; they could be reading, mathematics, citizenship, creativity, the ability to learn, critical thinking, appreciation of poetry, and tolerance of others, but schooling has to be *something* other than just sitting in school. Second, if the relationship between the school learning objectives and time in school is weak, as in Ghana, then expanding time in school doesn't help with the education goal that much. My use of the mathematics scores from TIMSS is not meant to argue for a "back to basics" approach to education in which math has priority, or to argue that TIMSS's approach to assessment is better or worse than any other, or even that "standardized testing" is the best way to assess student mastery. But schooling is the means, while education—however defined—is the end.

I can do similar calculations for other approaches to assessment with other subjects, such as with the PISA 2009 and 2009+ round,[12] and get the same basic results. As discussed in chapter 1, PISA is an age-based (not grade-based) test of enrolled students (not a cohort), so results show what fraction of the enrolled cohort is below any given standard, rather than the fraction of the total cohort that is below the standard. PISA data can be used to answer the question, if *all* students (including those who did not enroll or who dropped out) had the same distribution of performance of the *enrolled* students, what fraction would still be below a learning goal?

Figure 2-6 shows the fraction of enrolled fifteen-year-old students below level 2 learning in the most recent PISA results.[13] (This is the average fraction across reading, mathematics, and science.) Ten of the nineteen countries or states have half or more fifteen-year-old students—even of those still in school—with below level 2 proficiency.[14] Hence, even if all students stayed in school to age fifteen (at which age students are typically in grade eight, nine, or ten), at the same distribution of learning, less than half would be at a minimally adequate level of learning.

In using internationally comparable standardized assessments such as PISA and TIMSS, I am not arguing for a particular learning goal or standard based on the existing global comparisons. Exactly the same calculations of learning profiles that lead to learning goals could be done

12. See www.oecd.org/document/61/0,3746,en_32252351_32235731_46567613_1_1_1_1,00.html.

13. PISA classifies students by their level of performance based on their score, where levels have specific descriptions in each of the three subject areas. Subjects have either five or six levels.

14. All points on the graph represent countries with the exception of Himachal Pradesh, India (HP-Ind), Tamil Nadu, India (TN-Ind), and Miranda, Venezuela (MI-Vez).

Figure 2-6. Most students enrolled at age 15 in most developing countries are far from achieving adequate learning.

Percent of students below PISA level 2 proficiency, by country

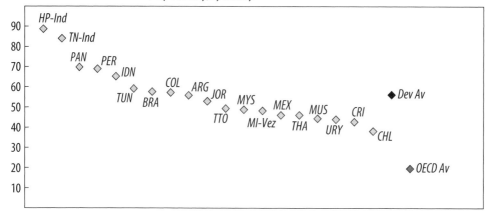

Source: PISA (2009, tables I.2.1, I.3.1, and I.3.4).

Note: Definition of "developing" for the developing country average (Dev Av) excludes all former Soviet or Eastern bloc countries, the high-performing East Asian countries (such as Korea and Singapore), wealthy Persian Gulf countries (such as Qatar and the United Arab Emirates), and the estimates for Shanghai, China. Developing country average is unweighted. Country codes are UN standard codes.

with national or regional standards. For instance, the Southern and Eastern Africa Consortium for Monitoring Educational Quality (SACMEQ) does reading and mathematics assessments of in-school grade six children in fourteen African countries. SACMEQ has devised its own scale and levels: eight levels for reading (from "pre-reading" to "critical reading," with level 3 as "basic reading") and eight for mathematics (from "pre-numeracy" to "abstract problem solving," with level 3 as "basic numeracy").[15]

15. The descriptions of these basic levels are as follows: Basic reading (level 3): Interprets meaning (by matching words and phrases, completing a sentence, or matching adjacent words) in a short and simple text by reading on or reading back. Example test items: (a) uses context and simple sentence structure to match words and phrases, (b) uses phrases within sentences as units of meaning, (c) locates adjacent words and information in a sentence. Basic numeracy (level 3): Translates verbal information presented in a sentence, simple graph, or table using one arithmetic operation in several repeated steps. Translates graphical information into fractions. Interprets place value of whole numbers up to thousands. Interprets simple, common, everyday units of measurement. Example test items: (a) recognizes three-dimensional shapes and number units, (b) use a single arithmetic operation in two or more steps, (c) converts single-step units using division (SACMEQ 2010).

The results of the 2007 round of assessments (SACMEQ 2010), presented in table 2-5, show that in mathematics, three quarters or more of sixth-graders do not reach above level 3 in Malawi, Zambia, Lesotho, Uganda, Namibia, or Mozambique. Nearly four in ten do not reach above level 3 in every country but Mauritius.[16]

What if SACMEQ participants expanded enrollment and grade attainment? These southern and East African countries have relatively high grade completion rates (compared to West Africa or the Sahel), so there is not much scope for gains in cohort learning goals from expansions in primary school completion. If one set a learning goal for primary schooling as mastering even above level 3 competencies, and even if these countries attained universal grade six enrollment, the majority of students would still fall short of a learning goal in mathematics; and a large plurality would fall short in reading.

For example, in South Africa, already over 90 percent of youth complete grade six or more, so reaching universal grade six schooling, even if it raised the non-completers to the level of capability of those in grade six, would, under the most optimistic assumptions, add only 3.2 percentage points to the fraction of the cohort with adequate skills. That is, suppose that all children who did not complete grade six did not attain above level 3 in mathematics. Then the cohort average would be 92.4 percent grade six completers times 30.8 percent of grade six completers at level 4 or above, plus 7.6 percent non-completers times 0 percent at level 4 or above, which equals 28.4 percent at level 4 or above. At a 100 percent completion rate, this would be equal to those who are now in grade 6, which is 30.8 percent. So reaching universal enrollment would add, at best, two percentage points to the fraction reaching an "above level 3 competence" learning goal. In contrast, in Kenya, 61.7 percent of enrolled students are at a level that is 30 percentage points ahead. Put differently, the difference between the percentage of students at mathematics level 3 or below is more than 30 percentage points higher in Kenya than in South Africa. So the gain to South African learning from having Kenya's learning profile is ten times as big as the predicted gain from expanding enrollment (a 29.7-percentage-point increase in the percent of students at acceptable mathematics competency) versus pushing for universal primary school completion (a 2.3-percentage-point increase in the percent of students at mathematics level 4 or above).

16. Comparisons with Botswana on TIMSS or Mauritius on PISA suggest these standards appear less stringent relative to grade level than the "international low benchmarks" of TIMSS or PISA (as many fewer are behind the level 3 levels than are behind comparable low benchmarks).

Table 2-5. Achieving universal primary schooling (grade 6) would not bring even half of students in most countries to regionally adequate levels in reading or mathematics.

Country/Region	Percent of 15- to 19-year-old cohort attaining grade 6 or higher (year)	Percent of students reading at level 3 or below	Percent of students achieving mathematics level 3 or below	Gains in the percent of a cohort at minimal competence (above level 3) in mathematics	
				Through universal grade 6 (upper bound calculation)[c]	Having Kenya's learning profile
Malawi	57.2 (2005)	73.3	91.7	3.6	53.5
Zambia	72.6 (2007)	72.7	91.8	2.2	53.2
Lesotho	75.6 (2009)	52.5	81.1	4.6	37.8
Uganda	54.1 (2006)	45.9	74.9	11.5	31.4
Namibia	82.1 (2006–07)	38.7	81.7	3.3	31.2
Mozambique	22.9 (2003)	43.5	74.2	19.9	29.8
South Africa	92.4 (2005)	48.3	69.2	2.3	29.7
Zanzibar	n.a.	21.4	73.4	n.a.	18.4
Zimbabwe	92.4 (2005–06)	37.2	57.3	3.2	18.2
Botswana[a]	n.a.	24.2	56.4	n.a.	11.3
Seychelles	n.a.	22	42.3	n.a.	3.1
Kenya	81.2 (2008–09)	19.8	38.3	11.6	0.0
Tanzania	78.0 (2010)	10.1	43.1	12.5	−2.5
Swaziland	75.2 (2006)	7	44.3	13.8	−3.4
Mauritius[b]	n.a.	21.1	26.7	n.a.	−5.2

Source: SACMEQ (2010) for learning levels, Filmer (2010) for cohort grade attainment.

a. Percent of grade 8 students below a low benchmark (400) on TIMSS 2007 Mathematics: 68 percent, versus 56.4 percent at or below SACMEQ level 3.

b. Percent of students age 15 below level 2 in PISA 2009+: Reading, 36.2 percent; Mathematics, 46.8 percent versus 21.1 percent; and 26.7 percent at or below level 3 in SACMEQ.

c. Assuming that zero percent of children completing less than grade 6 are at level 4.

n.a. = Not available.

Why Setting Education Objectives and Tracking Progress in Meeting Them Is Essential (and Why Specific Metrics Are Less So)

It is important to note that I have no particular stake in the particular calculations I have just shown. I don't care whether PISA or TIMSS or SACMEQ or any other particular international testing metric is used.

Nor am I advocating for the importance of mathematics or reading or science skills over any other skill set that schooling sets out to achieve. I use quantitative measures of standard skills because these are the data I have, not because I am pushing for achievement on *these measures* rather than on any other set of educational outcomes as the goals of education, such as the ability to work in groups, communicate effectively, or think critically. There are many who oppose "testing" because they feel that putting "high stakes" on certain dimensions of education goals will detract from other dimensions of education. But there is nothing intrinsic in a cohort learning approach that specifies which dimensions of competencies/skills/abilities are to be assessed, or how those could be assessed. And, as I will show, the "no assessment" option has risks of its own. If I had data for those outcomes, I would use them too, and I strongly suspect, for example, that "critical thinking" data would produce similar results. Unlike the debates in wealthy countries about the relative emphasis on different educational outcomes for students mostly already with mastery of basics, I highly doubt (but for lack of any relevant data cannot conclusively prove) that students in India who cannot read or count nevertheless somehow manage to excel at "critical thinking" or "creativity."

Data on reading, mathematics, and science are available because these domains are universally regarded as relevant in every education system. That is, every education system claims it teaches children reading and mathematics and science. If educational systems want to encourage students' ability to think creatively, analyze arguments critically, work with others from diverse backgrounds effectively, or any other new basic skill, there is no reason in principle these skills and domains could not be assessed and included in a country's learning goals.

I am not arguing for an international standard versus national or even regional standards, so I am not going to defend 420 versus 440 versus 380 versus any other level, nor am I arguing for any particular approach to assessment, such as the "curricular mastery" versus "life skills and applications" approach.

I am advocating for education systems to measure and work to achieve their *education* goals—whatever they are. And calculations like cohort learning profiles are essential to understanding what you are achieving. The basic finding I am highlighting with a variety of measures (such as ability to perform simple division versus mathematics versus reading) and at a variety of levels of mastery (using country, regional, international benchmarks) is robust: (1) the *education* objectives of *schooling* are not being reached at anything like the pace they need to for children to be equipped for their futures and (2) expanding years of schooling at the current pace of learning just won't help that much. This basic finding emerges no matter which subject matter or skill set is tested, no matter which method is employed, because schooling is already high and learning is still low. More schooling—which is the easiest thing for the existing educational organizations and the education movement itself to promote—will not solve the education problem.

The False Dichotomy of "Quantity" versus "Quality"

School is the fiercest thing you can come up against.
Factories ain't no cinch, but schools is worst.

GIRL WORKING IN A FACTORY IN EARLY TWENTIETH-CENTURY CHICAGO (TYACK 1974)

These illustrations of the relative impact of enrollment and attainment versus learning should not lead to simplistic interpretations or premature policy conclusions. A focus on cohort learning goals can restore the true purpose of education systems and obviate the false debate over "quantity" versus "quality." That is, many have legitimately opposed the view that to maintain quality for students already enrolled, the pace of enrollment expansion needs to be limited. However, in a cohort-based assessment of learning distributions, both quantity (moving along the learning profile by increasing attainment) and quality (raising the learning profile) are essential. With measures of the entire distribution of cohort learning, targets can be based on averages, inequalities, or minimal achievements to reflect any array of education goals.[17] Cohort-based measures of learning do not intrinsically favor quality over quantity, as both are fundamental to achieving universal learning goals.

Moreover, no one could sensibly argue for quantity if in fact learning profiles in all relevant domains, including cognitive and noncognitive skills, were truly flat. Some justify low performance on cognitive skills assessments by saying, "Well, it is okay if students are not learning much math or reading; the important thing is that they are in school." But no one wants kids to sit in a building called a school just because it is a building called a school. Some argue that through the *experience* of

17. There is a close analogy with the distribution of income across households. If one knows the entire distribution, then one can talk about goals for average income, for inequality-adjusted average income, for poverty (those in the distribution below a certain point), and so forth, all based on the same distribution.

school, children will acquire other traits societies or nation-states desire, such as a sense of appropriate behavior (for example, obedience to authority), social solidarity, national pride, religious faith, or admiration of Mao or Atatürk, even if they don't learn anything else. But what a cruel trick that is to play on children! That is, if year after year, schools pretend to teach math or reading or science while not really caring whether kids learn math or reading or science as these subjects are really only a pretext to achieve other goals, well, forcing that on kids is just plain mean.

When It Is (Nearly) All Dropout

In this chapter, I have developed scenarios using mechanical calculations to show the consequences of expanding enrollment without improving learning quality. Certainly when enrollment is limited by physical access or ability to pay, policies can expand enrollments even at constant quality. However, the massive success of expanding schooling facilities implies that pure access-based deficits in grade completion are mostly small. The question is why children drop out, and what can be done about it. If children drop out of school because of the low quality of the instruction, then the scenarios presented above for the scope for improvements in learning through enrollment expansion, even as small as they are, overstate the potential for quantity expansion, as you cannot get it without quality.

As I mentioned in the beginning of this chapter, and as shown in figure 2-1, attainment deficits around the world are increasingly the result of students dropping out, rather than nonenrollment. Countries like Mali, where less than 50 percent of children ever enroll or complete grade one, are thankfully a minority. Colombia is more representative of the majority. The grade completion profile of a fifteen- to nineteen-year-old female cohort in 1995 is shown in figure 2-7.[18] Nearly every child started school, but only 40 percent completed grade nine or higher. One can calculate the total deficit between years of schooling and grade nine completion. For example, those with no schooling would need nine years, those who dropped out in grade five would need four more years, and so on.[19] The obvious point is that in a country like Colombia, the "never enrollment"

18. I am using data from 1995 and for females only, since that is when the question about reasons for dropping out, used below in table 2-7, was asked.

19. The school year deficit can be decomposed into the proportion of the deficit due to nonenrollment and due to children who enrolled but did not reach grade nine.

Figure 2-7. Most of the attainment problem in Colombia is due to high dropout rates, not low enrollment.

Percent with grade completion or higher

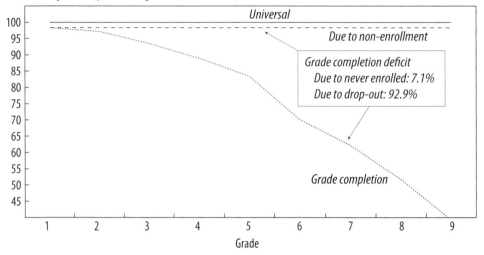

Source: Author's calculations, based on Filmer (2010) data.

problem is small, so the completion deficit due to those who never enrolled is also small (even though some children completely lack schooling). Thus, strategies to meet attainment goals should be focused on keeping kids in school and progressing through grades.

Looking at a handful of other countries, in table 2-6 I show the proportion of the total deviation from grade nine completion due to "never enrollment."[20] There is little remaining dropout in many countries where few children are meeting basic levels of proficiency. In middle-income countries such as Egypt, Indonesia, the Philippines, or South Africa, any reasonable calculation of learning goals would show that half or more of the cohort reaches the end of basic education ill-equipped for a future in the workforce or citizenry. But in these countries almost every child enrolls. For instance, in Peru, the PISA results show that two-thirds of a recent cohort—those in school—are below low international benchmarks

20. I chose grade nine because in many countries, schooling goals are moving to beyond primary school.

Table 2-6. In very few countries is much of the deficit in universal grade 9 completion attributable to children never having enrolled in school.

Selected countries	Percent of cohort aged 15–19 who completed grade 1 or higher	Total deficit from universal grade 9 completion (average years)	Proportion of the total deficit from universal grade 9 completion due to "never enrolled"
Peru 2004	99.4	0.8	0.07
South Africa 2005	99.0	1.0	0.09
Colombia 2010	98.9	1.1	0.09
Indonesia 2007	98.8	1.0	0.11
Philippines 2003	98.6	1.3	0.10
Mexico 2002	97.2	1.2	0.22
Egypt 2008	93.2	1.4	0.42
Tanzania 2010	91.7	2.6	0.29
Ghana 2008	91.6	2.3	0.32
Malawi 2005	91.4	3.3	0.23
Bangladesh 2007	89.6	3.1	0.30
India 2005–06	84.7	2.5	0.55
Nigeria 2008	80.0	2.8	0.64
Pakistan 2006–07	73.0	3.9	0.62
Mali 2006	42.7	6.3	0.80

Source: Author's calculations, based on Filmer (2010) data.

in reading, mathematics, and science. And yet few children never enroll—99.4 percent of the cohort aged fifteen to nineteen years in 2004 had completed at least grade one. This means that the issue of access is nearly irrelevant in Peru's deficit from any learning goal.

Even in relatively poor countries, such as Ghana, Malawi, or Tanzania, the proportion of the total grade completion deficit is less than a third. This means that two-thirds of the grade attainment deficit is due to children who attended school but dropped out before reaching grade nine. Of course, there are some places where access is still a major issue, as I illustrated above with Mali (see figure 2-1), but ever enrollment is not a major challenge to universal grade nine attainment in most countries.

The scope for expansion of schooling through expansion of physical access to schooling is nearing an end. Using regressions that predict child enrollment, Filmer (2007) estimated the relationship between child enrollment and distance to school in twenty-one low-income countries and calculated that even if an expansion in access meant the average distance to a primary school was zero, the typical country increase in enrollment would be less than one percentage point. This is not to say that expanding access isn't important in some places. Filmer estimated that in Mali, it would have gone up ten percentage points. There is no question that building schools expands enrollment when there has been a lack of physical access. But as a result of the tremendous success of the schooling agenda, those places are fewer and fewer. Recent rigorous evaluations have found that school construction, even when combined with school improvements, has mixed impacts. For instance, an evaluation of the construction of improved schools in Burkina Faso found a substantial impact on enrollments, attendance, and learning (Levy et al. 2009), but in Niger, a country with low enrollments, a program of school construction and improvement had very limited impact on enrollment (only 4.3 percentage points) and no discernible impact on attendance or child learning.

Nearly all of the expansion in schooling will be convincing children to stay in school (and their parents to keep them there). Do children stay in school when not learning?

Why Do Children Drop Out?

If you can follow what is going on, and perhaps even excel in the classroom, then school is fun. You get to do something you are good at, make progress, and get repeated positive feedback (and avoid other tasks, such as gathering firewood or tending goats). People for whom school is fun tend to do more of it, and many become researchers and professors. These people then write books about, among other things, education. The irony is that these people are the least likely to really "get" the retention problem. After all, how likely is it that a person who did ten more years of schooling than legally required will have good intuition for why others quit school? People adept at school find intrinsic enjoyment in it, in addition to its instrumental value, and thus have a hard time understanding why not everyone wants to go to more school.

In the perfectly legitimate interest of promoting schooling, advocates often lose sight of what a miserable and alienating experience school can be. Particularly for adept and intellectually brilliant researchers who attended excellent schools, it takes a tremendous leap of empathy from their own conditions to those of children in Uttar Pradesh. Imagine you are one of the half of the fifth-grade class that still cannot read. The teacher's writing on the board, textbooks, and workbook exercises on any subject mean nothing to you. You realize you are falling further and further behind but do not know what to do about it, nor does anyone seem to care. Worse, a recent survey found that 29 percent of children in India—and a much higher rate among the poor—were "beaten or pinched" in school in the immediate past month (Desai et al. 2008). A study examining "child-friendly" teacher classroom behavior in five states in India found that in less than a third of classrooms were students observed asking teachers questions; and in only about one in five classrooms was the teacher ever observed to "smile/laugh/joke" with *any* student (Bhattacharjea, Wadhwa, and Banerji 2011)—and if you are a low-performing student, perhaps with you least of all.

Being unable to follow the lessons, getting pinched or beaten, and not learning make school unpleasant at best. The Educational Initiatives study (2010) compared the language and math scores of students according to characteristics about themselves, the schools they attended, and their teachers. The simple cross-tabulations reveal that the single biggest factor associated with test scores was whether students found school "boring and not useful" (average test score 40.6) or "fun and useful" (average test score 56.4). Whether this is because bored children do not learn, or because if a child is behind and not learning, school is a boring place, one cannot say, but these definitely go together.

But what are the reasons for dropping out? Education studies are dominated by analysis of factors that "pull" children out of school— poverty, the need to work, or marriage. But this is perhaps because researchers like school and assume that others do too. Pull factors are indeed important. The Demographic and Health Surveys (DHS) in the 1990s asked girls why they dropped out of school. As shown in table 2-7, family reasons (about a quarter) and economic reasons (about another quarter) were, naturally, significant factors.

But "push" factors also influenced girls' drop-out decisions. In Colombia's 1995 DHS survey, the most frequent reason given for why girls dropped out of school, noted by 31 percent, was "did not like school." Simple arithmetic shows that not liking school is an enormously larger problem for expanding grade completion than is access. (Since I showed in figure 2-6 that 93 percent of the attainment deficit in Colombia is due to dropout and 7 percent is due to nonenrollment, 31 percent of the

Table 2-7. Worldwide, about half of girls report leaving school for reasons that pull them out, such as poverty or family, but many report leaving school because they just do not like it or they did not pass exams.

Country/Year	Reasons given for dropping out of school for those who had enrolled but did not complete secondary schooling (percent)					
	Family (got pregnant, got married, family needed help, taking care of children)	Economic (could not pay fees, needed to earn money)	Did not pass exams, done enough	Did not like school	School not accessible	Other/don't know
Median	24.5	25.6	6.5	16.0	2.4	10.0
LAC (6)	21.4	27.2	4.1	24.7	4.5	9.2
Middle East (2)	36.1	26.3	1.8	16.2	8.7	10.9
Francophone Africa (10)	18.1	19.6	25.1	18.7	1.9	13.8
East/Southern Africa (10)	32.4	25.6	6.2	5.3	1.4	9.7
Asia (5)	29.1	52.5	5.3	5.8	2.5	7.3

Source: Author's calculations, using DHS Statcompiler (http://statcompiler.com/).

93 percent of the attainment deficit due to dropout is bigger than 7 percent of the attainment deficit due to "never enrolled.") It is impossible to know more about why they did not like school, but it is conceivable that the frustration from low learning progression may play a big role.

The simple point is this: it is hard to make children who are not learning, and who know they are not learning, stay in school. The calculations above about how much could be done for learning with enrollment expansion alone implicitly assume that achieving universal grade completion is possible with unchanged learning. But this assumption is dubious. Conversely, almost certainly improving learning will keep more kids in school longer.

Keeping Kids in School—and Learning

Much of the recent education research has been devoted to two initiatives largely focused on expanding enrollments: eliminating charges for schools and conditional cash transfer programs (which started in Latin America and spread). Both these initiatives have been successful in putting more kids in schools, but neither has been shown to improve the learning

Table 2-8. Abolishing government primary school fees in Kenya in 2003 was associated with increased enrollment almost exclusively in private schools—which did not charge fees.

Type of school	Net enrollment (percent) 1997	Net enrollment (percent) 2006	Percentage point increase/decrease 1997–2006	Percent of total increase in enrollment rates by type of school
Government primary	71.2	71.6	0.4	7.3
Private primary	3.8	8.9	5.1	92.7
Total primary	75	80.5	5.5	100.0
Government secondary	14.2	17.1	2.9	67.4
Private secondary	2.4	3.8	1.4	32.6
Total secondary	16.6	20.9	4.3	100.0

Source: Adapted from Bold et al. (2011, table 1).

profile (Fiszbein and Schady 2009), and whether either one increases learning at all has found mixed results.

In January 2003, Kenya adopted a free primary education policy and abolished all fees in government-controlled primary schools, with the goal of increasing enrollments. Enrollments increased from 1997 to 2006, but nearly all of the net increase was in private schools, which did not eliminate fees. Moreover, the increase in the net enrollment rate in government primary schools, which eliminated user fees, was 0.4 percentage points, compared to 2.9 percentage points in government secondary schools, which did not eliminate user fees. One reading of this experience (Bold et al. 2011) is that the government's attempt to make the schools cheaper in the interest of expanding enrollment and attainment caused parents to think that quality had gone down (as many of the fees were locally controlled and used for school inputs). This led to weak increased demand for government-controlled schools, while the relative price in money terms fell; and enrollment in government schools fell precipitously for the children of higher-educated parents. Strikingly, the proportion of additional enrollment that went to government schooling was much higher for the secondary sector (67 percent) that did not eliminate fees than for the primary sector that did (only 7.3 percent) (table 2-8).

Malawi adopted free public education in 1994. The fraction of a fifteen- to nineteen-year-old cohort with no schooling fell from 26.4 percent in 1992 to 8.6 percent in 2005. During this same time period, the fraction of the cohort finishing grade six or above rose from 31 percent to 57.2 percent—a huge improvement. However, the SACMEQ 2007 results show that only 26.7 percent of those in grade six could read with even minimum proficiency, and only 8.6 percent had minimal numeracy skills (see table 2-6). If these additional 26.7 percent of grade six completers from free public education had average 2007 learning levels (which is an optimistic assumption), only an additional 7 percent of children reached a reading goal and only 2.2 percent reached a numeracy goal.[21]

Conditional cash transfers (CCTs) induce children to go to school by conditioning their household's receipt of targeted transfers on enrollment or attendance. This has become a popular policy tool, shown to increase attainment in a large-scale randomized experiment in Mexico (Behrman, Sengupta, and Todd 2005), and has spread from its origins in Mexico (where it was formerly known as PROGRESA and is now known as Oportunidades) and Brazil to more than thirty other countries. However, if the child dropped out because he or she was not learning in school, there is nothing about the program that helps that. Intriguingly, the initial evaluation of PROGRESA, which many cite in claiming that CCTs "work," found no impact on learning at all (Behrman, Sengupta, and Todd 2005).[22] Of course, if CCTs do nothing to raise the learning profile and the children who dropped out of school did so because they were not learning, then the increment in learning from a program that financially induces them to go back to those same schools so that their family might qualify for cash from the government could, unsurprisingly, be even less than that of the typical enrolled child. CCTs are a wonderful mechanism to transfer purchasing power to poor households, but at best, we should expect only modest impacts on learning.

The recent results of the centralized secondary school leaving examination in Tanzania illustrate a possible scenario. After implementation of a variety of policies for expanding schooling, the number of students sitting for the examination expanded massively from 2008 to 2011. Almost 200,000 more students took the examination in 2011 than in

---

21. Intriguingly, the 1998 version of SACMEQ found that 55 percent of Malawian students achieved level 4 literacy or above, and in 2000 the cohort had completion rates of 45.5 percent. So, if the tests are reliable and the comparison is valid (the tests are meant to be comparable), then the fraction of a cohort with adequate literacy may actually have *fallen* over time, as the increases in enrollment more than offset decreases in learning.

22. The findings on this subject are rare, as most studies evaluate only additional attendance (e.g., Glewwe and Kassouf 2010 for Brazil) and are mixed, as some more recent evaluations have found learning impacts (e.g., Baird, MacIntosh, and Ozler 2010).

Figure 2-8. From 2008 to 2011, the number of students in Tanzania who completed secondary school doubled, but in absolute numbers fewer passed the examination.

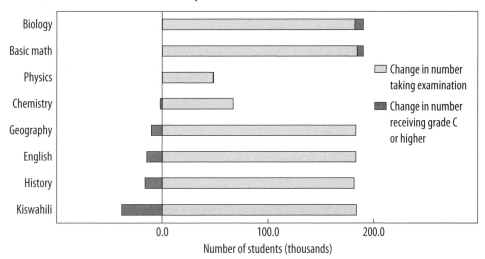

Source: Author's calculations, based on CSEE data (Tanzania Ministry of Education and Vocational Training, 2012).

2008. This rapid expansion might have kept weaker students in school all the way to schooling completion, so perhaps the *proportion* passing the examination would fall but the total number would go up. But that is not what happened. In many subjects (including compulsory subjects such as Kiswahili) the absolute number passing the examination at a grade C level or higher fell in absolute terms. In history, 151,000 took the exam in 2008, and 33,000 passed; in 2011, 332,000 (more than double the 2008 figure) took the exam, and only 17,000 passed (figure 2-8).

More Is Not Enough

More schooling is insufficient in itself to answer the need for improved basic education. The learning profiles by grade in the developing world today are just too flat. Reaching the Millennium Development Goal of universal primary schooling completion will not bring anything that could properly be called universal education. We know that with certainty, since many countries have met the Millennium Development Goal target and do not provide adequate education, with millions of children completing primary schooling lacking even literacy and numeracy. Moreover, even achieving universal basic schooling—or, at the shallow learning profiles often observed, even universal secondary schooling—would not bring most countries near a minimal threshold of learning.

This is not to say that aiming for universal enrollment and primary (and basic, and perhaps even secondary) school attainment is not important; of course it is. But as we near these goals, it is time to admit the world needs more than schooling, it needs more education. The difficult question is, can the same techniques that led to the success in expanding quantity work for learning?

CHAPTER 3

More of the Same Is Just More of the Same

It would be nice (and easy) if the goal of universal education could be met in the same way as the goal of universal schooling: apply more of the same, and eventually children will be equipped for the twenty-first century. If this were so, then the same coalition of advocacy, altruism, and self-interest could segue from a schooling goal, like the Millennium Development Goal, to learning and education goals without innovation, disruption, or change from the existing "access axis," which has been successful in putting together a powerful coalition for expanding schooling. But a wish is not a plan, much less a plan grounded in evidence about what "more of the same" would actually achieve. In this chapter I marshal evidence to show four things:

If their current pace of progress remains unchanged, most developing countries will take centuries to reach acceptable levels of student learning.

No developing country has an evidence-based plan for achieving significant progress in education. Nearly all countries have plans to spend more on inputs and will call that "quality," but none has a plan for increasing student capabilities.

Copying the educational fads of rich countries will not work: the pedagogical and educational problems of developing countries are entirely different from those of more developed countries.

System change and the diffusion of innovations, rather than just more of existing inputs, are needed to meet education or learning goals.

This is not to say that inputs cannot affect learning in developing countries; they do. But replicating or augmenting the external trappings of good schools does not make a good school. Without the animating drive that is at the heart of any functional school, adding more of one or another input won't make much difference. This is the lesson of Frankenstein: while most people have two arms, stitching arms on a cadaver does not make a living person; conversely, people can lose an arm and still be functional. Appearances can be forced from outside, but performance is driven from within.

The Current Pace of Learning Progress in Developing Countries Is Slow

Chapter 1 documented the magnitude of low learning in developing countries. But, it may be argued, although things are bad now, perhaps they are getting better. Perhaps the same "business as usual" approach that successfully expanded enrollments will also, just left to its own devices, lead to better learning outcomes.

Data that track learning over time are difficult to come by. However, the ASER data for India have been collected for the last seven years, and cross-country international assessments like PISA and TIMSS and SACMEQ test the same concepts with the same age or grade cohorts over time. All of these tell the same story: progress in the measured learning of children is often negative, and even when it is positive, the pace of progress is typically very slow. Only a very few countries show rapid progress. Extrapolating current trends shows that it will take anywhere from "forever" (for countries going backward) to a century or more for countries to reach minimally adequate levels of capability in basic literacy and numeracy.

ASER in India has been testing almost a half a million children a year since 2005. As figure 3-1 shows, things are getting worse. The percentage of grade five students who cannot read a story at the grade two level has been *rising* over the past seven years. The fraction of students in grade

Figure 3-1. India's progress is retrogressive: more and more children cannot read a story or do division, even as they reach grade 5.

Percent of grade 5 students who can . . .

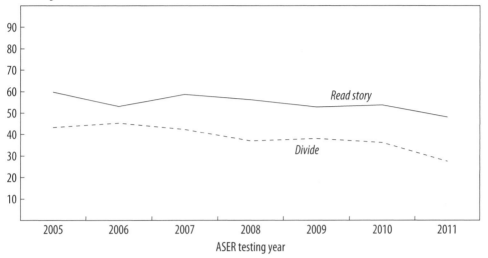

Source: Author's calculations with Barro-Lee data on years of schooling, POLITY IV for Democracy-Autocracy, ICRG for Control of Corruption, and Freedom House for Civil Liberties (see Data Sources).

five who cannot do division has stayed the same or gone up over the past seven years. Obviously, if progress is retrogress, it will take forever to reach learning targets.

Perhaps India is an exception. So we might ask, what is the pace of learning outside India? The easiest way to examine progress over time is to measure it using a student standard deviation or an international assessment (from PISA- or TIMSS-like instruments) student standard deviation (IASSD) because these normed scores are at least somewhat comparable across countries and time. On PISA and TIMSS, scores are normed so that the IASSD is 100 points for OECD students on a 500-point scale. As we saw in chapter 1, nearly all developing countries, including many middle-income countries, would need to gain at least 100 and sometimes 200 or more international assessment points to achieve the OECD learning level of 500.

Eight developing countries participated in the TIMSS mathematics and science assessment in either 1995 or 1999 and 2007. This amounts to only twelve (or eight) years of data, but it provides some sense of the direction and magnitude of change. In six of the eight countries, mathematics scores fell between the first available year, either 1995 or 1999, and 2007. In some countries, such as Jordan and Indonesia, the fall was

Table 3-1. Progress in learning achievement of grade 8 students on the TIMSS is slow (or moving backward) in many countries.

Country (year if not 1999)	Mathematics					Science				
	1999 (or 1995)	2007	Points per year gain (loss)	Years to gain 100 points (one SSD)	Years to reach a score of 500	1999 (or 1995)	2007	Points per year gain (loss)	Years to gain 100 points (one SSD)	Years to reach a score of 500
Colombia (1995)	332	380	4.00	25	30	365	417	4.33	23	19
Indonesia	403	397	−0.74	Forever	Forever	435	427	−1.06	Forever	Forever
Iran (1995)	418	403	−1.22	Forever	Forever	463	459	−0.34	Forever	Forever
Jordan	428	427	−0.10	Forever	Forever	450	482	3.92	25	5
Malaysia	519	474	−5.67	Forever	Forever	492	471	−2.70	Forever	Forever
Thailand	467	441	−3.25	Forever	Forever	482	471	−1.46	Forever	Forever
Tunisia	448	420	−3.44	Forever	Forever	430	445	1.92	52	29
Turkey	429	432	0.35	285	194	433	454	2.64	38	17
Median			**−0.98**	**Forever**	**Forever**			**0.79**	**126**	**55**

Source: Pritchett and Beatty (2012). Data from National Center for Education Statistics (http://nces.ed.gov/surveys/international/table-library.asp).

a small amount, but in some scores fell by more than 20 points (Thailand, Tunisia, and Malaysia). Intriguingly, in science, there were more countries with improvement, but learning fell in half the countries.

If mathematics capability in your country is moving at the typical pace observed in the countries that participated in the TIMSS, then your average score is *falling* by about one point per year (table 3-1). At that rate, your students will never catch up, and your country is falling further and further behind. At the pace of the median country's progress in science, with a gain of 0.79 points per year, a country would take 126 years to gain 100 points (or one IASSD). If your child is average, at 400, then perhaps her great-great-great-great grandchild will reach OECD levels of learning.

We used data from fourteen countries or regions in eastern and southern Africa that have been participating in regional mathematics and reading tests, the SACMEQ (Southern and Eastern Africa Consortium for Measuring Educational Quality), since either 1995 or 2000.[1] These tests are different from PISA or TIMSS in that they assess students earlier, in sixth grade, but are similar in that they are normed for the participating countries to have a mean of 500 and a student standard deviation of 100 (and hence these scores are not comparable in levels to PISA scores, as a SACMEQ score of 500 is just a regional norm; countries that have participated in both SACMEQ and PISA have PISA scores 100 to 200 points below the PISA norm of 500). Using these assessment data, we can make similar calculations and standardize the results to make comparative statements about the pace of progress.

In mathematics, at the current observed pace, it would take the fourteen African countries sixty-eight years to gain 100 points, and in reading it would take eighty-seven years. This means it would take three to four generations just to increase learning by one student standard deviation—and this would leave many countries still far from OECD levels in these subjects. In six of the fourteen countries the trend was negative in reading and in five countries it was negative in mathematics (table 3-2).

Alternatively, comparing the PISA results for reading from 2000 to 2009 for the nine countries with comparable reading scores yields a modestly more optimistic picture (Pritchett and Beatty 2012). The estimate is a 1.7-point gain per year, and hence only fifty-seven years are needed to gain 100 points. (For math, it would take 47 years.) Thus, if a child going to school now at age six has a child at age twenty-five, who has a child at age twenty-five, in most countries the great-grandchildren will be at OECD levels of capability when they reach age fifteen in the year 2071. And that is the most optimistic of scenarios.

Of course, this simple comparison over time of those who are tested (who may be in different grades or of different ages, according to the different assessments) mixes both changes in learning and changes in the composition of those tested. Part of the slow pace of learning may result from the influx of less learning-ready students attending school for the first time, which would mask underlying progress.

In some cases the deterioration in learning is so great that even though more students are in school, absolutely fewer students are at an acceptable level of performance. For instance, Tanzania has had a massive increase in secondary school attendance and hence a massive increase in the number

---

1. We did not use the data from Zimbabwe.

Table 3-2. Gains in reading and mathematics in southern and eastern Africa show several generations (68 to 87 years) would be needed to make 100-point gains in assessed learning.

Country (year if not 2000)	Reading				Mathematics			
	2000 (or 1995)	2007	Points per year gain (loss if negative)	Years to 100-point gain	2000 (or 1995)	2007	Points per year gain (loss if negative)	Years to 100-point gain
Botswana	521.1	534.6	1.93	52	512.9	520.5	1.09	92
Kenya (1995)	543.4	543.1	−0.02	Forever	563.3	557	−0.90	Forever
Lesotho	451.2	467.9	2.39	42	447.2	476.9	4.24	24
Malawi (1995)	462.7	433.5	−2.43	Forever	432.9	447	2.01	50
Mauritius (1995)	550.2	573.5	1.94	52	584.6	623.3	5.53	18
Mozambique	516.7	476	−5.81	Forever	530	483.8	−6.60	Forever
Namibia (1995)	473	496.9	1.99	50	430.9	471	5.73	17
Seychelles	582	575.1	−0.99	Forever	554.3	550.7	-0.51	Forever
South Africa	492.3	494.9	0.37	269	486.1	494.8	1.24	80
Swaziland	529.6	549.4	2.83	35	516.5	540.8	3.47	29
Tanzania	545.9	577.8	4.56	22	522.4	552.7	4.33	23
Uganda	482.4	478.7	−0.53	Forever	506.3	481.9	−3.49	Forever
Zambia (1995)	477.5	434.4	−3.59	Forever	435.2	435.2	0.00	Forever
Zanzibar (1995)	489.2	536.8	3.97	25	478.1	489.9	1.69	59
Median			**1.15**	**87**			**1.46**	**68**

Source: Pritchett and Beatty (2012). Data from SACMEQ.

of students taking the Central Secondary Education Examination (CSEE) in the mandatory subjects; that number increased by 180,000 students from 2008 to 2011. However, the proportion of students scoring a grade of C or higher fell so fast that in five subjects—Kiswahili, English, history, geography, and chemistry—the absolute number of students passing fell. The number taking the CSEE exam in Kiswahili increased from 155,000 to 339,000—about 185,000 more students sat for the exam in 2011 than in 2008. The number passing with a grade of C or higher fell from 65,000 to 27,000 as the pass rate fell from 41 percent to 7.8 percent in just four years. Had the pass rate stayed constant, the number passing would have risen by 80,000, instead of falling by 27,000 (see figure 2-8 on page 87).

All Countries Plan to Improve "School Quality," but No Country Has an Evidence-Based Plan to Improve Learning

To expand enrollments, education systems needed more schools, more inputs, and more teachers. So the natural extension would be that to improve the quality of schooling, systems need better schools—where "better" is defined as having more *infrastructure* (for example, more space, more rooms, playgrounds, toilets for students), more *inputs* (more chalk, more learning materials, more textbooks), more *teachers* (leading to smaller teacher-to-pupil ratios), and more formal *qualifications* and *training* of teachers (more years of pre-service training, more time in in-service training). This redefinition of quality from learning outcome to inputs is supremely convenient as it reduces the task to the logistics of expanding inputs.

A common component of school quality improvement, one that illustrates the typical approach of existing top-down bureaucratic spider systems, has been to create education management information systems (EMIS) to create and centralize information about schools. If the system's goal is to improve input quality (such as adding buildings, toilets, classrooms, books, desks, trained teachers, better teacher-pupil ratios), then EMIS can track these ingredients, school by school, in real (or at least realistic) time. This approach sees only the "EMIS-visible" information—those aspects of classrooms, schools, and teachers that can be coded into bits and bytes.[2] This is not to say that learning progress cannot be quantified and tracked, or become "visible" through an EMIS. But EMIS reduces schools and learning to "thin" criteria that can be tracked and "seen" by a spider bureaucracy. These cannot cope with the reality of the "thick" experience of actual learning. EMIS goes hand-in-hand with an input-oriented approach to progress in education.

The logic of these "quality" improvements is circular and hence internally unassailable. Progress is *defined* as schools having more inputs, and success is reached when every school is a "quality" school. Thus, school quality is achieved when the EMIS shows that schools have adequate infrastructure, teachers and inputs. Success is guaranteed when funds are available because budget improvements lead to measured input

---

2. This is in homage to James Scott's landmark *Seeing Like a State* (1998), which describes many "schemes to improve the human condition" based on making the complexity of life "legible" to nation-states that rely on "bureaucratic high modernism" for implementation.

improvements. Alternatively, when funds are not available, the EMIS documents the magnitude of the so-called quality deficit and hence the need for more education funding.

Suppose the input-oriented, EMIS-visible agenda were successful. How much closer would a country be to meeting learning outcome goals? Following the imagery introduced in chapter 1, we can think of a learning profile as a ramp that students walk up as they increase their capabilities through schooling. Improving learning entails steepening the ramp. Metaphorically, the EMIS approach steepens the ramp by adding input wedges under the ramp: more books, smaller class sizes, or more trained teachers.

How much steeper does the ramp need to be? If developing countries want to reach anything like developed countries' levels of learning achievement, the learning profile needs to be dramatically steeper. The number of wedges needed to raise the learning profile depends on the size of each wedge. How thick are the wedges? Suppose we divide the quality improvements into four EMIS-visible input-oriented wedges:

— *Physical infrastructure of the school and classroom,* or such things as walls, windows, a leak-proof roof, classrooms, toilet facilities (including separate facilities for girls), desks, chalkboards, and so forth.
— *Learning inputs,* ranging from simple needs like chalk and pencils, paper, workbooks, textbooks, and learning activity materials to more sophisticated inputs like materials for science demonstrations or experiments to computers.
— *Formal teacher qualifications and training,* including any variety of general level of education, pre-service training for teaching, and in-service training.
— *Teacher-pupil ratio,* which is related to available teacher time per pupil.

The thickness of each wedge is the simple product of two features. The wedge's size is in part determined by the *effect size,* which is the impact of the intervention—better buildings, more textbooks, smaller class sizes, more trained teachers—on the learning outcome, measured in student standard deviation units. So, think of two equivalent students finishing eight years of basic education, one of whom in each year had a trained teacher and one who never had a trained teacher. The wedge size would correspond to the differing learning outcomes as a result of being consistently exposed to trained teachers (or smaller class sizes, or classrooms with chalk, and so on).

The second determinant of wedge size is the *scope* for expanding the input. Often there is an upper limit either to usefulness of the input or to the range over which the input has meaningful impact. It is plausible that moving from no available textbooks to shared textbooks could improve performance, as would perhaps moving from shared textbooks to one textbook per student. But almost no one expects any additional learning impact from each student having his or her own textbook to each student having two of the same textbook. So the scope for learning gains from textbook provision is from none to one per student. Other inputs also have a natural upper limit. Having a leaky roof might inhibit learning, but once the roof doesn't leak, better and better roofs likely won't improve learning outcomes. Limits on the achievable scope also come from practical considerations such as cost. For example, class sizes could affordably be reduced from forty to thirty, but perhaps not from forty to twelve.

Let's take a simple illustration of a quality (in the above sense) improvement's effect on ramp height or the learning profile. Suppose the cumulative (by say, grade nine) effect size of a child's being exposed to a trained versus untrained teacher in each year of schooling is 0.2 (effect sizes mean the magnitude is expressed in student standard deviation units). What is the feasible gain to the average student from training teachers? If, say, 70 percent of teachers are already trained (and hence 70 percent of students are already exposed to trained teachers), then the additional gain from having teachers universally trained is exposing 30 percent of students to trained teachers. So the gain is a 0.2 effect size for each student exposed times the 0.3 students newly exposed to trained teachers, which means the increase in the average would be $0.2 \times 0.3 = 0.06$. Hence, in this super-simple and simplistic example, the gain from having all students taught by trained teachers would equate to a wedge height gain of 0.06 effect sizes toward the goal of increasing one effect size (one student standard deviation) in learning.

An evidence-based plan for achieving any learning goal based on EMIS-visible input expansion would have three parts:

— *Goals,* defined as student domain skills or competencies or capabilities or functioning (which could be anything from basic literacy to working in teams to thinking creatively and need not be assessed with a standardized examination; they could require sophisticated assessment tools) where each goal is described in terms of the *distribution* of student performance, such as the

Figure 3-2. An evidence-based, EMIS-visible plan for achieving learning goals based on improving "quality," or expanding inputs, is lacking everywhere.

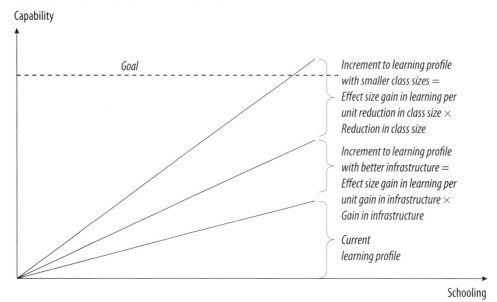

fraction of students above a certain minimal level, the performance of the average student, or reaching an ideal level.
— *Effect sizes* of EMIS-visible inputs based on a fair reading of the best available empirical evidence.
— Budgetary and logistically achievable targets for the expansion of the inputs that would reach the specified learning goals.

An example of an evidence-based input expansion plan is illustrated in figure 3-2. The goal is to improve mean student mathematics performance. The effect size target is 100 points, or one IASSD, to be derived from a reduction in class size and infrastructure expansion, accompanied by an implementation plan involving sufficient budget and capacity to execute. To be justified in terms of outcomes, an input plan must lay out the causal linkage (which has a magnitude) between the inputs and the outcomes.

No developing country in the world has an evidence-based plan for accomplishing any significant learning objectives through expanding EMIS-visible inputs.

I am not advocating the mechanistic, input-expansion approach described here; indeed, a major purpose of the entire book is to argue *against* this type of mechanistic input-output approach to education. With this illustration I am just making explicit the often hidden logic of the predominant current strategy to improve educational outcomes. The call to expand inputs—more toilets, more books, more teacher training—is never done for its own sake but with the often implicit claim that inputs will lead to better outcomes for students. This is not to say countries don't have plans to expand inputs. But plans to expand inputs lack one or more of the features that would make for a real plan for education.

First, very few countries have any articulated and measurable goals— that is, clear statements of the *magnitude* of the improvement in learning objectives that will be achieved by its plans for input expansion. Rather, nearly all plans are circular: quality will be improved when inputs are expanded because inputs *are* quality.

Second, no country has a plan that links plans for input expansion to learning objectives based on any evidence about effect sizes. While learning objectives may be mentioned, their magnitudes are not quantified. If you are a kilometer from your goal, it is critical to know whether your planned steps will move you closer by one centimeter, one meter, or a hundred meters. So, while some countries might pay some attention to evidence of which inputs are effective in moving some positive distance, none pays attention to magnitudes.

So far, countries do not have evidence-based plans to meet ambitious learning goals. It is not that they have "bad" or "wrong" or "inadequate" plans, they lack anything that even minimally qualifies as this type of plan. Which is not to say education ministries lack plans. Plans they have. They have plans for expanding schooling. They have plans for expanding inputs. They have plans for spending money. They have plans for training teachers. And it is not as if they don't have objectives. Objectives they have. What they don't have is (1) plans that link expanded schooling and input expansion to educational achievement, or, more important, (2) any kind of evidence-based plan for increasing the learning profile of students to meet specific and adequately ambitious learning goals.

The Learning Gap Cannot Be Filled with Inputs

Why does no country have an evidence-based, EMIS-visible input-based plan to meet learning goals? Because they can't have one. There is a fundamental contradiction between the best available evidence, which

Figure 3-3. Will expanding inputs be enough to meet learning goals?

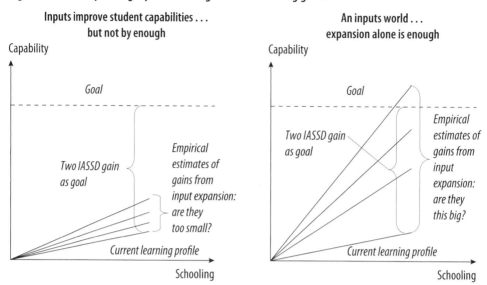

suggests input-based gains are small, and the need, which shows the learning gains to achieve adequate education are large.

The key question is, are the wedges produced from expanding EMIS-visible inputs just too thin to add up to any meaningful change in the steepness of a learning profile (illustrated on the left side of figure 3-3), or will input expansion be roughly sufficient to achieve learning goals (the right side of figure 3-3)?

No country has an evidence-based plan for expanding EMIS-visible inputs to meet learning goals because the weight of the evidence—from literally thousands of empirical studies—suggests that achieving learning goals through input expansion alone, without increases in the efficacy with which all inputs are used, is impossible. The input wedges are just too thin. I do not claim that inputs make no difference, or that a viable, learning-oriented plan will not involve the expansion of inputs. But the overwhelming bulk of the empirical evidence suggests input expansion, at the current level of efficacy in actual use, could constitute only a small part of countries' progress toward meaningful learning goals. Input-oriented plans alone cannot produce anything like the one or two IASSD gains that countries need for their students to be equipped for the twenty-first century. To illustrate this point, I draw on three literatures:

—Studies that compare student learning across schools with different levels of *inputs*

—Studies that compare learning achievement and *expenditures*

—Studies that track the *evolution* of learning achievement performance over long periods

Education Production Functions: Thin Wedges Do Not Add Up to a Steep Ramp

There is a massive literature investigating the links between educational inputs and learning achievement with literally thousands of studies.[3] These studies have compared learning performance and exposure to inputs across students, across schools, across districts, across states or provinces within countries, and across countries. Many of these studies use nonexperimental data and statistical procedures to try to eke out the causal effects of inputs, all else equal. This is what I call the "education production function" literature. I start with this literature because it has the elements to put together an evidence-based, input-driven learning plan because these studies look at the association of lots of different inputs in the same study. (More recently, randomized experiments have been very popular, and I will come back to them, but they tend to focus on one or at best a few inputs at a time.)

All these studies seek to compare the learning achievement of students over time, looking at some portion of the learning profile, either by tracking the same students as they progress in school (which is rare) or by comparing student achievement at a point in time.[4] The learning profile for any given student might be steeper if the student is in a learning environment with more inputs. How big are these effects? Are they big enough such that EMIS-visible input expansion or "more of the same"

3. The most recent review (Glewwe et al. 2011) found over nine thousand studies looking at the link between inputs and learning, just between 1990 and 2010.

4. I want to stress again that while most of the literature relates educational inputs to learning in subjects that are easy and lower cost to measure, such as reading and mathematics, citing studies that examine learning in these subjects does not imply a "back to basics" approach that asserts that reading and math are the only or even most important elements of schooling. The process of education has a large number of important goals, such as socialization and the development of skill sets, that are not well measured on the typical standardized exam, but there is no evidence to suggest that gains to these harder-to-measure education objectives are different in their relationship to inputs.

could steepen learning profiles enough to meet learning goals? How much higher could a student's *cumulative* mastery be from exposure to more inputs?

Any estimate of how schools or school inputs affect learning must account for other factors that affect student outcomes, such as family background, motivation, and innate abilities. One can only estimate the incremental impact of schools or inputs on a child's learning "all else equal." Nearly all empirical studies find that the "all else" about *students* matters, a lot. The single most consistent empirical finding in the education production function literature is that student performance differs enormously, even among children with nearly identical schooling experiences, and that differences in performance are robustly associated with student and parental background characteristics. It should surprise no one that children of better-off, better-educated, and more achievement-oriented parents tend to perform better in school. This is important to keep in mind as, if these student background characteristics matter (and they do), and students with similar background characteristics tend to cluster in schools (and they do, either because of patterns of residence or because of school choice), then there will be large differences in the observed performance of schools that have nothing to do with the school's causal impact on student performance. Moreover, to no one's surprise, schools with students with rich and well-educated parents tend to be schools with lots of inputs, and hence the naïve association will show that schools with good inputs have good learning outcomes—but this association reveals nothing about what would happen if inputs were expanded.

I use three examples that are typical of the massive existing education production function literature to show the limits to the gains achievable from expanding inputs. The first example is a study from Jamaica that did a careful job of measuring not just EMIS-visible inputs but also pedagogical practices, school organization, and community involvement (Glewwe et al. 1995). The study included fourteen EMIS-visible components, including school facilities, the availability of instructional materials, student-teacher ratios, teacher qualifications and training, and school-level pedagogical inputs, each of which is an element of most plans for school improvement,

In examining mathematics, the authors found that seven associations were positive and seven negative—exactly what one would expect from pure chance. For reading achievement, the effects of eight inputs were positive, the effects of six were negative, and only one was statistically

Figure 3-4. Empirical estimates of the maximum possible gain from EMIS-visible input improvements on learning is small: four examples.

Student standard deviation

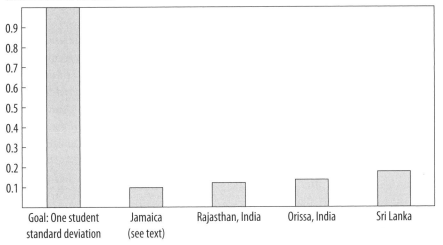

Source: Author's calculations, based on work cited in the text. The spreadsheet is available at cgdev.org/rebirth-of-education.

significant (at the 5 percent level).[5] Moreover, the effect sizes even for many of the variables that were statistically significant were small, as the very largest was 0.2.

Finally, the scope for expanding or enhancing the inputs that were positively associated with learning was limited. For example, the study estimated that textbooks arriving two months later than when they were needed was associated with less learning, in both math and reading. However, this creates the possibility of a one-off improvement to deliver textbooks on time, not something that could be continuously improved to reach higher and higher achievement. Similarly, the number of students with desks had a big effect size of .2—but has a maximum of 100 percent—and 85 percent of students already had desks. So the maximum gain—the effect size times the scope—from moving to the best possible scenario (100 percent of students with desks) is about one-tenth of one standard deviation for reading, and even less for mathematics (figure 3-4).

5. Pedagogical processes, school organization, and community involvement also showed similar results, demonstrating that the lack of effects is not just true of inputs. Out of the ten non-input measures, only one was significant at the 5 percent level for math, while for reading, three measures were significant at the 5 percent level.

What if we used these empirical results from this study to achieve an EMIS-visible input fantasy, that all of the inputs achieved their best possible values? What if all teachers had diplomas, all teachers had undergone training in the last three years, all students had desks, the class size was twenty-five, all schools had reliable electrical services, all textbooks arrived on time—*everything* was done? How much of a one standard deviation gain (on this particular test) in math and reading (averaged) would the input expansion produce? The optimistic estimate is that this EMIS-visible fantasy input expansion would produce about one-tenth of one student standard deviation.[6] So a massive program of input expansion, which would be fiscally very costly and would likely take a decade to achieve, would be (generously) predicted to have an impact of 0.1 student standard deviation.

A second example in the education production function literature is a Sri Lankan study that measured learning achievement of grade four students in mathematics, English, and the child's first language (Aturupane, Glewwe, and Wisniewski 2006). The study collected student performance data, detailed information about children's backgrounds (such as parents' education, resources in the home, and participation in private tutoring), and data on a rich array of variables intended to measure school quality, including infrastructure, teacher training, characteristics of teachers and principals, and so forth. In total, thirty-five inputs were measured.[7]

The authors used standard statistical techniques to estimate the association between the three learning achievement measures (math, English, first language) and child-, household-, and school-level variables. Nearly all inputs were dismissed in one telling sentence: "Variables with no explanatory power in any of the tests are dropped." Of the thirty-five input variables, twenty-eight were never statistically significant in any specification for any learning measure (not math, not English, nor first language). Only one-fifth (seven of thirty-five) of the EMIS-visible inputs had *any* demonstrable association with *any* learning outcome, and the magnitude of the effect sizes was empirically tiny (and inconsistent in sign). As with the Jamaica study, even where there were strong associations, the available scope for expanding the input was modest. The

6. This is optimistic because the puzzling result is that the predicted gain from the EMIS-visible fantasy is modestly *negative*—scores would fall. This result is because one input is estimated to have a large negative effect. So to get any positive impact at all we have to just rule that one out and say it must be a fluke.

7. This study also collected measures of pedagogical processes based on observation of teachers in the classroom.

school characteristic with the largest impact was all students having adequate desks (the analysis used either a zero or a one for each school). Providing adequate desks to all schools would (if the effect were causal) add 8.1 points to student scores, so the effect size is substantial. But there was a limited scope for desks to improve performance, as 58 percent of schools already had adequate desks. The gain from moving to 100 percent of schools is $8.1 \times 0.42 = 3.4$, which is good, but we are looking for a gain of 100 points, so this will at best get only a tiny part of the way.

Again we calculate the EMIS-visible input fantasy plan—that each of the seven statistically significant input variables was expanded to its maximally feasible scope. What is the gain? (And keep in mind this is already biased by the exclusion of the variables that were not statistically significant, as some of those might have been positive, some negative). The total gain is 0.18, which is undeniably something, but also undeniably not anywhere near 1.

What are the plausible upside possibilities and downside risks of an input expansion given the imprecision with which the impact of each input is measured? If each of the input impacts were one standard error below the point estimate, then the total possible scope for input expansion would be 0.03 (almost nothing). Alternatively, if the impact of every variable were larger than the point estimates, then even the maximum possible EMIS-visible expansion (at a uniformly optimistic assumption about impact) produces only about one-third of one student standard deviation.

To illustrate the third type of education production function research, I use studies from two Indian states, Rajasthan and Orissa, that examined the connection between learning achievement and the standard inputs such as teacher salary, teacher qualifications, teacher training, class size, and whether schools have multigrade teachers. Setting up the same thought experiment with the maximally feasible expansion of these inputs—that is, giving each grade a dedicated teacher with ten fewer students in each class, and with all teachers having degrees—I found total gains from 0.12 to 0.13 student standard deviations. Again, the combination of all possible input enhancements is nowhere near 1 (see figure 3-4).

These are just four specific studies in four specific regions, but I could do calculations like this all day (see my review of this literature in Pritchett 2004). These studies are typical of an enormous education production function literature. I encourage interested readers to do this too. The book's website (cgdev.org/rebirth-of-education) provides the spreadsheets used for these calculations and a template that can be used with any empirical study desired (www.cgdev.org/rebirth-of-education). One need only enter the effect size and the scope, then multiply and sum, and the total gain is given.

One very difficult technical issue is how to treat these estimates of the impact of inputs on students' scores in a particular year, either as the *cumulative* impacts from exposure to the school, and associated inputs up to the point the student is now (such as grade five or grade eight), or as just representing the gain from one year of exposure to the particular level of inputs. In the latter case, one could imagine multiplying the effect size by the number of years of school, since the gains could be replicated in each year. However, there are good arguments that when students are tested in grade five and the results are associated with school effects, this already estimates the cumulative effect, whereas some of the classroom-specific effects could represent the impact of just that classroom exposure (and hence might be multiplied by five in calculating the potential total gain). On the other hand, the recent literature on the "depreciation" of one year of exposure with respect to long-run learning gains suggests that the long-run impact of one year of exposure is very much smaller than the one-year impact coefficient (for example, while being in a small class in grade three might raise learning in grade three, this learning gain mostly evaporates in grades four and five). With high levels of depreciation, the one-year gains would have to be sustained in each year for the one-year effects to be cumulative. In the calculations above I treat the reported estimates as representing cumulative gains.

Beware of evidence-based plans using cherry-picked estimates. There are many technical issues with estimating the causal impacts of inputs on student learning, and hence for many researchers, education production functions are out of style. However, the alternatives run the risk of cherry-picking the data to produce the results one hopes to derive.

First, using all the estimates from the *same* study (for example, in Sri Lanka or in Jamaica or in India) prevents someone from scouring the existing literature (which consists of literally thousands of studies) and picking the largest-ever reported effect size for books, the largest-ever effect size for class size, and the largest-ever effect size for teacher training, and then producing an "evidence-based" plan on those estimates. The danger is that publication bias (in all its many forms) already actively promotes a certain amount of cherry picking, so basing plans on selective reviews of an already selective literature can be massively biased.

Second, the fashion for relying only on "rigorous" estimates of causal impacts based on randomized (or well-identified by natural experiments) studies is not really an alternative, for three reasons. One, there are just too many inputs for which there are no randomized (or even rigorous studies). Two, the external validity problems are insurmountable—already there are rigorous estimates of the causal impact of class size that span the range from zero to quite large, so the hope that more "rigorous" methods will produce more consensus estimates has already evaporated (Pritchett and Sandefur 2013). Three, it is extremely unlikely that randomization will, on average, produce bigger estimates than the nonexperimental literature. The bias from nonexperimental evidence can go either way and make the non-experimental effect size estimates either too large or too small. The most recent review of the literature (Glewwe et al. 2011) suggests that the more rigorous the method, the *less* likely it is that a study provides support for a large causal impact of inputs, which is most researchers' intuition.[8]

How Much Will Meeting Learning Goals Cost?
All You Have—or Nothing at All

Evidence as to the futility of just adding more of the same inputs also comes from studies that compare budgets. The link between evidence about inputs and evidence about budgets takes a bit of arithmetic and a few definitions, but is worth pursuing. To make the arithmetic easy, I'll assume a linear relationship between learning outcomes and the four types of EMIS-visible inputs: infrastructure (IF), learning inputs (IP), teacher training and qualifications (TTQ), and teacher-to-pupil ratios (TPR), so that the expected learning outcome (L) gain (of "plan" over "base case") from a plan of expansion of these inputs is given by:

$$L^{Plan} - L^{Base\ Case} = \beta_{IF} \times (IF^{Plan} - IF^{Base\ Case}) + \beta_{IP} \times (IP^{Plan} - IP^{Base\ Case}) + \beta_{TTQ}$$
$$\times (TTQ^{Plan} - TTQ^{Base\ Case}) + \beta_{TPR} \times (TPR^{Plan} - TPR^{Base\ Case}),$$

where the β values for each input are scaled in effect sizes.

8. The natural assumption is that most nonexperimental settings make input use look bigger than its true impact because inputs and unobserved factors are positively correlated. That is, suppose that motivated parents/students are both more likely to be in schools that use inputs and more likely to perform well at any level of inputs. Then, if "motivation" is not measured in a nonexperimental study, this positive association of inputs and the omitted variable of motivation will cause estimates of inputs to be larger than their true causal impact because statistically the motivation impact, which goes unmeasured, gets falsely attributed to inputs. In contrast, pure measurement error of any input produces attenuation bias.

The cost of this plan is just the sum of the cost of expanding each type of input, which is just the magnitude of the change in each input times the unit cost (UC) of the input. This expression is simplified using just four aggregates, but it can be built up from the educational plan that specifies each input and its cost:

$$Plan\ Cost = \left(IF^{Plan} - IF^{Base\ Case}\right) \times UC_{IF} + \left(IP^{Plan} - IP^{Base\ Case}\right) \times UC_{IP}$$
$$+ \left(TTQ^{Plan} - TTQ^{Base\ Case}\right) \times UC_{TTQ}$$
$$+ \left(TPR^{Plan} - TPR^{Base\ Case}\right) \times UC_{TPR}.$$

Two ratios make things clear. The *cost-effectiveness* of a given input is just the ratio of its effect size to its unit cost, or how much it costs to achieve learning through the expansion of that input:

$$Cost\ Effectiveness_{Input} = \frac{\beta_{Input}}{UC_{Input}}.$$

The second is just the share of the total cost that is devoted to any given input:

$$Cost\ Share_{Input} = \frac{\left(Input^{Plan} - Input^{Base\ Case}\right) \times UC_{Input}}{Plan\ Cost}.$$

The overall cost-effectiveness—or learning gain per additional expenditure for an input-driven plan—is just the sum of the cost-effectiveness times the cost share of each input. Put differently, cost-effectiveness is the cost-share-weighted average of the cost-effectiveness of each input:

$$\frac{Learning\ Gain}{Total\ Cost} = CS_{IF} \times CE_{IF} + CS_{IP} \times CE_{IP} + CS_{TTQ} \times CE_{TTQ} + CS_{TPR} \times CE_{TPR}.$$

These few simple equations allow us to link the literature on education production functions, which connects inputs and the learning outcomes of various inputs, with the also voluminous literature that relates spending per student to learning outcomes.

From this simple equation we already know two things to expect from this literature on the association between spending and learning outcomes: first, anything can happen from increasing spending, and second, mostly nothing does.

Anything can happen in associating learning outcomes and expenditures across jurisdictions (schools, districts, states or provinces, countries)

Table 3-3. How to understand associations between learning outcomes and spending: anything could happen . . .

What could happen	Empirical result	Relation to underlying inputs and outcomes
Some schools face higher prices for inputs, but all schools use the same inputs.	No association between spending and outcomes is discernible.	Higher-spending schools are less cost-effective on average because unit costs are higher.
Higher-spending schools spend incrementally more on highly cost-effective inputs.	Higher spending is associated with higher learning achievement.	The *composition* of spending (cost shares) is better in higher-performing schools.
Higher-spending schools spend more on inputs with zero or small cost-effectiveness (at the same unit costs).	Higher spending is only weakly associated with higher learning achievement.	The *composition* of spending by cost-effectiveness is worse in higher-spending schools.
Cost-effectiveness is high across all inputs.	Higher spending is strongly associated with learning outcomes.	The composition of spending doesn't matter (much) because all inputs have high cost-effectiveness.
. . . but mostly nothing does.		
Cost-effectiveness of most inputs (at existing levels of utilization and efficiency) is low	Higher spending is only weakly associated with learning outcomes.	The composition doesn't matter (much) because either (1) nearly all inputs have low cost-effectiveness at the overall effectiveness with which resources are used or (2) most resources are spent on expanding inputs with low cost-effectiveness.

or in the same jurisdictions over time. Anything can happen because estimates of the relationship between budgets and outcomes are just recovering some mix of the underlying cost-effectiveness. As table 3-3 elucidates, this means that if the incremental spending is on cost-effective inputs, then spending can have a big impact on outcomes, whereas if the incremental spending falls on inputs that are not cost-effective, then it will have no association with learning.

But mostly nothing does. A massive literature exists comparing levels of learning achievement and spending per pupil at many different levels—across countries, states or provinces within countries, smaller jurisdictions, and schools. And there is a literature comparing performance at these different levels over time. The finding, again and again, is that resources per se have little to no statistically significant impact on measured learning

Figure 3-5. Even if Mexico increased spending fivefold, it would not be predicted to attain OECD learning levels.

PISA 2009 average (reading, math, science) score

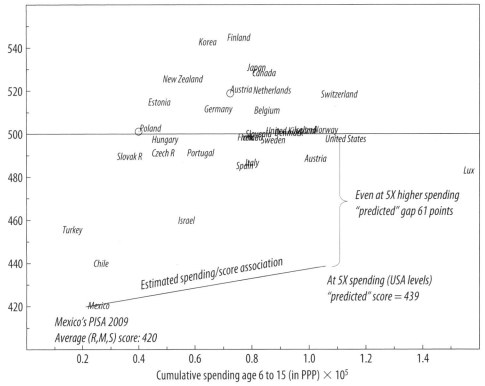

Source: Author's calculations, based on PISA 2009 (OECD 2010) data.

outcomes. But as with the impact of inputs, the question is not statistical significance but the *size*: how much can spending do?

While there are many sophisticated ways of attempting to use cross-national data to tease out the impact of resource expansion, the basic data tell the big-picture story: countries have *exactly the same* measured learning results with *very different* levels of spending. And countries have *very different learning outcomes* with exactly the same level of spending. Figure 3-5 shows PISA 2009 results (averaged across all three domains, math, science, and reading) and cumulative educational spending on a child from age six to age fifteen (in comparable purchasing power parity, or PPP, units). It doesn't take any fancy statistical procedures to see that the United States spends PPP $105,000 per child and Poland spends PPP $39,000, and they get nearly the same results. Conversely, Spain spends PPP $74,000 and Finland spends slightly less, PPP $71,000, yet Finland outperforms Spain by 50 points (half a student standard deviation).

Suppose we estimate the simple bivariate association between spending and these measured learning outcomes using OECD data (excluding Mexico, since I do the thought experiment for Mexico) and ask, if Mexico's learning outcomes were to increase with spending in exactly the same pattern as learning is associated with spending across the other OECD countries, how much spending would it take to reach an OECD-based learning goal? Not surprisingly, Mexico will never reach such a learning goal through spending alone. The score gap between Mexico and other OECD countries is 75 points (425 versus 500), and each $10,000 of cumulative student spending is associated with 2.2 additional PISA points. So an amazingly large increase in spending—say, a 50 percent increase from Mexico's base of PPP $21,000—would lead to a gain of two points. Suppose Mexico were to double spending from PPP $21,000 to PPP $42,000—which would entail massive fiscal costs—the estimated gain would be 4.6 points. Even in the absurd scenario that Mexico reached U.S. levels of spending, five times Mexico's current spending level, the predicted impact is still only 14 points of the 75-point gap.

Extending this analysis beyond the OECD, and comparing other countries around the world, I find the same pattern—countries with the same performance at very different levels of spending, and conversely, countries with very different performance at the same levels of spending. The overall learning outcomes-to-resources relationship is weak. Figure 3-5 uses the cognitive skills estimates that Hanushek and Woessmann (2009) produced using all available, internationally comparable assessments and compares them with UN data on education spending as a fraction of GDP. Brazil's cognitive skills estimate is 364 and Korea's is 540, or 176 points higher, but both spend roughly the same fraction of GDP on education.

Suppose this cross-national pattern revealed the typical path a country would take if it expanded spending. Suppose Brazil expanded from its current levels of spending and reached the *highest* level of spending as a fraction of GDP in the world (that of Denmark, which spends more than 8 percent of GDP on education). This would increase Brazil's performance by only about 21 points, which would still leave Brazil 115 points below the OECD norm (figure 3-6). Remembering that the relationship

Figure 3-6. If Brazil increased education spending as a fraction of GDP to Denmark's spending levels, Brazil would still not increase learning enough to achieve an OECD average.

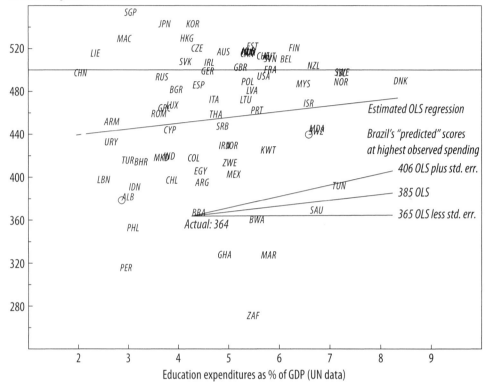

Source: Author's calculations, based on data from Hanushek and Woessmann (2009) and UNESCO UIS data from http://stats.uis.unesco.org/unesco/TableViewer/tableView.aspx?ReportId=172.

between spending and learning is statistically weak, let's suppose, for argument's sake, the estimate of the association is one standard error larger, meaning we were optimistic about the impact of spending expansion. Even if Brazil were the world's highest-spending country *and* the impact of this additional spending were at the high end of the range consistent with cross-national patterns, this would still get Brazil only to 406 points, still almost one full IASSD below the OECD average. Conversely, at the low end of the range of the association, doubling spending as a fraction of GDP would gain Brazil only one point.

The usefulness of the arithmetic above is that we know that associations between spending and learning outcomes do not reveal some deep underlying hard technical facts about the world, but rather the opposite. Arguing about the causal impact of additional spending is pointless. The evidence suggests that the cost-effectiveness of spending, including the individual impact effects of various inputs, varies widely around the world.

In many physical sciences there are hard physical facts, like the mass of a proton or neutron. We know that if one atom has exactly one more proton than another atom, its mass is higher by exactly that amount, in Kenya, India, or Tennessee. But everything important about education involves human beings—as students, as teachers, as parents, as principals—and human beings are not reducible to physical facts because they have hopes, fears, identities, likes, tastes, motivations. Human beings choose. Therefore the impact of learning from adding a teacher to a classroom is not a fixed quantity, like proton mass, but rather is determined by the behavior of people.[9] Studies measuring the impact of interventions such as lowering class size or adding resources or increasing teacher salaries do not reveal *the* impact of class size—they reveal *there is no such thing* as the impact of class size (Pritchett and Sandefur 2013).

What appears to constitute the major difference in the performance of educational systems in producing outcomes is the effectiveness with which people in those systems—students, teachers, administrators, parents—use resources. In low-effectiveness systems, no amount of additional resources that is not accompanied by a substantial increase in the effectiveness with which people work can achieve the education countries strive for. We can draw an analogy between spending on educational inputs and releasing water into a canal to provide irrigation for farmers in a desert. We know that water is needed to grow plants, but that doesn't mean that pouring more water into the canal will increase the growth of plants. What if the canal might be breached so that water leaks out? In this case, releasing more water at the head of the canal just leads to more water spilled, not more crops grown.

The West Does Not Know Best

Follow the leader makes some sense. Nearly all of the international assessments put countries into four groups: (1) East Asian countries, which have the highest scores, (2) most of the OECD countries, tightly

---

9. In research with Deon Filmer (Filmer and Pritchett 1999), I have shown that the education production function literature reveals more about the politics of spending than about the pedagogical value of inputs.

clustered around the OECD mean of 500, (3) East European countries and former Soviet bloc countries, which are also mostly near the OECD mean, and (4) the rest of the world, mostly developing countries, which score around 400 or below. Therefore, a natural policy recommendation for developing countries might be to attempt to follow the same path as most OECD countries. Perhaps even education experts from the high-performing countries could teach developing countries how they achieve scores of 500.

The problem with learning from the West is that no living Western education expert has led, participated in, or lived through a truly major national improvement in measured student achievement. (In this case, "Western" excludes Finland, to which I return later.) Except for the United States the evidence is indirect, but it strongly suggests that all of the currently high-scoring educational systems in OECD countries were already high-scoring forty years ago. This means even a very experienced education expert, say, someone sixty years old, who finished his or her education training at age twenty-five in 1975, has never seen his or her country make a major improvement in average performance on measured learning outcomes. Such an expert's lived expertise therefore can include many issues, such as dealing with racial and gender inequalities, expanding reach to learning-disabled students, and coping with fractious social issues, but does not include creating a high-performance system.

This long-run stagnation in scores also means that the massive expansion of "more of the same" in OECD education systems—much smaller class sizes, much higher real spending per child, much higher levels of teacher educational qualifications—*followed* rather than preceded the achievement of high learning performance.

How do I defend this claim about the performance of the West? Nearly all schooling systems are much too clever to allow their performance to be tracked consistently over time. That would provide precisely the information needed to judge whether the improvements provided were really useful, and for what objectives. On this score, it pays to be ignorant (Pritchett 2002). By not tracking achievement over (a very long) time, the system is freed to follow the internally circular legitimization that more is better just because more is better.

The United States, however, consistently tracks performance in reading and mathematics using the National Assessment of Education Progress (NAEP). The really astounding result of the NAEP assessments is that over the thirty-three-year period from 1971 to 2004, the average reading score of seventeen-year-olds in American schools did not change at all. In 1971 the scaled score was 285 and in 2004 the scaled score was 285. Moreover, while there have been many socioeconomic and population composition changes in the United States since the 1970s that might have affected the national average, if we limit the time series comparison to just "advantaged" students (e.g., white students with a parent who graduated from college) the same trend holds (over the shorter period for which the data are available). In 1980 these students scored 305, and in 2004 they scored 303.

What would progress—for example, scores improving a student standard deviation in a generation—look like? As we have seen, the actual numerical scaling of learning assessments is just a convention, and on the NAEP, a student standard deviation in 2004 was 43, so a student standard deviation gain among the privileged students over this period would have taken scores from 305 in 1980 to 348 in 2004. This pace of progress in reading is illustrated in figure 3-7 as a hypothetical pace. While any education data are subject to quibbles, we can be confident that progress in the United States over this period was far, far, far less than a gain of one student standard deviation.[10]

While this lack of progress has occasioned massive debate in the United States, it is not a uniquely U.S. phenomenon. The U.S. rate of improvement is roughly the same as much of the OECD countries. Three German researchers, Eric Gundlach, Ludger Woessmann, and Jens Gmelin (2001), realized that although the United States was unique in tracking its own performance over time, many countries participated in a variety of international comparisons that compared their national average scores to those of the United States in reading and mathematics. Therefore one could link the assessments to estimate the speed of progress in countries that were not measuring their own speed. A simple analogy is to imagine you are watching a marathon. As long as two runners remain the same distance apart, if you know the speed of one, you automatically know the speed of the other. In the same way, if the United States measures its progress over time using one instrument, and Germany measures its position relative to the United States at various points in time, even using a different instrument, we can estimate the pace of progress in Germany by comparing its position relative to that of the United States. If it gained, it was improving faster; if it fell behind, it was improving more slowly. Woessmann

---

10. For the same population (seventeen years old, white, at least one parent a college graduate), mathematics scores increased from 319 in 1978 to 322 in 2004.

Figure 3-7. Average and "advantaged" children in the United States made nowhere near a student standard deviation progress in reading achievement over the past 40 years.

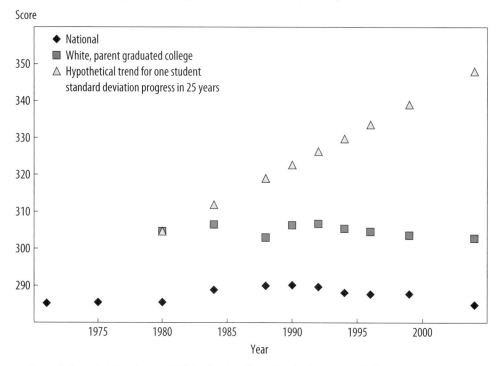

Source: Author's calculations, based on NAEP data from http://nces.ed.gov/nationsreportcard/lttdata/.

has updated these calculations recently with Eric Hanushek (Hanushek and Woessmann 2009) using this simple concept, while making adjustments for the different subject domains, student populations, and assessment designs.

The results from this line of research reveal three important facts.

First, all fifteen OECD countries for which Hanushek and Woessmann had data were at or above 500 by 1975. These countries achieved roughly their current learning levels *before the 1970s*. This means no living education expert from the West has had experience implementing programs or practices or activities that led to the type of massive learning improvements that developing countries aim to achieve today. Instead, all existing education experts inherited systems with high learning performance. Therefore, their professional experience is in operating or improving functional, high-performing systems, not in building them.

Second, as Gundlach, Woessmann, and Gmelin (2001) show for the period 1970 to 1994, there have been massive increases in real education expenditures in every OECD country—in most countries, expenditures per pupil doubled or even tripled over this period. Moreover, all measures of the standard EMIS-visible inputs—infrastructure, supplies, teacher training and qualifications, reduced class sizes—also greatly increased over the same period. Whatever the gains from such increases in real education expenditures (and I am not debating whether there might not have been other valid educational gains from increased spending and inputs), however, the post-1970 improvements in spending per pupil neither account for the current OECD educational advantages nor appear to have led to substantial learning gains in the standard subject areas.

Third, countries that wish to increase learning outcomes cannot rely on imitating the current OECD pace of learning. The average gain in learning outcomes in the fifteen countries measured is 10 points over twenty-five years, only 0.4 IASSD a year. But 0.4 points a year is at the low end of the ranges we saw above for developing countries, based on PISA, TIMSS, and SACMEQ scores. This observation suggests that, while OECD countries are ahead, they are not systematically making faster progress.

Suppose we just do the mechanical exercise done in the opening of the chapter of asking, if developing country X were to achieve the pace of progress of the OECD, how long would it take that country to reach the current OECD level of learning achievement? Table 3-4 shows that it would take a very, very long time. We may take as an example Indonesia, a middle-income country with a growing economy and an average 2009 PISA score of 385. At the pace of 0.39 points a year, it would take almost 300 years (115/0.39 = 298) to reach the current OECD levels of learning achievement.

Some advanced countries have made more progress than others. For instance, Finland has been widely acknowledged as exhibiting rapid improvements. Between 1975 and 2000, Finland improved at about 1.2 points a year, almost three times faster than the OECD average. This is terrific, and later in the book I'll discuss more about how the country achieved that pace. But even at Finland's pace, Indonesia would take one hundred years to reach average OECD levels.

The reason I highlight the irrelevance of the pace of learning in OECD countries relative to that in developing countries is that debates about educational policies in poor countries often become about the educational fads in rich countries. But these are, for the most part, completely

Table 3-4. Developing countries would take hundreds of years to reach OECD learning levels if they were to achieve on the pace gains in learning of the rich countries.

Country	PISA 2009 average score (reading, science, math)	Years it would take the country to reach 500 if the country improved at the pace of . . .	
		At the average pace of 15 OECD countries between 1975 and 2000 (500 to 510, 0.4 points/year)	At the pace of the three fastest OECD performers (Finland, Canada, Netherlands, 1.13 points/year)
Kyrgyzstan	325	454	154
Peru	368	342	116
Panama	369	340	116
Qatar	373	329	112
Albania	384	300	102
Indonesia	385	298	101
Azerbaijan	389	289	98
Tunisia	392	280	95
Argentina	396	270	92
Kazakhstan	399	263	89
Colombia	399	263	89
Brazil	401	257	87
Jordan	402	253	86
Montenegro	404	249	85
Trinidad and Tobago	414	224	76
Mexico	420	208	71
Thailand	422	203	69
Romania	427	190	65
Uruguay	427	190	65
Bulgaria	432	176	60
Chile	439	157	54

Source: Author's calculations, based on PISA 2009 data and estimates from Hanushek and Woessmann (2009, table B.3).

immaterial to solving the learning challenges of poor countries because OECD countries and poor countries are not tackling the same problem.

Why am I devoting so much time and intensity to the negative message that expanding inputs or spending alone cannot be the centerpiece of a strategy to improve learning? Because the first step to success is admitting failure. Thomas Edison and his team created a commercially viable electric light bulb by testing thousands and thousands of different materials and their shape. But this innovation was possible only because of three things: (1) he was looking for a new source of light, not content with existing sources; (2) he knew what he wanted; and (3) he was willing to admit failure and move on.

The next chapter discusses why all three things are difficult under the existing educational systems in most of the developed world. Major gains will have to come from *system* or *structural* changes that either produce more with existing inputs or accelerate the process of discovering and adopting new learning-achievement-improving innovations.

CHAPTER 4

Camouflage of the Spider and Dangers of Centralized School Systems

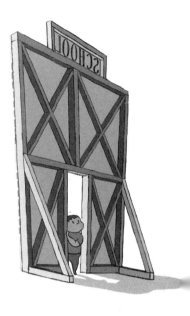

But it will do *some* good, and what harm can come of it? This is the common reaction to the arguments of chapter 2 and chapter 3 that just expanding years of schooling and education management information systems (EMIS)–visible inputs alone will do little to raise student learning. Once the problems of learning achievement are recognized, the instinct is to do *something* to address the problem, and expanding inputs is readily at hand and easy to adopt as *the* solution. Arguments against input expansion are seen as pessimistic and fatalist: "Don't just do something, stand there!"

Doing the seemingly useful might not just be futile, it can be dangerous. Taking a placebo can be dangerous if it prevents you from seeking out the right diagnosis and pursuing a real cure. Pursuing an agenda of "quality improvement," defined as exclusively expanding "known" and EMIS-visible inputs, perpetuates an illusion of progress. This illusion protects dysfunctional systems against creating the space for new innovations, against the freedom to experiment, and in particular against the disruptive innovations that ultimately can lead to rapid and sustained pace in improvements in learning.

Evolution has produced an animal world full of deceit and deception. Things are often not what they seem. Camouflage is common. Many animals blend into their surroundings to make it difficult for predators or prey to spot them. Salamanders change color to maintain invisibility. Puffer fish move slowly but are able to blow themselves up to appear much larger (and spikier) than usual.

Camouflage that enhances an animal's survival value by mimicking another species is called isomorphic mimicry. The eastern coral snake is highly poisonous and brightly colored, with black, red, and yellow stripes. The scarlet king snake is not poisonous; it is really just a harmless creature, but it too is brightly colored, with black, red, and yellow stripes. The scarlet king snake enjoys the evolutionary advantages of signaling that it is dangerous without the bother of actually being dangerous. Some species of flies have evolved to look like bees, and even to make a bee-sounding buzz as they fly. The survival pressure of natural selection at times produces mimics, species that derive a survival value from imitating other species' forms or appearances without any real function attached to that appearance.

The deception of camouflage also works for organizations. Sociologists borrowed the idea of animal isomorphic mimicry and have applied it to organizational ecosystems to describe how many organizations behave (DiMaggio and Powell 1983). Organizations, particularly in fields in which the desired outcomes are complex to produce and hard to assess, can enhance their organizational survival by adopting "best practice" where it doesn't really matter. Such reforms can make them *look* like functional organizations. Adopting the forms of best practice without any of the underlying functionality that actually characterizes the best practice can produce quick and easy gains in perception. Such organizations can look like successful organizations while lacking any real success.

In this chapter, I argue that many education systems around the world, especially those spider systems dominated by large, top-down ministries of education, are garbed in camouflage and actively seeking to hide disastrous levels of underlying dysfunction. Unfortunately, the camouflage has been effective. By pretending to adopt the pursuit of quality education through the expansion of EMIS-visible inputs, more training, and more formal qualifications, these systems are able to fend off challenges, resist innovations, and delay core reforms integral to improved learning. Some schooling systems are like a Bollywood set, just realistic enough to create the illusion of glitz and glamour for a movie, but nothing more than a façade. Buildings that look like schools but don't produce learning are a façade that deludes children and parents into believing they are getting an education while depriving them of real opportunity.

Chapter 3 argued that the dominant approach to improving school quality in developing countries has been to expand known inputs, leading to higher per student costs, but with little impact on learning outcomes. But state-of-the-art research shows that *organizational* and *systemic* changes that change the scope of action, incentives, and accountability of agents in education are vastly more cost-effective in producing higher learning than increasing inputs.

— A large-scale experiment in Andhra Pradesh, India, showed that community-hired teachers produced equivalent (or better) learning outcomes for students, even while earning salaries one-fifth or less the salaries of civil service teachers (Muralidharan and Sundararaman 2010b).

— In Kenya, within the context of class size reductions (from, on average, eighty-two to forty-four students), locally contracted novice teachers on one-year contracts earning one-fourth of what civil service teachers earn substantially outperformed their civil service counterparts (Duflo, Dupas, and Kremer 2012).

— In two states in India, low-cost tutors who taught the lowest-performing students for part of the school day produced substantial gains in performance at very low cost (Banerjee, Cole, et al. 2010).

— Putting cameras in classrooms and requiring teachers to take date- and time-stamped pictures increased student attendance and raised scores substantially at very low cost in NGO-run schools in India (Duflo, Hanna, and Ryan 2010).

— In Punjab, Pakistan, private schools outperformed public schools on measures of mathematics and language performance by a full student standard deviation—even for similar students, at much lower cost (Andrabi et al. 2007).

— Private schools in Kenya outperformed public schools on the standard school leavers' examination by a full student standard deviation (or more)—even when adjusting for student composition (Bold et al. 2011).

Community-hired teachers. Tracking by ability. Tutoring low-performing students. Low-cost yet high-performing private schools. Simple technological mechanisms to ensure teacher attendance. What is most striking about these innovations that cost-effectively improve student performance is that none is on the "quality improvement" agenda of government school systems in nearly any country in the world. In fact, many of them are viewed by the old-school schooling establishment as a problem (such as the rise of private schooling) or as backward (such as hiring community teachers with less training) or as not quality oriented (such as remedial teaching) or as "old-fashioned" (such as student tracking). But how much of the opposition by education establishments to these innovations is evidence-based and how much is isomorphism?

Value-Subtracting and Rent-Extracting School Systems: Illustrations from Punjab, Pakistan, and Uttar Pradesh, India

One fundamental feature of modern organizations is that people working together, with structured roles and assigned tasks, can, through specialization, cooperation, and coordination, produce a whole that is much more than the sum of its parts. Indeed, one might say, along with venerable authorities like Max Weber, that the essence of modern life is the rise of the bureaucratic organization. This is true in the private sector through the modern economy of "scale and scope," made real in the early twentieth century in railroads, oil, and banking (Chandler 1977, 1990). The rise of the public sector bureaucracy was a parallel evolution through professionalized armies and autonomous bureaucracies (Carpenter 2001). Even in the nonprofit sector the growth of large-scale political and social and humanitarian organizations led to large organizations and institutionalized bureaucracies. What can now be accomplished by individuals because of the increased value added and productivity made possible by being embedded into large organizations staggers the imagination.

But what if organizations are value subtracting?[1] What if hundreds of thousands of people work together in organizations that look modern, with organizational charts, bureaucratic offices, and rules and procedures, yet all of these features are merely a façade? If such bureaucracies are shams, could these workers, such as teachers, be more productive working outside a ministry-run school than in it? Could the whole be much less than the sum of its parts, such that organizations are not just rent extracting (producing less with inputs than possible) but actually value subtracting? Yes. Organizations, including school systems, can be

1. The idea of value-subtracting organizations discussed in this chapter comes from conversations with Devesh Kapur.

so bad that teachers are absolutely less productive at helping their students learn when trapped inside the spider bureaucracy than when acting completely on their own.

Before moving to rigorous evidence, let me tell a story, perhaps apocryphal, but told to me in the first person by a member of the prestigious Planning Commission of India. As a member of the Planning Commission, he was allocated a government-owned flat with a yard and garden, and was assigned a gardener to keep it up. During his first year of residence he enjoyed the garden, and the gardener worked diligently. At the end of the first year the gardener came to the Commission member and said, "Sir, I am sorry to say you will have to get a new gardener." "I am sorry to hear that; you have been a good gardener. Are you moving?" "No, sir. I will be starting a new job." "Oh, that is wonderful. What is your new job?" "Well, I have been gardening your garden as a contractor, and now I have been finally officially hired as a full-time employee of the government." "Again, that is wonderful; what is your new assignment with the government?" "Ah, sir, I have been assigned to be *your* gardener, but now that I am assigned as a government servant, you will need a new gardener as a contractor to actually do the work."

Value-Subtracting Government Schools in Punjab, Pakistan

The LEAPS (Learning and Educational Achievement in Pakistan Schools) study is the result of an unprecedented exercise in Pakistan of measuring school and teacher characteristics and grade three to six student learning, including tracking students across grades (used to calculate the learning profiles shown in chapter 1), with detailed collection of data on schools and their operation in Punjab province. While much useful and relevant research has emerged from LEAPS, one unexpected finding is the proliferation of low-cost, nonreligious private schools. Nearly all of these new schools are not part of any larger organization but rather are stand-alone mom-and-pop operations.

The LEAPS data present a unique opportunity to examine the value added of government education organizations by comparing learning in government schools with all of the *potential* value added and higher productivity in a formal organization: procedures for hiring teachers, requirements for pre-service training and in-service training, guidance in curriculum, systems of supervision and quality control, economies of scale and scope in inputs, and governmental financial support that allows teacher wages to be independent of student ability to pay. All of this potential value added can be compared to the typical productivity of an independent person with no expertise or experience trying to run a school on his or her own. The main finding is that the government organizations not only do not add value, they subtract it, on three levels.

First, the performance of students in government-run schools is worse: equivalent students learn *massively* less in government schools than in low-cost private schools. While the LEAPS data are not the result of an experiment, they contain an abundance of information on students and schools, providing estimates of the average learning of the "same" (that is, observationally equivalent) students in government versus private schools (Andrabi et al. 2011). Compared to the gains from inputs in the previous chapter, where the total scope-for-learning gains from all potential EMIS-visible input increases were on the order of 0.1 to 0.2 effect sizes, math learning in private schools was 0.7 effect sizes higher than math learning among equivalent students in public schools. The gaps in English were even higher (in Urdu modestly lower), but the researchers found that the private-public gap was roughly an entire student standard deviation. This gap between the private sector and the public sector is much larger than differences on any other school or household characteristics, such as the gap between children with literate versus illiterate mothers or between poorer versus richer students.

Second, government schools are substantially more expensive, as total costs per student are higher. The average cost per student in government schools is roughly twice as high as in private schools (2,000 rupees per child versus 1,000 rupees per child). This difference is primarily the result of teachers in the public sector making substantially more. The study estimates that an equivalently qualified teacher would make 5,299 rupees in the public sector and 1,619 rupees in the private sector.

Lower learning at higher cost implies even lower efficiency. As a crude measure of learning productivity, the private sector spends 1 rupee per percent correct on the LEAPS assessment while the public sector spends 3 rupees. Thus, the cost per unit of learning is three times as high in government-run schools as in private schools.

Third, and perhaps most striking, the *inequality* of school quality across schools is much higher in the government-run schools than in the private schools. One thing you might expect large spider bureaucracies to produce is uniformity. Many think one advantage of a top-down spider system is that it can ensure equality across schools so that, while public schools might be mediocre, they are at least uniformly mediocre. But this is not always so. As it turned out, many of the best schools were public sector schools, but *all* of the worst schools were public sector schools.

When spider systems turn dysfunctional the variance increases, as some schools retain some elements of functionality while the worst become beyond bad.

The striking thing is that not only are government schools rent extracting, or paying more for inputs and teacher wages than needed, they appear to be actually value subtracting: a teacher in the government system does absolutely worse at producing child learning than a teacher completely on his or her own. The learning gains from moving children from organized public schools to completely unorganized, mom-and-pop private schools are roughly the equivalent of two full years of schooling. And these gains are cheaper than free. If there are roughly 12 million children enrolled in government schools, then these learning gains would save $200 million a year. Government schools, with hearty bureaucracies and much more means to attract qualified teachers, produce worse results than teachers just setting up their own schools.

Value-Subtracting School Systems in Uttar Pradesh

Uttar Pradesh is a populous state in northern India (with nearly 200 million people, it would be the world's fifth largest country). As the state has been expanding schooling rapidly, it has been hiring both regular civil service and contract teachers. Contract teachers are usually granted one-year contracts, subject to renewal. These contract teachers have, on average, less formal education and less pre-service training than civil service teachers, are not hired through standard civil service procedures (they are instead hired at the school or village level), are more likely to come from the villages in which they are teaching, and are generally paid less than civil service teachers. In 2009, civil service teachers were making around 11,000 rupees a month, compared to contract teachers at 3,000 rupees a month.

Recent research (Atherton and Kingdon 2010) used unusually detailed data on learning conditions and teaching practices to investigate the relative performance of contract teachers versus civil service teachers. The authors compared the learning of students who had contract teachers with that of children who had civil service teachers, controlling statistically for all other factors that affect student learning, such that their estimates are plausibly the causal impact of an equivalent student being randomly assigned a contract teacher versus civil service teacher. Atherton and Kingdon (2010) found that students taught by contract teachers learned twice as much per year of schooling as students taught by civil service teachers. Going from second to fourth grade with a contract teacher versus a regular teacher added about 0.4 effect sizes of learning (if linear, about 0.2 effect sizes of learning per year). The typical year in schooling with a civil service teacher produced total learning of about 0.2 effect sizes. So the learning impact of having a contract teacher versus a civil service teacher added about 0.2 effect sizes of learning, equivalent to an entire additional year of schooling.

The learning and cost implications of these findings are staggering. Suppose that Uttar Pradesh could replace all civil-service teachers with noncivil service teachers at the same cost and effectiveness of current contract teachers. If feasible, this act alone would double student learning—which is larger than the promise of any combination of expensive, cost-raising, EMIS-visible input increases—and would put Uttar Pradesh on par with the best-performing Indian states. Using illustrative numbers,[2] in 2009 there were roughly 600,000 primary and upper primary grade teachers. The annual wage difference between civil service and contract teachers was U.S. $2,100 (11,000 rupees less 3,000 rupees times twelve months, divided by an exchange rate of 45 rupees per U.S. dollar), which I round to $2,000 a month. The annual cost savings would be $1.2 billion, or $30 per household per year in Uttar Pradesh (which is 3 percent of the average Uttar Pradesh household's total income). In fact, the wage premium—the excess that civil service teachers were paid over what teachers doing a better job were paid in 2009—was ten times the total expenditure of the median rural household in Uttar Pradesh.

If teachers were doing the same work but for more money or less work for the same money, then this evidence would be just another example of a common phenomenon (in both public and distorted private markets) of rent extraction. But this evidence suggests that the government organization of schooling in Uttar Pradesh is *value subtracting*. The expectation is that the education institutions, through teacher training, peer coaching, mentoring, providing teaching resources, and so forth, allow individuals to reach higher potential as teachers than they could independently. Yet a person with lower credentials and operating with little to no institutional support does an *absolutely better* job teaching students at lower cost if *not* hired into the civil service. Is it that the array of departments, councils, and bureaucracies, whose nominal purpose is to promote education, is actually doing the opposite? The evidence suggests that indeed these

2. This is the illustration of a scenario, not a policy proposal, so rough figures will serve the purpose.

government schooling organizations are deeply *antiteacher*—people working there are worse teachers than they would be if they set out to teach the same students independently.

Highlighting the terrible performance of Uttar Pradesh's civil service teachers is not antiteacher. It is the government institutions of education that are antiteacher and antiteaching, on several levels.

One major problem is that the system does not enforce compliance even on fundamentals. As the comedian Woody Allen points out, 80 percent of success is just showing up. Yet teachers don't even do that. The UN's 1996 *Public Report on Basic Education in India,* better known as the PROBE report, whose senior researcher was Jean Dreze, documented the shocking state of elementary education, including lack of facilities, low enrollments, high dropout rates, and high levels of teacher absence in several weaker-performing states in North India (UNDP 1998). In part because of the report, teacher attendance garnered widespread, high-level attention and political concern from the left, middle, and right of the political spectrum.[3] The PROBE team returned to the field in 2006, a decade after the original fieldwork had been conducted. During the course of this decade the government had made massive investments in schooling and focused attention on reducing teacher absenteeism. The follow-up study found significant improvements in EMIS-visible inputs: more classrooms, more desks, more teachers, more kids in school. But the teacher attendance rate was roughly the same as ten years before, a fact that has been documented by every independent study of actual teacher attendance since 1996.[4] Absence rates of 25 percent that persist for a decade or more suggest not a crisis (which would imply some urgency for action) but rather a system that is comfortable with dysfunction.[5]

And it gets worse. Data from the 2005 India Human Development Survey (Desai et al. 2008) show that 29 percent of parents reported their child was "beaten or pinched" in government schools in the previous month. Worse still, this abuse in government schools discriminated

3. I emphasize this to stress that this evidence about the dysfunction of government education systems is not a "partisan" or left-right ideological issue, as Jean Dreze is a committed lifelong socialist.

4. Teacher absences have been documented by studies done by the World Bank (Kremer et al. 2005), by the regular ASER surveys, and by detailed studies of classroom practices (Bhattacharjea et al. 2011).

5. The problem is worse than just physical absence, as even when present, teachers often are not actively teaching. One study documented that less than half of teachers were engaged in teaching activity at the time of a random visit during the school day (Chaudhury et al. 2006).

against the poor. A child from a poor household was almost twice as likely to have been "beaten or pinched" as a child from a rich household. (Private schools, by contrast, while still using physical abuse as discipline, at least show no income favoritism in beatings, which is thanking heaven for small favors.)

Shockingly, the public system in Uttar Pradesh is producing a schooling experience of such low quality that half of urban parents do not send their children there even though it would cost them nothing, choosing instead to pay out of their own scarce resources for private schools. Even in rural Uttar Pradesh, one of the poorest places in India, ASER 2011 data showed that 45.4 percent of all rural children ages six to fourteen were enrolled in private school, compared to 46 percent in government schools (ASER 2012). Parents are using extremely scarce resources (57 percent of the average rural household's budget in Uttar Pradesh goes to food) to avoid government schools.

This government apparatus for schooling in Uttar Pradesh is an example of a value-subtracting organization. Teachers do an absolutely worse job when inside the organization than what they could do just working alone. The whole is well less than the sum of the parts.

The hard question is, how do public sector institutions and organizations survive with such dysfunctional performance? How do they maintain their legitimacy as organizations when they are not just ineffective and rent extracting but apparently value subtracting? And amazingly, despite its dysfunction, public education is not just surviving but in some ways thriving. During the decade from 1996 to 2006, real per student spending on government primary education in Uttar Pradesh more than doubled, and the centrally sponsored scheme to improve basic education was widely hailed both within India and by external agents as a success.

These two examples are just examples, not evidence that governments always, or even typically, fail. But these examples raise questions about failure. What happens in response to failure? How do failing schooling organizations and systems persist?

Isomorphic Mimicry: Camouflage for Failing Spider Systems of Education

An ant colony is a social world with an emergent order. Different ants play different roles in the social order, and they do so by following very simple biochemical scripts. This differentiation allows ant colonies to be tremendously successful in evolutionary terms, as the colony can act in complex ways even in the absence of a centralized intelligence directing each ant. However, natural evolution produces survival, which sometimes comes with what we regard as amazing features, such as the cheetah's speed or the eagle's eye, but it also produces bizarre behaviors. As Holldobler and Wilson (1990) recount, one species of beetle has evolved to emit the right chemical marker that makes worker ants believe that the beetle is actually an ant larva needing to be fed. So the worker ants will drag the beetle into the ant colony and feed the beetle as long as it continues to emit the right chemical signals. This happens even though the beetle looks nothing like ant larvae—the beetle is many times the size of an ant larva. The simple chemical mimicry of the beetle keeps the ants busy feeding a worthless beetle lout because they are following some simple preprogrammed scripts, and no individual ant is equipped to step back and say, "Hey, that doesn't even look like one of us. Why are we feeding it?"

If an ecosystem is configured so that parasites will survive, then parasites will emerge. The pressures of survival and evolution produce both thriving species and parasites thriving on those species. One species of fungus has evolved to take over an ant's body, including using mind control to cause the ant to become a zombie that serves as a vehicle for the survival of the fungus—with the ant killing itself in the process.

Given the deficiencies in learning and school systems outlined so far, one might hope that natural pressures on organizations would lead to improvements. The natural world's evolution metaphor, that weaker species die off and are "naturally" replaced by those better adapted to excel in an environment, suggests that low-performing organizations would die off and be replaced by high performers. Similarly, business market metaphors, or even political or policy metaphors for good ideas, suggest that weak organizations would die off and reform pressures would produce better outcomes.

But this hasn't always happened. In many countries, we observe persistently bad organizational performance, yet no discernible trend for the better. In fact, as we saw in chapters 2 and 3, the empirical learning profile has become worse over time in some countries, has stagnated in others, and has improved in only a few.

The deep question is, what is it about the ecosystem for basic schooling that allows the persistence of organizations that produce disastrously bad learning? How do ministries of education manage to maintain legitimacy and attract continued internal and external resources, despite continued failure?

My argument is that the key to this perverse success of failure in educational systems is isomorphic mimicry. Just as the beetle benefits from the ants by mimicking their larvae, failing public systems survive, and even thrive and attract more resources, by striving simply to look like functional school systems.

Ecosystems That Lack Evidence-Based Decisionmaking Encourage Camouflage

In a highly influential work on the behavior of organizations, the sociologists Paul J. DiMaggio and Walter W. Powell (1983) identified isomorphism as an organizational strategy. They argued that organizations often adopt "reforms" that have little or no demonstrated connection to the organization's goals but rather serve to provide the organization with legitimacy from key stakeholders, and with that legitimacy, increased support and resources. These actions do not touch the core of the organization but rather deal with peripheral functions in the organization.

Knowing that organizations engage in isomorphic mimicry leads to the question: What are the *system* conditions in which isomorphic mimicry is an attractive or even optimal *organizational* strategy? In what man-made ecosystems does organizational isomorphic mimicry thrive?

The schematic in figure 4-1 shows the characteristics of ecosystems for organizations and how those affect the strategies of organizations and agents in the ecosystem (Andrews, Pritchett, and Woolcock 2012; Pritchett, Woolcock, and Andrews 2012). Drawing on the work of Carlile and Lakhani (2011), this figure highlights two key features of an ecosystem of organizations: the space for novelty, and how novelty is evaluated.[6]

The *space for novelty* in figure 4-1 ranges from open to closed. How easy is it to attract the resources to do something innovative, particularly something with the potential to scale up? Some systems make it easy for new entrants to come in and try, while others have barriers—legal, social, political, operational—to entry.

---

6. I follow Carlile and Lakhani (2011) in using the word "novelty" rather than "innovation" as "innovation" has acquired, in many contexts, a positive connotation such that "innovation" is taken to mean "something new and positive" as opposed to the more neutral meaning of "something new" that "novelty" preserves.

Figure 4-1. System characteristics determine the possibilities for failing organizations to persist through isomorphic mimicry.

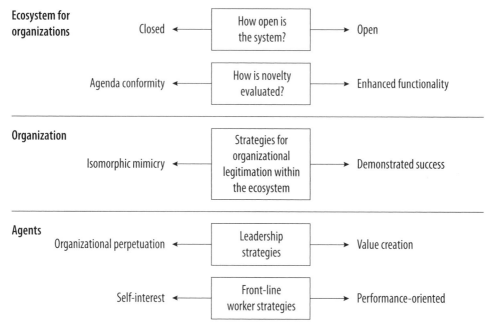

Source: Adapted from Andrews, Pritchett, and Woolcock (2012).

The *evaluation of novelty* ranges from agenda confirmation to demonstrated functional success. Often innovations are simply new ways of doing the same thing and pose no threat to the core of the system. For instance, if in-service teacher training is done once a year, then someone could propose doing it twice a year. Or the content of teacher training could be altered to cover new subjects. Or teacher training could be done with active versus passive pedagogical techniques. In most educational system these "novelties" will be adopted, or not, for reasons unrelated to whether they lead to higher or lower student learning. An alternative way to evaluate a novel approach would be evaluate it based on functional success.

The basics of any evolutionary ecosystem, whether natural or man-made, are two features: *a source of variation* and a *survival* function for variation (see table 4-1). These combine to produce the dynamics of an evolutionary system. With no source of variation, there can be no dynamics. But variation alone is not necessarily a good thing. Nearly

Table 4-1. Combinations of "space for" and "evaluation of" novelty (new ideas, innovations) make up the ecosystem for innovations.

| | | Space for novelty | |
		Open	Closed
Evaluation of novelty	Demonstrated functional success	Ecological learning takes place. New organizations emerge and rise; horizontal spread of ideas occurs as other organization adapt new ideas.	Very few new ideas are generated at scale, but evaluation plays some role in what is scaled. Only organizational learning is possible.
	Agenda conformity	Ample experimentation is potentially possible, but all within the existing paradigm as tweaking around the edges (e.g., more instructional days, smaller class sizes, different kinds of teacher training), but innovations spread based on fashion, not on demonstrated performance.	Little or no ecological learning takes place. Large mainstream organizations can use isomorphic mimicry to appear to implement agenda-conforming "best practice" but actually resist organizational learning. Innovation by small players is "effervescent" and does scale, either vertically or horizontally.

all genetic mutations are harmful, so variation without a survival function that differentiated on some criteria generates only observed variation, but no progress.

When an organization, such as a Ministry of Education, is embedded in an ecosystem that both is closed—so that the organization is never under serious existential threat from a competitor—and does not have its performance evaluated according to any agreed-upon outcome metric of success but rather on "compliance," then progress is doubly hard. Isomorphic mimicry can easily become the most desirable strategy. After all, organizational learning is hard even in the best of circumstances, when performance metrics are clear and pressure is on. When innovations are threatening to the status quo and meet strong internal and external resistance, and there is little or no consensus about their payoff, then avoiding hard changes while pursuing simple, cosmetically attractive, camouflaged objectives is a compelling approach.

This camouflage gives rise to an intellectual atmosphere in which creating functional standards and expectations for child learning is regarded as retrogressive and anti-education. In one of the saddest ironies of our era, the systems around "basic education" are ignorant of their own impacts. Without standards, there can be no measurement, and without measurement, there is no evaluation of success and failure. Luis Crouch's description of the predicament of the educational system in Peru, as he found it in 2006, is perfect, and poignant (see World Bank 2007).

> The need to create standards is related to the need for developing a culture of evaluation in Peru. There is currently a pervasive fear in Peru's education sector of anyone being evaluated. This creates a vicious cycle. The fear of failure creates a fear of evaluation, but the lack of evaluation condemns almost all efforts to failure, because there is no serious way to detect when anything is going wrong. Failure and lack of evaluation against any kind of standard become self-fulfilling prophecies of each other, and create an environment of intense pessimism, fatalism, and lack of accountability. The fear of evaluation and standards has been turned into a virtue, and it has become popular to question evaluation and measurement as intellectually suspect, non-modern, regressive, or inequality-inducing.

Saying that educational systems are anti-evaluation is not synonymous with anti-novelty—quite the contrary. If you criticize any education system in the world, you will quickly be pointed to how they are changing and improving. Often this evidence will be data on the expansion of EMIS-visible inputs, but there will also be pedagogical and organizational innovations. But if you ask for *evidence* that these innovations are successful, you will be accused of not understanding how complex educational processes are and of pushing narrow criteria of standardized testing that would reduce the quality of the "true" educational experience.

The problem is not the lack of change or innovation but how the innovations are chosen, evaluated, and scaled. Innovations that reinforce existing agendas are always welcome. Moreover, every innovation can be successful if each is allowed to declare the performance against which it will be evaluated as an innovation. Circularity abounds, as mere adoption of the innovation is itself defined as success.

My argument is that a huge amount of what passes for improving the quality of schooling and even education reform is window dressing. Such reforms have no plausible evidentiary basis and do not include a plan for generating evidence about performance. The real purpose of reform efforts is to create certain appearances to legitimate failing and flailing systems, without making demands or threatening existing political interests.

The camouflage of reform has only gradually been revealed because many conventional schooling innovations were functional for the *goal* of *schooling: getting children into seats* (for example, building more schools, providing basic inputs, and hiring minimally equipped teachers). Whatever quality agenda existed also confirmed the schooling movement agenda and found ready acceptance and adoption, without any requirement for evidence. Whatever challenged the "more is better" belief system had a difficult time penetrating the closed space for public funding (which still dominates) and had to push uphill against existing incumbents, because there was no consensus view on the desired educational outcomes that would allow innovators to prove success.

The concern with innovation goes beyond organizations, as systems can produce scaled innovations as an outcome of a system in which no individual organization learns. In nature, the average fitness of organism in an ecosystem might improve even if no single organism learns, so long as organisms that better fit the ecosystem are more successful in reproducing. Thus, there is an important distinction to draw between *organizational* learning and *ecological* learning within a system. When productivity in a sector goes up over time, this is measured as the average productivity of all existing firms weighted by their size. Productivity could go up because existing firms get more productive (organizational learning) or because new firms that are more productive enter the sector and get bigger and bigger (ecological learning), or some combination of both. Economists often refer to ecological learning as "creative destruction," after the economist Joseph Schumpeter, who emphasized that the success of capitalism was due to both the birth and the death of firms, as often new ideas are incompatible with the structures of old firms, so that new ideas lead to the shrinking and even disappearance of firms that are unable to adapt.

In market economies, there are sectors that illustrate both organizational and ecological learning. For instance, in retailing there have been several waves of creative destruction as new technologies made possible new ways of retailing. In the United States, for instance, the rise of low-cost train and truck transport and reliable nationwide mail delivery systems led to the rise of the firm Sears, Roebuck. This mail-order retailer blew gales of creative destruction across America as mom-and-pop retailers could not compete with the ability of people to order the latest of everything, from fashion to tools, straight from a catalogue. Sears became a huge firm that moved markets and was headquartered in the Sears Tower, at the time the world's tallest building. Leading business schools studied cases describing the keys to Sears's fantastic success.

No reader younger than I (fifty-four in 2013) can remember when Sears was a powerhouse, because, as recounted in Donald Katz's gripping account, *The Big Store* (1987), in the mid-1980s low-cost retailers eroded Sears's advantages. Of course, the company responded in various ways, but organizational learning is difficult even in high-pressure market environments, and Sears began a slide as a retailing organization. Lower-cost retailers such as Kmart that weakened Sears were themselves eventually confronted by new competitors like Wal-Mart, which has grown to over two million employees. (In a borderline ironic development, Kmart emerged from bankruptcy and bought Sears.) But these retailers are in turn under threat from both specialty superstores and online retailers such as Amazon.com. Retail marketing has gone through several generations of innovation now, and productivity is much higher. This is ecological learning. But the e-tailing world is dominated by Amazon.com and not Sears.com or Kmart.com or even Walmart.com because ecological learning can happen even when organizational learning is hard. This is particularly true when the innovation that is needed is inconsistent with the existing organizational culture and requires "disruption."

What is the point of a vignette about American retailing in a book about education in poor countries? The gains in productivity in American retailing did not come about through the application of strategies thought up by the best and brightest managers in the best and biggest companies. Rather, productivity gains were the result of an ecosystem in which consumers could vote with their feet, creating a functional evaluation of innovations and a market system in which new entrants could attract resources to expand. The *system* produced the result through *ecological* learning, not the learning in the organizations.

Weak Systems of Accountability Produce Isomorphic Mimicry by Organizations and Agents

Whenever a tire is flat, the flatness is manifested at the bottom of the tire. But the hole isn't always at the bottom. In education, the evidence about teacher and student performance is generated at the school level. The temptation is to blame the teachers or school-level factors for inefficiencies or poor performance. However, in a system of accountability, the problems that are visible at the school level may have causes that are far removed. It is easy to say, "Children are learning so little because teachers are absent." And since teachers are the agents choosing not to attend or not to exert effort, it is easy to pin the blame on teachers. However, teachers are often themselves trapped in systems designed to induce and encourage bad outcomes. For instance, in political systems driven by patronage, in which politicians are rewarded for giving teaching posts to supporters rather than providing better education, the insulation of schools and teachers from performance responsibility is not a flaw but woven into the design. In education bureaucracies that rely on top-down control of rules and procedures, even positive deviations are squelched, not rewarded.

To switch metaphors, if your electric toaster does not work, your bread does not get toasted. However, without further investigation, it is impossible to tell whether the toaster doesn't work because a wire inside the device is broken, there is a fault in the wiring going to the outlet inside your house, the power is out in your entire neighborhood, or there is a regional blackout. If the power is out citywide, then trying to fix your toaster because your toast doesn't brown does no good at all. Moreover, there could be multiple failings, and *every* fault in the critical path has to be fixed for the toaster to work—the power has to make it to your house, the house wiring has to get power to the outlet, and the toaster has to be plugged in, and a heating device has to turn power into heat (and turn off).

The problem with government schooling is not that it is government schooling, it is the *governance* of schooling. The best systems of basic education in the world are predominantly government systems. Moreover, countries with predominantly publicly financed and controlled systems of schooling have discovered many different ways to be successful. Germany, France, and the Netherlands each have systems of basic education that produce (near) universal completion and high levels of learning, but they operate under fundamentally different institutions of governance. But what high-performing, publicly produced education needs is a coherent system of accountability, which can be embodied in many different institutional arrangements.

The World Bank's 2004 World Development Report, *Making Services Work for the Poor,* created an overarching framework for analyzing systems of accountability.[7] I cannot hope to do justice with a summary of

7. I was one of the team members and co-authors of that report, including its chapter on education.

Table 4-2. Performance accountability in "long-route" systems for the public production of schooling can go wrong in many ways.

Design elements of accountability	Three accountability relationships in the "long route"		
	Politics (Citizens to the state)	Compact (Executive to Ministry of Education)	Management (Ministries to teacher)
Finance	No link between taxes and services makes political feedback loops on taxes and demands for spending separate.	Financing is too little and too overly structured (e.g., too much to wages, too much control at too high a level).	Teacher compensation is inadequate (too low) or adequate but badly structured for performance, or both.
Delegation	It's hard to make quality education electorally salient.	Overambitious and vague goals are pursued, such that measurement is impossible.	Process compliance. Too many pressures on vague goals.
Information	Information is scarce, secret, and manipulated.	Little relevant, reliable, regular information is available except on process or logistics.	Measures of inputs and process at best. No ability to distinguish good from bad teachers and classrooms.
Enforceability	Pure electoral mechanisms are infrequent and weak.	Hard to judge the performance of monopoly provider (or monopoly recipient of public funds).	Job tenure is inviolable. Seniority is the main mechanism of reward. There is no upside potential.

that report, but want to draw on a few details using that framework. The report argued that a coherent system of accountability for the governance of schooling is one in which three functional relationships of accountability, namely, politics and voice, compact, and management, and the four design elements of any relationship of accountability, namely, finance, delegation, information, and enforceability, work together.

For governments to drive the traditional "long route" of public sector production of schooling to success, they have to create conditions in which all the relationships of accountability work, at least tolerably well, in each of the elements of accountability (this is called the "long route" precisely because it involves multiple different accountability links to work). Table 4-2 lays out the many ways in which the traditional long-route accountability approaches go wrong in centralized spider systems in developing countries.

Accountability is a *system* property. Strong accountability requires the integration of each of the design elements. Unfortunately, facile advocacy seizes on one element of the problem, with proponents then declaring they have found the elixir. For instance, many focus just on the element of enforceability, and claim the source of weak accountability is that you cannot do anything about poorly performing teachers. As this simplistic reasoning goes, if you could only fire at least some bad teachers, then all teachers would get the message and improve their performance. In this view, the villain is often the teachers' union, which blocks performance accountability for teachers.

This logic might get it exactly backward. There is no successful educational system anywhere, of any kind, that attained excellence by being hostile to teachers. Moreover, reducing the accountability of teachers to prescribed Taylorist controlled work environments and procedures as a way to hold them accountable is inconsistent with the nature of teaching as an intrinsically creative activity. Teachers' unions and their behavior are the result, not the cause, of spider educational systems. That is, the top-down, public production systems turn the craft and profession of teaching into a cog in a bureaucracy. If there is only one, monopoly financer of education, then teachers are at the mercy of that organization. If this organization treats teachers like automatons who are expected simply to follow rules, overly structures their work environment, and does not create a positive sense of teaching as a vocation with learning as the goal, then naturally teachers will respond by creating countervailing pressures through their own political organization.

Alternatively, suppose that these advocates triumphed and the system could fire teachers (or there were stronger "enforceability" as an accountability design element in the "management" accountability relationship between organizations and front-line workers), but the overall system of accountability were deficient in its other components—like "delegation" and "information"? Well, first of all, whom would you fire? Obviously, low performers. But when the *delegation* relationship is weak, so that teachers are overburdened with too many vague goals and given no support in achieving those goals, termination is manifestly unfair. Moreover, since delegation is weak, there is little or no reliable *information* on which specific teachers are or are not contributing to achieving education goals. Allowing organizations to fire teachers may result in completely arbitrary decisions, as teachers who are unorthodox in their approach but successful get fired for noncompliance with processes and procedures unrelated to actual goals. Worse, without the constraints of clear delegation and reliable information, imposing more enforceability on teachers may lead to good teachers being laid off just so that they can be replaced with a local patronage hire. So the very civil service protections that now thwart accountability were once seen as huge gains to prevent abuse.

The point is, you cannot fix organizations or expect very different behaviors from front-line agents unless you fix the system. That this is a system problem is too bad, because none of us are very good at thinking about system problems. Most of us are experts (of a sort, at least) at thinking about objects and agents because we need to be experts at objects and agents just to get by with life. None of us can be very success-ful at life without having pretty good theories about how objects—bricks, tables, shirts, pots and pans—will behave. We know what is solid (bricks) and what isn't (water), and we hence know that kicking a brick will hurt more than kicking water. Similarly, none of us can be very successful at life without having pretty good theories about how other agents (espe-cially people) will behave. We have pretty good ideas about what noises will get another agent to pass us the salt, what actions will make people angry, and what will make people happy. These are incredibly sophisti-cated mental feats for which billions of years of evolution have equipped us, and hence as humans we operate pretty well our whole lives with the dualistic mental ontology of stuff and agents we master by the time we are two-year-olds.

In contrast, most of us are completely worthless at thinking about system problems, because we almost never need to. In Howard Garden-er's (1991) evocative phrase, we live with an "unschooled mind" about systems. People live in incredibly sophisticated modern economies and have absolutely no idea how they work. And that is mostly OK, because the beauty of emergent orders in self-organizing systems is that no indi-vidual agent has to understand how the whole system works in order for the whole system to work (Seabright 2010). The problem is that when people do think about systems, they tend to extrapolate their expertise in objects and agents. In other words, they tend to anthropo-morphize and tell narratives and reason about systems as if a system were an agent.

But in complex adaptive emergent orders the system can have outcomes that no agent in the system intended. Two examples of complex adaptive systems in which outcomes emerge are evolution and economics.

If one asks questions today about the natural world, such as why an elephant has a long trunk, the answer will be that it is the result of evolutionary processes. This is a shorthand way of describing a system in which there is (1) a source of variation and (2) a mechanism that essentially evaluates variation, in that some variants are more like to replicate than other variants. No central planner ever designed an elephant's trunk based on its optimality criteria. No elephant ever chose its trunk size. The explanation for the wonders of the animal kingdom is that things just happened that way: stuff at the basic biological level (such as genes) interacted with system constraints, and the outcome was an elephant's trunk.

The essential insight of economics is perhaps still best expressed by two passages from Adam Smith, *The Wealth of Nations* (1776):

> Give me that which I want, and you shall have this which you want, is the meaning of every such offer; and it is in this manner that we obtain from one another the far greater part of those good offices which we stand in need of. It is not from the benevolence of the butcher[,] the brewer, or the baker that we expect our dinner, but from their regard to their own interest.

> As every individual, therefore, endeavours as much as he can both to employ his capital in the support of domestic industry, and so to direct that industry that its produce may be of the greatest value; every individual necessarily labours to render the annual revenue of the society as great as he can. He generally, indeed, neither intends to promote the public interest, nor knows how much he is promoting it. By preferring the support of domestic to that of foreign industry, he intends only his own security; and by directing that industry in such a manner as its produce may be of the greatest value, he intends only his own gain, and he is in this, as in many other cases, led by an invisible hand to promote an end which was no part of his intention. Nor is it always the worse for the society that it was no part of it. By pursuing his own interest he frequently promotes that of the society more effectually than when he really intends to promote it.

When this is simplified into mathematics, economists can show that some equilibrium allocations have a property called "Pareto optimality" (after an Italian named Vilfredo Pareto), which is that the allocation is "efficient" in the sense that there is no other allocation of consumption or goods that makes *everyone* better off without making someone else worse off. The most important point is not defending markets in the real world but the deep conceptual point that one can formally model complex adaptive system and show that the system has properties, desirable properties in the this case, that no agent in the system intended or sought. This is an emergent property of the system itself and cannot be explained in baby ontology categories of why things happen.

I am going on at length about this because this book is about explaining and fixing poor learning outcomes by fixing broken systems, not fixing people. But I have to go on about this because system explanations just have no appeal to people, myself included. Agent-centered explanations are powerfully appealing to us, on a very deep level. Believe me, if your child says, "Daddy, tell me a story," you can be sure he or she wants a story with *agents*, heroes and villains who have goals and make plans and overcome obstacles. Even economists when they try to explain Pareto optimality resort to making the ontological unfamiliar seem plausible by invoking "an invisible hand"—and hence making it seem familiar. "Oh," say sophomores on hearing the invisible hand metaphor, "like an agent with a hand willed it. Now I get it"—and hence deeply don't get it. But even as an economist who loves system explanations in the domain of my expertise, I am bored silly by historians who tell the stories of structures and institutions and geographic constraints (I have never been able to make my way through any small part of the French historian Braudel, for instance, though I often think that I should). I love a good yarn about American independence that does not involve the carrying trade but does involve George Washington and his bravery. The appeal of agent-centered, human narrative explanations over systemic explanations is why no one—except perhaps you—is reading this book.

This is because nearly all of our success as organisms is driven by understanding stuff and agents. Just as none of us really needs to understand quantum mechanics or general relativity to live our whole lives as successful, fulfilled, productive individuals, the number of times any of us needs to understand systems is vanishingly small. You can have a successful professional career without understanding systems. You can have a happy marriage without understanding systems (perhaps more likely, in fact: try asking your spouse sometime about the system of marriage—such as "Why did monogamy as an organizational form of the family triumph over polygamy?"—and see how that works for you). You can raise lovely children without understanding systems.

You just never need to really understand systems, until you do. Because even though life is always really about agents, it is also really always about systems.

Dangers of Isomorphism I: Good Ideas Can't Succeed in a Camouflage System

The first danger of isomorphic mimicry in spider school systems with weak accountability is that good ideas imported from elsewhere become irrelevant or even bad ideas, as they are used to prevent needed system reforms. Implementing "best practice" gleaned from the superficial comparisons of the forms of schooling around the world can even lead to perversity, and "best practice" can make things worse if form and function have diverged.

What passes for advice is looking at the success of the Finnish schools and recommending to others, "Do what the Finns did." The reality is that what countries need to do is not what the Finns did but rather they need to do what the Finns did. Yes, I know, sorry about that sentence; I'll try again. What countries need to do is not what the Finns did; rather, they need to *achieve* what the Finns *achieved*—which might require doing the opposite of what the Finns *did*. That is, the problem is not adopting the forms of what the Finns did but rather solving the problems the Finns solved to produce functionality—which is what the Finns did—but that approach may not at all produce the same forms the Finns ended up with.

Camouflage Protecting Organizations Rotten at Their Core

Students of organizations traditionally identify five elements of organizational structure (e.g., Mintzberg 1979). One is the technical or operational core, which is where the value added of the organization happens. For a manufacturing firm, this would be the factory floor; for a hospital, it would be the care provider-patient interactions. Around the technical core are other elements of the organization: top management, middle management, technical support, and administrative support. Ideally, in a schooling organization or system, the technical core would be the classroom interactions between teachers and learners (and among the student learners themselves). The rest of the organization would include technical support for training and supervision, administrative support for procuring materials, and the human resource functions of hiring and allocating teachers, as well as middle management and top management. These components would provide support to those in the technical core (teachers) to improve their productivity in educating children.

How do we explain the survival of organizations like school systems that are value subtracting (or even ineffective or rent extracting)? How can an organization be sustained if teachers, part of the organization's core, are less productive at achieving learning goals inside the organization than if they were to have no association with the school system? If organizations survive, it is because they create value for *someone,* and hence the question is, what is the *real* operational core of dysfunctional schooling systems?

Moreover, what happens to the human resource functions of recruiting, hiring, and assigning teachers to classrooms in value-subtracting school systems? In a functional schooling system, these are "support" or administrative functions that contribute to the operational core by making sure that each classroom has a teacher with the capacity to help students learn—the value-creation function of the organization.

At their worst, the only value schooling systems create is contracts for school builders and jobs for those hired. In a dysfunctional system, hiring and allocating people to civil service protected posts becomes *the rotten technical core* of a rent-extracting—and even value-subtracting relative to its putative purpose—organization. The people who control the allocation of those jobs (including hiring and assignment) are afforded a lot of power and value. Imagine that I get to hire teachers who are paid 20,000 rupees a month, but many people with the same qualifications would take up an equivalent teaching job at equivalent quality for 2,000 rupees a month. I am controlling 18,000 rupees per month of potentially extractable rents.

The problem then becomes that the perversion of purpose of the school system—rent extraction—is camouflaged by the pretense that it is really creating learning. It is essential that it go through the motions so that it looks like an educational organization, even though it really isn't an organization about education at all.

Central to this camouflage is the resistance to changes in the ecosystem that would reveal the true technical core of the organization (rent extraction). Therefore it is essential that *outcomes*—actual student learning—*not* be measured in a repeated, regular, and reliable way that would allow easy comparisons of the value added of the organization with other alternatives. It is also essential that innovations be contained strictly within the organization so that the space for novelty (especially novelty that receives public support) is limited.

Input Improvements as Camouflage Do No Good—and Protect Harm

The danger of isomorphic mimicry is that elements that really are part of a successful education system are used tactically by dysfunctional systems as camouflage. Education initiatives that really can improve student learning are copied and implemented in such a way that they do not have any impact on learning and instead protect and further the noneducational objectives of the dysfunctional organization. Here are three examples of improvements that work in functional systems yet don't work in isomorphic mimicry systems.

Smaller Class Sizes

There is no question that reductions in class size can improve student learning. At the extreme, one-on-one or one-to-few tutoring is widely regarded as an ideal learning situation (as evidenced by its use to educate elites for millennia prior to mass schooling). There is also no question that reductions in class size alone, when implemented with no other changes to systems or accountability, might not result in learning gains. And now there is no reasonable doubt that class size reductions alone in some situations do not work because the huge literature on the topic, with debatable internal validity due to nonexperimental data, has been added to by rigorous randomized experiments.

For example, a recent experiment in Kenya, carried out by researchers from Harvard and MIT, featured the government randomly granting permission to some schools (or rather their parent-teacher committees) to hire an additional teacher, reducing class size—often from very high levels of one hundred or more students per class. Students in schools receiving a contract teacher were randomly assigned to the contract teacher or a civil service teacher. The new contract teacher's salary was one-fourth that of the civil service teacher's and the contract teacher's contract was subject to school committee renewal, while the civil service teacher had the normal civil service protections. As shown in figure 4-2, students gained 0.13 effect sizes more in learning in both math and literacy if they were assigned to a contract teacher in a school with school-based management improvements. On the other hand, if they were in a class of reduced size with a civil service teacher the students got absolutely no benefit from that (Duflo, Dupas, and Kremer 2012).

The mechanism of the differential impact on learning of contract teachers versus civil service teachers is not difficult to discern. The civil service teachers reduced their attendance as a result of having a contract

Figure 4-2. In Kenya, reducing class size with contract teachers, but not with civil service teachers, produced gains.

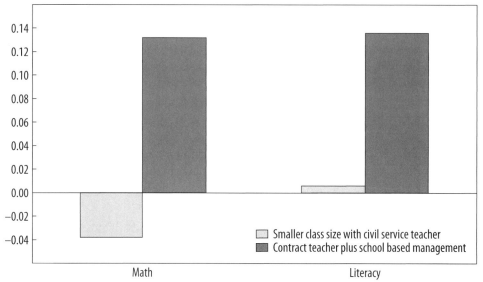

Impact (effect size) one year after program

Source: Adapted from Duflo, Dupas, and Kremer (2012).

teacher assigned to their school. Just as in the story of the gardener above, once there was more help, the civil service teachers did not utilize the additional help to improve performance but rather used it to do less work.

The idea behind using solid research methods (such as randomization) is to prove what works so that these new ideas can be scaled up. What is interesting is that this study (the results of which were available in roughly their current form in 2007) has produced two additional actions, both of which illustrate the dangers of isomorphic mimicry.

First, researchers tried to replicate the findings that additional contract teachers would improve student test scores at a larger scale than the original study (Bold et al. 2013). In doing so they replicated the process using both the Kenyan Ministry of Education and an international NGO, World Vision. Bold and colleagues found that when the original policy of contract teachers was implemented by the NGO, it had exactly the same impact, with relatively big effect size learning gains for students exposed to contract teachers. But when the Ministry of Education was responsible for implementation, even of the same design and using contract teachers, the impact on student learning was zero. So the Ministry appeared to be adopting a best practice of policies that had been "proven" by "rigorous research" to work, but it did not have the same impact.

Second, given the long lag of busy researchers in producing papers, one can see isomorphic mimicry play out in real time. Duflo, Dupas, and Kremer (2012) conclude their report with the following statement:

> Subsequent to our study, the Kenyan government, which had long had a freeze on hiring of new civil-service teachers, hired 18,000 contract teachers. Initial plans included no guarantee of civil-service employment afterwards. However, the Kenyan National Union of Teachers opposed the initial plans and under the eventual agreement, contract teachers were hired at much higher salaries than in the program we study, hiring was done under civil-service rules heavily weighting the cohort in which applicants graduated from teacher training college rather than the judgment of local school committees, and contract teachers hired under the program were promised civil service positions.

So all the key features of the contract teachers program that were "proven" to work were undermined politically and organizationally by pressures of isomorphism: formal training was valued over local judgment in hiring, civil service protections versus accountability for performance, and higher salaries over market-based wages.

The difficulty is that reductions in class size contribute more salaries for teachers—and hence to possible rent extraction by a rotten core—whether or not they contribute to learning. *Both* performance-driven *and* rent-driven systems will want to reduce class size at times, the former to improve learning and the latter to extract more rents, achieved under the camouflage of purported improved learning.

Teacher Training

An evaluation of decades of in-service teacher training in Indonesia found little or no impact on student learning, or even on teacher practices. How is it that this technical support, an element of any organization, has no impact on the performance in the technical core of the classroom? Because the technical core in dysfunctional systems is not supporting performance in the classroom but rather focusing on rent extraction. Close examination of most teacher training in Indonesia in the period under review found that the system was really designed to channel funds to teachers through excessive reimbursement of training costs rather than to provide training.

One anecdote from my experience living and working in Indonesia (which is dated and possibly not relevant to Indonesia today) illustrates three ways in which substantial budgets for training were used to extract rents. First, training sessions were usually three days, so that each participant received three days of per diem and two nights of accommodation. But the first day's training consisted of only one session, at night, and the third day's training consisted of only one session, in the morning, with just one full day of training in between, on the second day. Second, the hotel would give receipts for one rate but charge teachers another (with a kickback for the hotel) so that each night's accommodation was profit to the teachers (and the hotel owners). Third, often one teacher would attend and sign for other colleagues, so that one teacher attending one day of training would collect the per diem and accommodation fees for two or three colleagues. The administrative records of in-service training for an education project would show lots of budget spent, lots of man-days of training received, lots of curricula covered—but underneath, it was all a charade. The fact that empirical studies found no impact of this training should not have surprised anyone who knew the system. Teacher training *could* have impacts, but what happened in Indonesia was camouflage called teacher training.

Camouflage also plagues pre-service training. There is little empirical evidence of impact from pre-service training, even though subject matter knowledge and formal education tend to be associated with student learning. Does this mean pre-service training isn't important? No. It indicates that the pre-service training that exists is for the most part just isomorphic mimicry that looks like training.

Warwick and Reimers (1995) examined teacher training in Pakistan and found that all parties, trainers and trainees, were just going through the motions, and, not surprisingly, teacher training had no impact on student achievement. The authors' review of two teacher training institutes concluded:

> Most inmates of this system have no respect for themselves; hence they have no respect for others. They mock at the system, laugh at their own foibles. They don't trust each other. The teachers think the students are cheats, the students think the teachers have

shattered their ideals. Most of them are disillusioned. They have no hopes, no aims, no ambitions. They are living from day to day, watching impersonally as the system crumbles around them. If there is a major cause of self-destruction, it is this: each lifts a finger to accuse the other. Everyone thinks of themselves as a victim.

Yet even in this condition, when this is the description of the system for training new teachers, experts recommend that more teachers need pre-service training. Why? Because everyone "knows" that good education systems have trained teachers, so the camouflage value of teacher training trumps over the reality.

Teacher Salaries

The dangerous thing about isomorphic mimicry is that by imitating functional systems with a patina of formal structures and rules, dysfunctional education systems look to naive outside experts as places to implement best practice. So international experts come with advice that works in functional systems that may backfire because piecemeal advice doesn't take into account how the entire system is wired.

Often, experts give advice by examining top performers and telling others, "Be like them." For instance, a recent report aimed at improving teaching quality in the United States compared the United States to "high-performing" systems (Singapore, Korea, Finland) and found much greater fractions of teachers in those countries were in the top third academically. Thus the report recommended that the United States attract academic high performers into the teaching profession through better compensation, as is done in "high-performing" systems (Auguste, Kihn, and Miller 2010). In the end, no matter how subtle the original message and no matter how focused on just the United States, the take-away lesson is that higher teacher pay leads to better performance.[8] This naturally strikes a welcome chord with key education constituencies. With such evidence, it becomes possible to treat raising teacher's salaries as not just politically expedient but actually best practice because it is what high-performing education systems do.

8. In the category "you cannot make this up," literally a week before my last edit of this chapter (April 2013) I was discussing organizational performance in India generally (with some references to education), and afterward someone said to me, "Don't we learn from the Finnish experience that you just need to pay teachers well and you'll get the highly qualified as teachers?" They obviously knew nothing about India or what teachers actually were paid in India but "knew" the "lesson" of high performance. Sigh.

The easily recognizable problem is that systems operate as systems, and merely imitating one component of a system without the other components will not necessarily lead to the same outcome—in fact, it could make the outcome perverse. The organizational economist John Roberts (2004) emphasizes that compensation schemes are complementary with other dimensions of firm organization, and so introducing a bonus system within a firm may or may not increase worker productivity, depending on how the bonus interacts with other elements of the organization of production.

Here is the kicker about the Uttar Pradesh evidence that opened the chapter: despite the evidence that civil service teachers were massively overpaid relative to their contract teacher or private sector counterparts, and despite the evidence that, on average, students taught by civil service teachers versus contract or private teachers learned less, the pay of civil service teachers was raised. So while the study in 2009 found civil service teachers making almost four times the wage of contract teachers (which was itself higher than the private sector wages) of 11,000 rupees a month, the current average pay for civil service teachers is 23,000 rupees a month.

This high pay has led to perverse results: the appeal of the higher salary has made the demand for civil service teaching jobs so great that the profession attracts people who have no interest in teaching but rather join, often using bribery or political connections to do so, *because* of the high salary and low accountability. So the combination of (1) high pay with (2) systems that are ineffective at hiring the best teachers (as opposed to those with appropriate credentials and political connections) and with (3) systems with weak local accountability (which is exacerbated by hiring teachers more powerful than the village leaders in communities to which they are posted) leads to even worse problems. As I have argued elsewhere, this combination has led in India to a "perfect storm" in which costs are high, learning is low, students are unhappy, parents are unhappy (and moving to private schools), and teachers themselves are unhappy with their working conditions, despite the high pay (Murgai and Pritchett 2006).

And yet people use the evidence of best practice as an isomorphism to push for even higher salaries (and sometimes get them). Popular education reforms, even ones that are proven to work in some circumstances in which ecosystems create performance pressures, when implemented without consideration of the ecosystem of accountability and innovation will just fail.

Dangers of Isomorphism II: Resisting Disruptive Innovation

Animals go extinct not because their genes change but because their environment does. When the climate changes or when a new predator is introduced, survival requires animals to change or die. Mostly they die. The result of rapid environmental changes is usually not the learning of species but monumental declines in the population, or even extinction. This is because the stability of the genetic code, which is a boon in stable times, cannot change fast enough to adapt to changed conditions.

Spider education systems are both incapable of making the changes needed to pursue the learning agenda and block the viable space for innovation. The dysfunctional spider systems found in the developing world lack accountability structures that would allow them to respond effectively. The systems of education have created a cocoon in which isomorphic mimicry, which allows schools to look like good schools without being good schools, is a strategy that safely provides success at every level. Systems that promote isomorphic mimicry through a closed set of possible innovators (only the top) and through weak performance of innovations on the basis of demonstrated functionality effectively deflect disruptive innovation.

The second danger of isomorphic mimicry is that there is no room for the innovation or reform that leads to improved learning. Spider systems may have a constant stream of "innovation" and "reform," but the system does not choose which "novelties" to scale based on their functional performance, nor does it have an effective mechanism for the diffusion and scaling of a novelty that has proved successful. The camouflage protects the organizations from failure and delegitimation, but at the cost of only being able to continue "business as usual." Once the ecosystem is aligned into isomorphic mimicry mode, then even well-meaning leaders or bold outside reformers have a difficult time getting productive ideas up.

Even Innovative Leaders Can't Implement Innovation in Isomorphic Systems

Education system leaders can choose between activities that push the functionality of the organization and activities that promote the organization's narrower interests in perpetuation and expansion. In isomorphic systems, leaders who provide more of the same are lauded and rewarded. Expanding budgets, raising teacher salaries, hiring more teachers, and expanding enrollments are the outcomes that the system is set up to track and measure, and hence these are efforts that bring immediate rewards, even if they do not address any of the system's problems or improve outcomes in education or learning.

Improving organizations can be very painful, particularly in organizations in which norms of front-line workers are entrenched and expectations are low. Sustaining core reforms that change front-line worker behavior typically requires a strong political authorizing environment (e.g., Moore 1995) and at least a minimal inside coalition of support (e.g., Kelman 2005).

This is not to say there are no reforms—quite the opposite. A common complaint among teachers and principals is reform overload. Every few years a new fad comes along, and teachers are expected to adopt this new idea into their classroom practice. But in a closed system without the ability to differentiate functionally, these innovations do not necessarily improve outcomes. Innovative organizational leaders often get crushed because the existing system has no way of acknowledging success, even on the items already on the organization's agenda. Without some way of demonstrating success on established consensus goals, potentially successful reforms can get reversed under push-back from outside and inside before they have had time to take hold and establish themselves.

In a system with no consensus about standards of performance or rigorous, real-time measures of what would constitute demonstrated success, then the *optimal* organization strategy may well be business as usual in the core activities, even if they are dysfunctional, combined with isomorphic mimicry of best practice activities that do not threaten fundamentals on the surface as camouflage.

Effervescent Innovation: Challenges to Scaling in Isomorphic Systems

One of the most puzzling aspects of schooling is the magnitude of innovation. The field of education is always abuzz with the latest thing. The problem is that many ideas, including ideas with compelling evidence on their side, don't scale. If the survival function is not strongly related to performance, then in a closed system, these new ideas do not attract more resources and grow across schools.

Think about a glass of Coke as a metaphor invoking "effervescent innovation." Pour out a glass of Coke and bubbles pop up off the surface. But, once poured, the level of Coke is at its maximum. The bubbles are a transitory phenomenon, rising and fizzling back to the initial beverage level.

You can travel to any country in the world and see educational innovation—someone can take you to a great school, or a great initiative.

If you come back in five years and ask to see educational innovation, you will see it again—someone can take you to a great school, or a great initiative. Five more years, more good schools, more great innovations. But has any of this led to replicated changes at scale such that you can see more good schools, more great innovations, such that *system* productivity has increased? Have any of the bubbles risen beyond where the Coke was originally poured? Crouch and Healey (1997, 2) described this problem perfectly:

> There is a particular irony to education reform. Pockets of good education practice (such as enlightened and effective classroom management, novel curricula, and innovative instructional technologies, many of them cost-effective) can be found almost anywhere, signifying that good education is not a matter of arcane knowledge. Be it the result of maverick teachers, the elite status of the parents, enlightened principals, and/or informed communities, these localized pockets of effective educational innovation can be found throughout the developing world, sometimes in poor material circumstances. Yet the rate of usage of the available knowledge, and the rate of spread of effective practices, is depressingly low. As a result, these innovations exist on a very small scale—the number of schools affected by these reformist innovations is minuscule relative to the total number of schools. Moreover, these innovations often have a short half-life. Either the maverick teacher leaves the system, the enlightened principal gets burned out, or the informed community simply loses interest after finding no echo of support in the bureaucracy.

When the public sector has a monopoly on support to basic education and when it is organized hierarchically, there is only one way for system scaling in a spider system. Information about the efficacy of the innovation travels up a chain of decisionmaking, then the head makes the decision to adopt, then instructions proceed down the chain of command with instructions for others to adopt the prescribed innovation. The difficulty with this approach is that this mode of innovation works for only a very few elements of education, typically EMIS-visible elements.

One education reform initiative sought to tackle the issue of system reform and developed a threefold approach of "clearing space, filling space, and developing reform support infrastructure" (DeStefano and Crouch 2006). Even failing systems, however, can be successful at maintaining their closed ecosystem and preventing any clearing of the space for innovation by pretending to adopt best practices and resisting innovations by not allowing functional evaluation.

Spider Systems Don't Allow for Disruptive Innovation

Spider systems use the camouflage of isomorphic mimicry to look like successful systems, and thus are able to prevent learning failures from creating threats to their legitimacy. This camouflage, unfortunately, can be sufficiently distracting as to prevent scaling up even attractive innovations, as the very mechanisms that prevent attack also prevent progress. The lack of regular, reliable reporting on outcome measures prevents external attack, but also leaves the system without internal yardsticks by which it could assess innovations. This means that innovations are adopted in part based on how much they look like whatever best practice the system is imitating, independent of whether that practice works in a given context. The quest to mimic best practice retards innovation generally, but it particularly blocks disruptive innovation.

The idea of disruptive innovation, popularized by Clayton Christensen (1997), is to distinguish cutting-edge innovations (those that advance the technological frontier) from innovations that, in appearance, are low cost and meet the needs of users at a lower level of performance. The intellectual puzzle that Christensen sets for himself is why perhaps the most wildly popular management book of all time, Peters and Waterman's *In Search of Excellence* (1982), which sold three million copies in its first three years and was the most widely held library book in the world for decades, got it so wrong. The book is premised on choosing "excellent" companies with consistently good management and performance, and then deducing from how these companies operate the principles of good management. Christensen's archetypal example of disruptive innovation is the advent of the personal computer: many that were the paradigms of excellence ended up in the dust-bin of failed companies (Wang Labs, Digital Equipment Corporation) or the companies suffered large-scale, embarrassing reversals (such as the vaunted IBM). Many companies no longer with us made the obviously wrong choice of not betting on personal computing. Why?

One might hypothesize that all of sudden, smart management got stupid, or that somehow the track record of excellent management disappeared as the company stopped pursuing the principles that brought them success. But Christensen has a much more interesting explanation: it was precisely sticking to the principles that brought the firm to excellence that brought failure. The same principles that make for excellent management if one is pursuing advancement of the cutting-edge frontier make for disastrous management when one is responding to the emergence of disruptive innovation. That is, firms whose internal vision and mission were driven by being on the cutting edge of technology, defined in terms of capacity to compute, were unable to see how a low-cost, kludge technology like a personal computer was consistent with their firms' vision as technological leaders, and hence lost sight of the entirely new potential for low-cost computing to take on a new range of functions. The engineers building computing machines to send rockets to the moon could not be bothered with a hobbyist's tool to do word processing. Oops.

Christensen has since explored the role of disruption in other industries such as steel (where initially low-cost, low-quality producers from scrap disrupted high-quality, high-technology integrated steel mills). With co-authors, he has also examined the implications for health care (Christensen, Grossman, and Hwang 2009) and education (Christensen, Johnson, and Horn 2008) in the United States.

Disruptive innovation's relevance to education in developing countries should be obvious. The coalition of professional education schools, donors, advocates, and elite policymakers in developing countries promotes the adoption of best practices. That is, the response to low learning is to strive to imitate best practice *schools* instead of the *ecosystem conditions* that created those good schools. This leads to isomorphic mimicry in which potentially disruptive innovations are rejected as not meeting the best practice model of "good schools" in developed countries, even when these disruptive possibilities are rigorously proven to promote learning and to be cost-effective. I give three examples of disruptive innovations proven rigorously to work but that cannot clear the space to move to scale because they are disruptive to existing agendas: alternative modes of teacher employment, remedial instruction, and technology.

Disruptive Innovation versus Isomorphic Mimicry: Community Teachers

One innovation, successful in a wide variety of contexts, is simply to avoid the centralized bureaucratic process of hiring and assigning teachers based on degrees and allow communities to hire local, often less-qualified teachers. Inevitably, education experts and the vested interests of teachers' unions protest this lowering of the "quality" of teaching. But what happens when one allows quality to be defined by performance, not just circularly defined by degree? One finds these community teachers perform just as well as the supposedly high-quality teachers. But contract teachers rarely get adopted at scale. And even in the rare cases where they are scaled, they don't last as a system for hiring, assigning, and retaining teachers. Eventually these informal teachers are reabsorbed into the regular teaching force and the performance benefits disappear.

In Andhra Pradesh, India, a large experiment compared the performance of contract and civil service teachers. Contract teachers were paid around five times *less* than civil service teachers. No matter how one slices the data, the learning from these informal contract teachers was at least as high as from the civil service teachers (Muralidharan and Sundararaman 2010b).

These rigorous experiments just confirm what has been found again and again in a variety of places and with a variety of evidence. In Madhya Pradesh, India, an innovative chief minister launched an education guarantee scheme (EGS). Communities over a certain size that lacked a school could build one independently and the government would pay for the teacher (at a reduced rate relative to rates for civil service teachers), and the community could manage the school. This program was a success, with an impressive expansion in enrollment. An evaluation of the program found that, while these EGS schools lacked the trappings of "good" schools with "qualified" teachers, their learning performance was just as good as government schools', at much lower per student costs (Leclercq 2003). However, eventually the combination of the education bureaucracy, the teachers' unions, and political pressures from the new teachers, who naturally wanted the higher wages, combined with the view that these alternatives didn't *look like* good schools, led to an end to the program.

In India, there have been at least ten separate experiences with some form of contract teacher, all of which had the same trajectory of success followed by political pressure ending success, followed by reabsorption of the innovation back into the spider, followed by disappointment and cynicism on the part of all involved. I am not arguing that countries should replace their current modality of teacher employment with a system of all contract teachers on year-to-year contracts. Of course not. But I am pointing out that the disruptive innovation of contract teachers is not allowed to evolve from a pilot into a full-fledged, alternative system. Disruptive innovation cannot survive because in the ecosystem of dominant isomorphic mimicry, illustrated on the left side of figure 4-1, closed systems have no functional assessment of novelty and hence no room for novelty to flourish and scale by demonstrating its functional superiority.

The example of contract teachers in India illustrates three points, which are typical more broadly. First, there is no consistent, reliable system of reporting on basic schooling learning quality. All of the official goals are enrollment, input, process, and compliance driven. Therefore, even though outsiders like researchers can generate evidence that these innovations work (using the researchers' metric of learning performance), there is no one who can say that contract teachers improve officially measured performance. Since the system has no learning measure as part of its official definitions of functionality, the system officials can simply ignore or deny the researchers' results.[9]

Second, part of "agenda conformity" in education is that no one inside the education system pays attention to costs except to increase them. After all, a performance metric is the total expenditures, both as a political symbol of commitment to schooling (not education) and as a bureaucratic measure of power and legitimacy. Therefore, a disruptive innovation that produces the same outcome with fewer resources has zero traction. The facts that the typical Indian citizen is very poor, devotes over half of his or her budget to food, and has many competing uses for scarce resources have zero traction inside education systems. Not only are there no metrics of learning effectiveness, there are especially no measures of cost efficacy. I am not arguing that funding be reallocated from education, but with the savings from a systemic implementation of contract teachers, a lot of other education challenges could be addressed. But this cannot get onto the agenda.

Third, India has two education systems: a perfect isomorphic mimic (the government sector) and an almost completely unregulated starfish system of private schools. Among private schools, naturally, "contract teachers" is the basic model and has expanded like wildfire. Since parents with even modest means can vote with their feet, they are in effect "disrupting" in the way the PC disrupted the dominant providers. But the

9. I speak from experience. I was attending a seminar with top national Indian Ministry of Education officials in charge of implementing the billion-dollar flagship program, Sarva Shiksha Abhiyan (SSA). When researchers were scheduled to present their results about impacts on learning, the top bureaucrat asked, "Was this research financed by Indian government funds under SSA?" When told that it was done by the state, and not the central government, the official walked out of the room, claiming that evidence about learning performance had nothing to do with her, the government, or the billions being spent on the SSA program. As long as SSA was compliant with administrative procedures, the question of whether it led to learning was not on the table.

government of India, unlike Wang or DEC or IBM, is in the position of forcing people to pay, and hence can delay reform much longer.

Disruptive Innovation versus Isomorphic Mimicry:
Overambitious Curricula and Remediation

One of the first of many recent rigorous field experiments carried out in the developing world took place in the Busia district in western Kenya. Researchers Glewwe, Kremer, and Moulin (2009) tested whether providing additional textbooks to students, in a situation where only a fraction of students had even one, would raise learning. The proposition that having a textbook would raise learning seemed so obvious as to hardly be worth going through the effort and expense of a randomized, controlled trial, but, as they say when the underdog wins, that is why they play the game. As it turned out, the "treatment" group, students who were provided textbooks, had on average no better assessed learning outcomes than the students in the "control" group. After combing through the data to understand how that could be, the researchers found that only the very top students—those in the 80th percentile or above on the initial (pre-intervention) examination—had statistically significant gains. Further investigation revealed that the textbooks were just too hard for the typical student, so that more instructional materials, even if they were in accordance with the curriculum, did no good for the typical student.

Recalling the learning profile results from India in chapter 1, it is interesting to contrast what students can *do* in grade five with what the educational "experts" in India stipulate as Minimal Learning Levels (MLL) for grade five students. As shown in table 4-3, these supposed "minimal" levels of learning are far beyond what the typical child has learned as he or she reaches grade five. As we saw in chapter 1, only about half of students master even the most simple and rote arithmetic operations, and very few have command over even rudimentary concepts of measurement or weight, much less fractions. Nevertheless, just in mathematics, and just in the component of mathematics for "fractions and decimals," there are fourteen distinct objectives—when less than half of students can identify a figure that is a quarter shaded.

It might seem that it can do no harm to be ambitious, and that schooling systems should have high expectations of all students. But the combination of overambitious curricula and weak teaching can destroy learning. Common sense and pedagogy agree that student learning decreases with the distance between students' actual level of skill and the level at which the material is being taught. This is a commonplace of any instruction,

Table 4-3. The curricular expectations are completely out of touch with actual student learning in India.

What fifth-graders in Andhra Pradesh know		What the "minimum" levels of learning say children in grade 5 should know about fractions, percent, and decimals
Test question	Percent answering correctly	
What part of the figure is shaded?	48	4.5.1. (e.g., area 4 of Mathematics, grade 5, item 1) Arranges simple proper fractions in ascending or descending sequence with denominators not exceeding 10 4.5.2. Reduces simple fractions to lowest terms 4.5.3. Adds and subtracts fractions and mixed numbers with denominator not exceeding 10
Which figure has $^1/_5$ apples?	38	4.5.4. Solves daily life problems involving comparing, addition, and subtraction of fractions and mixed numbers with denominator not exceeding 10 4.5.5. Adds and subtracts mentally in daily life problems involving some combinations of fractions which occur frequently (e.g., $^1/_2 + ^1/_4 = ^3/_4$)
Which is larger: $^2/_3$ of 4,500 or $^1/_6$ of 6,000?	25	4.5.6. Multiplies and divides two fractions with denominators up to 10 and expresses the answer in its lowest terms
Rama ate $^1/_3$ and Rita ate $^1/_4$ of a piece of a chocolate. Who ate the larger piece of chocolate?	9	4.5.7. Adds and subtracts decimals up to three decimal places 4.5.8. Expresses units of length, weight, and capacity in decimals up to three decimal places. 4.5.9. Multiplies and divides a decimal number up to three decimal places by a single-digit number 4.5.10. Solves daily life problems involving length, weight, capacity, etc., involving comparing, addition, subtraction, multiplication, and division of decimals up to three places 4.5.11. Converts fractions and decimals into percentage and percentage into fraction in lowest terms and decimal 4.5.12. Finds required percentage of a given number or measure 4.5.13. Solves simple daily life problems involving application of percentage 4.5.14. Converts mentally frequently used percentages into fractions and vice versa (e.g., 50% = $^1/_2$, $^1/_4$ = 25%, etc.)

Sources: Pritchett and Beatty (2012), based on APRESt data, and the official Ministry of Human Resources website www.education.nic.in/cd50years/r/2S/99/2S990404.htm.

Figure 4-3. The learning profile flattens and children make little progress when the curricular pace of learning exceeds the actual pace of learning.

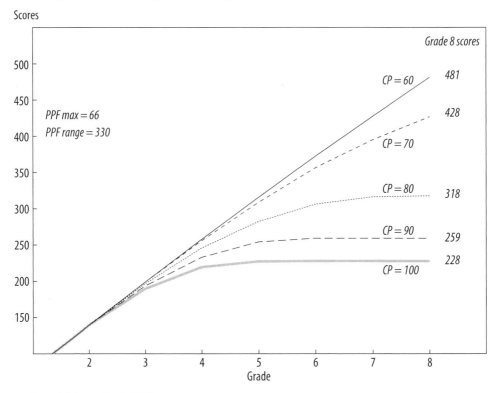

Source: Pritchett and Beatty (2012).

from piano lessons to sports to language to mathematics. It does no good to confront piano students with the full score of a Beethoven sonata before they can even read notes; instruction has to build level by level. In a paper with Amanda Beatty, we simulated the consequences of a curriculum that moves ahead at a pace faster than the pace at which student skill is progressing (Pritchett and Beatty 2012). As the gap between the curriculum for the grade and student skill for the grade widens, the fraction of students learning anything falls. When more and more children are left behind, the learning profile flattens. As figure 4-3 illustrates using a simulation model of student learning, if the speed of the curriculum (called curricular pace, or CP) doubles but the pace of actual learning remains constant, the learning profile is almost entirely flat by grade five, since students just cannot grasp the material being presented.

Recent reforms in India, Ghana, and elsewhere have shown that remedying the problem of overambitious curricula is relatively simple, as the problem is not with the children. The problem is with the system. Efforts at remediation that move lessons to the level of students have been shown in rigorous studies to have enormous impact (e.g., Banerjee, Cole, et al. 2010). The example of remedial teaching by tutors (*balsakhi*) above demonstrates how significant gains are possible if teachers shape lessons to students rather than sticking to a curriculum too difficult for students to follow.

In addition to spearheading and evaluating the tutoring program, the Indian NGO Pratham also experimented with recruiting "typical" teachers to teach Pratham's simplified curriculum in an unpressured environment, summer school. This was to demonstrate that the problem was not the teaching skill of civil service teachers but rather the curriculum, absenteeism, and other pressures faced by civil service teachers. Government teachers[10] in Bihar and Uttarakhand taught low-performing children in grades three through five for four hours a day for a month. Reading levels improved. A child attending gained on average more than half a level in reading (out of five levels) in just a month.[11]

Despite demonstrated evidence of the efficacy of low-cost interventions such as tutoring or curricular reform, amazingly, closed spider systems manage to resist these innovations. Those who monopolize public sector systems find it easy to block such reform agendas by claiming they "dumb down" the curriculum or focus too much on basics and not enough on creativity or the "construction" of learning. This keeps outside innovations from moving to scale. Simple goals with simple techniques cannot scale in closed, public support systems because such systems judge innovations only on whether they conform to a predetermined elite agenda.

Overambitious curricula are another example of the triumph of isomorphic mimicry over functionality. The education bureaucrats, "experts," and elites would rather have school systems that look like good schools on paper, with "best practice" and "global standard" curricula,

10. Participants were mostly teachers newly appointed by the local government. Such local *panchayat* teachers are government teachers, different from state teachers, who are paid much more.
11. The experiment had some challenges with targeting, as Pratham and researchers hoped to recruit more low-performers. Seventy-four percent of the children who attended the summer camp were in grades three through five, but only 39 percent were in the low-performing target group.

than have children in those schools learning (Banerjee and Duflo 2011). By creating a system in which no achievable goals are set and in which learning isn't measured in ways that are high stakes for the system, the schools get away with creating curricula and standards that are mere agenda confirmation.

Disruptive Innovation versus Isomorphic Mimicry: Technology

There is often enthusiasm about how the latest technology, combined with rigorous evidence of its impact, will transform the education process. In 2012, commercials for the iPad tell us that it will reinvent the world of learning, as will use of the Internet and other kinds of tablets. There is always something latest and greatest in technology, but there has been something latest and greatest in technology for a long time without these technologies delivering on the promise that they will improve education.

In 1976 in Nicaragua, the government tried out broadcasting lessons over the radio. This innovation was evaluated using a randomized, controlled trial to scientifically test the learning gains of students exposed to the radio-based instruction versus those who were not. The study, published in 1981, proved conclusively that radio-based instruction was more effective in absolute terms than traditional classroom-based pedagogy and was wildly more cost-effective.

So the end of the story was widespread adoption of broadcasted lessons, followed by improved average test scores in Nicaragua, followed by adoption and adaption for other places in the world, right? Wrong. Radio-based instruction did not meet the standard of isomorphic mimicry—it didn't look cool. The cool, richer countries in the education world didn't use radio-based instruction, so why should Nicaragua? Of course, Nicaragua soon thereafter entered into a long period of civil war and political strife, so the counterfactual of what could have been is impossible to predict.

Reviews of the impact of technology on learning are strikingly mixed, with some claiming huge success but many interventions showing little or no impact. My reading is that when computers are used in an EMIS-visible fashion, as just another way to soak up resources and promote more inputs advocacy, they have no impact on learning. Many initiatives around the world that have been rigorously evaluated find no impact at all, despite the hype. However, technology could be potentially a disruptive innovation that changes the way schooling and instruction are organized. This, however, would require an ecosystem in which innovations were adopted and scaled based on their impacts on learning, not merely on how attractive they were from an agenda confirmation point of view.

The world changes. The very same organizational survival strategies that worked to create and expand the infrastructural conditions for universal schooling, one of the triumphs of humanity, are now, ironically, counterproductive. The same strategies that worked for logistics are now blocking the space in the educational ecosystem for the rebirth of education.

CHAPTER **5**

Why Spiders Came to Dominate Schooling

If it ain't broke, don't fix it! Chapter 3 argued that "more of the same" is not on track to reach meaningful learning goals. Chapter 4 argued that the existing large, top-down, input-oriented ecosystems of schooling (metaphorical "spider" systems) present solutions as problems and hence bring as many problems as solutions. But this leaves the question of why countries have the school systems they have. Before entertaining notions of sweeping systemic reform, we ought to have a good account of why things are the way they are. In Voltaire's *Candide*, Dr. Pangloss's narrative—that things are the way they are because this is the best of all possible worlds—might just be right, even if the best of all possible worlds is pretty mediocre. It's a pretty good rule of thumb not to mess with things you don't understand. Before moving on to a chapter laying out new approaches, I owe you an answer to the hard question: if spider systems are so terrible at providing learning, why do so many countries still have spider systems?

Three big questions about schooling are:

—Why has the expansion of public schooling been so universally successful?

—Why does government directly *produce* (and not just provide through financing) so much of basic schooling?

—Why does the government produce schooling in spider systems: top-down, hierarchical organizations of massive scale?

Perhaps the answers to those questions are really simple:

—Because schooling is so good and is universally recognized as such.

—Because governments are the best at producing schooling.

—Because big is the best size for schooling systems.

If this is the right account, then fixing schooling to meet the learning gaps will not require fundamental change, just trying harder. Perhaps more of the same, but done better, and with more money, really is the solution to all ills.

However, this simple Panglossian account of the rise of government-owned and government-operated spider systems as the dominant system of basic education has very little going for it. An alternative account capable of explaining the historical rise of government-operated schooling, its successes in mass expansion, its present features, and how it functions as a spider system, as well its failures, has three essential elements:

—The inculcation of beliefs—or socialization—is not third-party contractible.

—Nation-states care about, and act to control, the socialization process, through the direct production of schooling.

—Isomorphic mimicry is a powerful force in shaping the diffusion of institutional organizations across nation-states.

With these three analytical pieces in place, I can explain everything we observe about education systems in the world today. I can also dismiss for what it is the Panglossian nonsense that gets said about these questions. Once we have cleared the debris of the false necessity for the way things are, we can move on to discussing in the next chapter the essential characteristics of an alternative to spider systems: open-structured, performance-pressured, financially supported, locally autonomous starfish systems of schooling.

The Inculcation of Beliefs Is Not Third-Party Contractible

I don't care too much for money,
Money can't buy me love.

THE BEATLES

The Beatles knew, as everyone does, that money can't buy you love. Why not? If I tried to buy love, I could never be sure the person was not faking it. Someone could act like she loved me but just be pretending. Love is not observable. Moreover, a market in love would require that love not only be observable between two people but also be verifiable. Could a third party reliably settle a contractual dispute between two parties over whether money had bought love? Could a paying lovee who felt defrauded by a contracted lover successfully get her money back? Love, being neither observable nor verifiable, is not contractible.[1]

In Vienna, Virginia, a perfectly ordinary suburb of Washington, D.C., Robert Hanssen lived the apparently perfectly ordinary life of a career bureaucrat for the FBI. Perhaps his most remarkable characteristic, those who knew him said, was that he was a fervent conservative Catholic, attending mass daily at 6:30 a.m. (and often again during the day) and sending his daughters to an Opus Dei–operated private school, where his wife taught religion. The reality was apparent to no one: Robert Hanssen was a spy for the Soviet Union, then for Russia, and remained so, off and on, during nearly all his FBI career from 1979 to 2001, when he was caught. This outwardly fervent anticommunist was perhaps the most damaging U.S. double agent in the history of the Cold War, playing a role in the loss of nearly every active U.S. asset in the Soviet Union in the period 1985–1986. Love is not the only thing that can be faked. So can loyalty.

If money cannot buy you love or loyalty, can it buy the teaching of love or loyalty—or of any belief or mental disposition, for that matter? I have a friend who is an excellent musician. He is also, as am I, a Mormon, a historically quirky American denomination with doctrinal beliefs far from the Christian mainstream. My friend worked his way through a PhD in choral conducting as the director of music for a local Catholic congregation. He had responsibility for the Sunday service music (playing the organ) and for directing the congregation choir, including its Christmas and Easter concerts and teaching the youth choir to sing. It is

---

1. The material in this section draws on earlier work of mine (Pritchett 2002; Pritchett and Viarengo 2008).

unremarkable that a Catholic congregation would hire a Mormon music director. But if the same congregation were to contract out to a Mormon the teaching of the youth Sunday School classes, it would be remarkable? Why can money buy teaching religious music but not the teaching of religion?

Suppose a student learns to speak Swahili and after a period of instruction can carry on a conversation with a native speaker and can read texts in that language. If the student reports to a friend, "They think I have learned Swahili, but I really haven't, because I don't believe in Swahili," most people would regard this as an exceptionally odd statement. Perhaps he might not enjoy Swahili or have the disposition to speak Swahili, but a person's functional mastery of Swahili can be separated from any mental states he might have about it.

Now suppose the same student is being taught to pray. For instance, suppose he has learned the series of words Christians call the Lord's Prayer, has learned to say those words with appropriate inflection and affect, and has learned the appropriate circumstances in which to repeat those words. In fact, imagine the student could pass any conceivable external assessment of his ability to pray. If the student reports to his friend, "They think I have learned to pray, but I really haven't, because I don't believe in praying," in this case he is right—he has not learned to pray.

I define a *skill* to be something for which the demonstrable performance is everything, while for a *belief,* a person's mental state is independently important. The distinction is not between those things that are physical and those that are mental, as skills run the gamut from weight-lifting or tennis to algebra or chess. The key analytical difference for which contracts and transactions are possible is that no one can pretend to have a skill he or she does not have (though of course, people can pretend not to have skills they do have), whereas people can, and do, pretend to hold beliefs they do not hold.

Skills are observable and verifiable. Hence skills are contractible and instruction in skills is directly contractible. Most important, instruction in skills is third-party contractible.

The distinctions between contractible, directly contractible instruction, and third-party contractible instruction can be elucidated using foreign language skills as an example. Suppose an American organization wants employees who can speak French. There are well-developed rankings of language proficiency and established expertise in language skill assessment. In an hour or less, any organization can reliably assess a person's maximum language proficiency (again, a person can fake not speaking French, but not vice versa). Speaking French is observable. Objective assessment is also verifiable such that, if an employee felt the organization were attempting to cheat on a promised incentive for speaking French, a third party could adjudicate whether or not "This person speaks/understands/reads French at the specified level of proficiency," and hence could enforce that contract. This means organizations can contract for speaking French by, say, hiring only people who speak French at a given level of proficiency or by paying a wage premium that is based on the level of language skill, with higher bonuses or any of a variety of incentives.

Language instruction is also directly contractible. That I don't speak French is observable (either painfully or laughably so for my French-speaking friends, depending on their sensitivity), but were I to want to learn to speak French, I would have an array of contracting options. I could hire a tutor, I could buy a commercial "teach yourself" service advertised in airline magazines, I could enroll in a course from any of a variety of institutions, I could try to teach myself with an online course. Since I can have my language proficiency objectively assessed at relatively low cost, I can easily assess my progress and switch among providers of instruction depending on my progress.

The most interesting case is if an organization wants to encourage its existing employees to acquire French skills by subsidizing instruction in French. This creates a "make versus buy" decision for the organization. The organization could "make" French instruction by hiring an employee to offer French instruction to the organization's employees free. Alternatively, the organization could engage in third-party contracting with its employees by agreeing to subsidize some portion of the cost of French instruction. This could be as simple as allowing employees to use work time to receive tutoring (from their choice of tutor) on-site. Or the organization could agree to pay a flat rate of X dollars of the employee's instruction from any authorized course of French instruction (allowing employees to "top up" by choosing more expensive courses if they choose). There is a wide array of organizational strategies, from just paying for skills and not subsidizing skill acquisition at all to a variety of ways of encouraging instruction. The optimal organizational choice will be a complex function of how costly it is to observe the skill, how fungible the skills are outside the organization, the determinants of skill acquisition in relation to the individual's own ability and effort, and the risk aversion of employees (what if employees pay out of pocket for instruction but fail to reach the wage bonus threshold?).

ble 5-1. Why money can't buy love and why governments do not give vouchers for schooling,
in one table.

	Skills/Factual knowledge (Foreign language, algebra, music, tennis, chess, test prep)	Beliefs/Attitudes/Dispositions (Love, loyalty, faith, duty, honor, patriotism)
ntractible (observable d verifiable)?	Yes (Hiring or incentive mechanisms exist, based on pay for demonstrated skills.)	No (All implicit, based on inferences from behavior; arm's-length transactions are seen as suspect.)
struction directly ntractible?	Yes (Thriving markets exist for instruction in skills through multiple modalities— tutors, classes, assisted own instruction.)	Yes (Individuals can choose their own instruction in beliefs because as they are direct participants, the instruction is observable.)
struction *third-party* ntractible?	Yes (Organizations have an array of "make" versus "buy" choices.)	No (Organizations must "make," not "buy," to avoid "insincere teaching.")

Whether or not third-party contracting for instruction in French skills is the organizationally optimal choice, it is a choice, because the skill and instruction in the skill are contractible and incentives can, in principle, be constructed such that the individual's, the instructor's, and the organization's incentives are aligned. Moreover, in my analysis of the organization's incentive structure for French skills, the organization's fundamental goals did not really matter: one can imagine the Catholic Church, the U.S. Marines, Wal-Mart, and Amnesty International all sending their employees to the same class in conversational French (table 5-1).

Organizations typically want long-term employees to be personally committed to the vision, mission, and mandate of the organization. The Catholic Church wants priests and nuns who believe in God, the U.S. Marines wants soldiers who believe in the Corps, Harvard University wants faculty who believe in the value of research (if not in Harvard itself), Amnesty International wants workers who believe in human rights. These beliefs come with a variety of descriptions: faith, duty, loyalty, commitment; but all of these traits have in common that they are neither directly observable nor verifiable in that they cannot be reliably assessed at a feasible cost or time in an intersubjectively reliable way.

The example of double agents in the world of espionage is exotic but nevertheless instructive. Robert Hanssen rose to be one of the top FBI officials for ferreting out double agents in the U.S. intelligence community on the basis of his apparently sincere anticommunism and loyalty, while in fact he was the double agent. The counterpart in the world of skills is simply impossible to conceive of. Imagine discovering that the top cellist for the New York Philharmonic cannot really play the cello. An all-time great tennis champion like Andre Agassi can write a memoir telling us he hated the game of tennis, but he could not possibly reveal he could not play superb tennis (although, lamentably, that could be in my memoir). Double agents illustrate there is no cheap and reliable way to observe or verify loyalty. Therefore, simple incentive schemes for contracting or for third-party contracting of instruction, such as paying a wage premium for those who speak French or paying for French instruction, are not possible. The elicitation and demonstration of commitment to the core values of organizations require much longer periods of observation—and typically lower-powered incentives.

Beliefs are not contractible because only I know (if only imperfectly) what I believe. Speaking for myself, I know that I mislead others about my true beliefs all the time ("Have you lost weight, sir?" "Your child's cello playing was wonderful." "My, what a lovely baby." "Loved your recent paper"), but I know what I really think. However, for that same reason, instruction in beliefs actually is directly contractible: as the intended recipient I both completely observe all of the instruction and can make some, if only imprecise, estimates of its impact on my beliefs.

Third-party contracting for the inculcation of beliefs, however, runs the danger of a collusive contract between instructor and student to produce insincere teaching—and hence thwart the interests of the third party who is paying for the instruction. Suppose, as is true in many politicized environments, that my career depended on being a loyal Baathist, or loyal Communist, loyal environmentalist, or, in a religious regime, a devoted follower of this or that denomination, or, in a secular regime, not having a religion at all. Then I would have the incentive to engage an instructor with the following contract for insincere teaching: "Teach me how to appear to be a loyal follower of ideology X, while reminding me periodically that ideology X is a crock."

More mundanely, consider an organization's "make versus buy" decision for instructional activities intended to build commitment to the organization's vision and mission. Could the organization just "buy" such instruction by giving employees a subsidy for "loyalty-augmenting" instruction that the employees themselves contract from third parties? Third-party instructors may maximize their attendance by offering the following deal: "I will really maximize how much fun you have during my course, and allow you to retain whatever bitter and cynical attitude you have about your organization, but I will also teach you how to plausibly pass an assessment of loyalty." For the organization to prevent this insincere instruction in beliefs when the organization's incentives and the employees' incentives differ in the desired outcome of instruction, the organization must exert more direct control of the process of instruction. In the limit, they want instructors who are themselves sincerely loyal to the firm or, at the very least, whose incentives are completely controlled by the firm, rather than instructors whose incentives are to please the market of employees who self-select.

Even outside formal schooling there are instances in which the make versus buy choice for instruction is based on the difference between skills and beliefs. The U.S. Army, for instance, contracts out the instruction of officers in some skills (language training, economics) but controls directly all the dimensions of training intended to induce service loyalty and unit cohesion. Many churches contract out child care in church-owned facilities or musical skills such as organ playing to people of different faiths, but few mainstream churches contract out Sabbath Day sermons or religious instruction to outsiders.

Priests and Marines and Wal-Mart employees might end up in the same courses (real or virtual) for skills like speaking French or how to use a spreadsheet. But churches will contract out music but not sermons. The U.S. Marines contract out skill acquisition but not their basic training—even branches of the U.S. armed forces don't share basic training. Wal-Mart employees have motivational programs run by Wal-Mart.

Instruction in beliefs is not third-party contractible, so organizations will choose to make, not buy, the inculcation of beliefs.

The Rise of Schooling: Origins of the Modern

An "official" educational enterprise presumably cultivates beliefs, skills, and feelings in order to transmit and explicate its sponsoring culture's ways of interpreting the natural and social worlds.

JEROME BRUNER, *THE CULTURE OF EDUCATION*

When I was a teenager my father used to tell me, "Whenever anyone tells you anything, your first question should be, 'How would they be better off if you believed them?' " My first reaction was that my father was a cynical old coot. My second reaction was to think he only wanted me to think that so that I would listen to him more and to others less—which showed I understood his fundamental lesson, perhaps even too well. But it turns out my father only appeared to be a cynical old coot because he was not a French intellectual. Michel Foucault, quite possibly the most influential intellectual of our times,[2] was saying nearly the same thing, but in less penetrable philosophical terms (and in French): that behind discourse we should look for power, that "reality" is not "discovered" but rather is socially constructed, often to serve the ends of powerful forces. The fun part of deconstruction is recovering the reality that existed before the dominant social construct became the "common sense" that now constrains discourse.

In the aftermath of the Meiji Restoration there were quite widespread popular protests with the slogans, "Down with conscription! Down with the solar calendar! Down with public schools!" In our current reality it is hard to entertain the idea that "Down with public schools!" was the slogan of a popular protest movement that the authorities suppressed with military force.

Public schooling, like any truly successful institution, projects its own inevitability into the fabric of language itself. The Millennium Declaration was signed by 147 heads of state as a consensus about the goals of development, and part of this consensus became elaborated into the Millennium Development Goals, which are to "achieve universal primary education," for which the target is "all children can complete a full course of primary schooling." But nothing could be more obvious than that education, defined as the preparation of children and youth to take on their social, political, and economic roles as adults, has always been universal in every society. Following the advice of my father and Foucault, you should ask yourself, why did 147 heads of state, ranging from democratically elected visionary leaders to generals to autocrats to kleptocratic thugs, all agree to conflate the obviously different concepts of "schooling" and "education"?

Returning again to the chapter's three big questions: Why has the public school as an institution been so successful? Why are so many schools run directly by governments? Why are the government organizations that run schools so large? Or, wrapped together into one question: how did governmental spiders become the dominant and successful system for schooling?

2. While many think that economists have been intellectually influential, the most cited academic economist in Google Scholar, Gary Becker, has half the citations of Foucault.

The answer for the "first movers" (those countries that built and expanded systems of universal basic schooling in the era from 1870 to the 1920s) is easy and was recognized as such during the time. Only our historical distance from schooling's origin has allowed mythic narratives to replace the contemporaneously obvious facts. The answer is that the rise of the modern economy, with the shift from traditional agriculture and craft production to larger organizational units of production carrying out new activities, implied that more and more parents felt their children needed more exposure to formal schooling as part of their education. At the same time, the consolidation of the modern nation-state as a mode of political organization required an extended process of socialization to mold the new citizens.

That is, if there were to be an extended period of schooling in which skills and beliefs were produced together, then the elites and leaders of the consolidating nation-states understood that the state must control that socialization, and understood too that this control required not just that the state support schooling but that, since the inculcation of belief was not third-party contractible, the state had to directly produce schooling. The political leaders understood that the fundamental contract had to be not directly between parents and teachers but between the state and teachers.

The resulting modern systems of schooling depended on how the various ideological struggles over the control of socialization between nation-states and parents played out. Since the most important competitors for the socialization role of education before the state were religions, the contest between and among state, society, and religion determined the ultimate size of the governmental units that controlled education. A series of vignettes from various countries illustrates how these forces played out. Notice that in none of these narratives do any Panglossian elements (elites providing schooling as a response to popular pressure, a benign state, the superior technical efficacy of the mode of the organization of schooling to produce greater learning of skills) play any role in the determination of the system of schooling.

Japan in the Early Meiji Period

In administration of all schools, it must be kept in mind, what is to be done is not for the sake of the pupils, but for the sake of the country.

MORI ANORI, JAPANESE MINISTER OF EDUCATION, 1886–89

Before the Meiji Restoration in 1868 there was a mix of schools and schooling that, with almost no direct influence or support of the national government, had already achieved quite high enrollment rates, estimated at 79 percent for boys and 21 percent for girls in 1854–1867. In 1873 the new government launched a new centralized school system (modeled on the French system) in which the national ministry dictated curricula and texts. This was not primarily an expansion of schooling but a bid to control the existing schooling. While compulsory, this schooling was not free: there were individual tuitions to be paid, and nearly all of the costs of basic schooling were locally borne. This new system was not popular, and riots broke out sporadically around the country between 1873 and 1877 that had to be put down with force. Whatever the motivation of the disturbances, the slogans often focused on three resented features of the new regime: conscription, public schooling, and the solar calendar. Over the decades of the 1870s and 1880s, as the public schools grew, three-way ideological debates raged among those emphasizing utilitarian skills (and Western ideas), traditionalists emphasizing Confucian training, and nationalists emphasizing loyalty to the nation-state (as embodied in the emperor). By the 1890s the nationalists were transcendent, promoting a dual educational system that had a "compulsory sector heavily indoctrinated in the spirit of morality and nationalism."[3]

Turkey and Atatürk's Republic

The Turkish education system aims to take the Turkish people to the level of modern civilization by preparing individuals with high qualifications for the information age, who . . . are committed to Atatürk's nationalism and Atatürk's principles and revolution.

TURKISH MINISTRY OF EDUCATION, 2007

In March 1924, barely six months into his presidency, Mustafa Kemal (Atatürk) launched the opening of the Grand National Assembly with a speech that announced three bold strokes: "safeguarding" the new Republic, abolishing the caliphate, and introducing the reform of education. The Law of Unification of Instruction placed all educational institutions—religious, private, and foreign—under the control of the Ministry of Education. This was indeed a bold stroke in a country whose population was overwhelmingly Islamic (and considered itself a, if not the, center of the Islamic world) and where the greatest part of education had been undertaken in schools controlled by religious authorities. Once education came under the control of the Ministry of Education, religious lessons were first made voluntary, then abolished at the secondary level,

3. Passin (1965, 88–89).

and then abolished altogether in primary schools by 1932. Just how unpopular this move, undertaken by a small "modernizing" secular and nationalizing group, was is difficult to gauge, as from March 1925 to March 1929 the government operated under the Law for the Maintenance of Order that provided for "extra ordinary and, in effect, dictatorial powers" (Lewis 1961, 266). As democracy has returned to Turkey, Islam has returned to Turkish schools. Since 1950 students in grades four and five have received religious instruction (with a chance to opt out), and religious instruction was reintroduced into secondary schools in 1956–1957. Nevertheless, as late as 2007 the Ministry of National Education openly proclaimed its fundamental goals for skills and socialization as a commitment to Atatürk's nationalism and the revolution.

France and the Laicism of the Third Republic

Let it be understood that the first duty of a democratic government is to exercise control over public education.

JULES FERRY, FRENCH MINISTER OF EDUCATION (1879–83)

France is the clearest example of the struggle between the religious—in this instance, Catholics—and the secularists over the control of schooling, which necessitated increasingly central control to resist the localities in which religious instruction in the schools was popular. The Ferry laws mandated free instruction in 1881, but, as many communes met their obligation to provide schooling by allowing the local Catholic parish school to be the "public" school, the law of 1883 mandated that all public education be secular. Not only that, but the threat of "insincere teaching" led to a ban on any cleric teaching in any public school.

The centralizing tendencies that result from a geographically widespread conflict between a secularist nation-state foundational ideology and a relatively homogeneous religious or cultural alternative is, of course, not the only possible outcome. Sometimes religion wins.

The Netherlands and Belgium

The former Low Countries, Netherlands and Belgium, today have respectively 68 percent and 54 percent of primary school enrollment in the private sector. The Dutch levels of private schooling are twice as high as in the next highest European country, Spain. The basic system has money follow the student. While the government produces schooling, parents choose their school freely from among available suppliers, and the state provides payments directly to schools on a funding formula that treats publicly operated and privately operated schools—including religious denominational schools—on an equal basis.

The lack of a public monopoly is not for lack of effort: the state did in fact try to secularize schooling, beginning in 1806, when Holland was "liberated" by the French. However, Holland had a long history of religious toleration and was deeply, and nearly evenly, divided along religious lines between Catholics and various denominations of Protestants. No religious denomination would trust a public school system to be either fair to religion (given the secular values of those allied with the French) or neutral between denominations. The compromise eventually reached was that schooling was compulsory but that religious schools "counted" as official education. By 1889, religious schools were receiving financial support, and full equality between public and private in funding was codified in the constitution of 1917.

In Belgium in 1879 a Liberal government adopted a school reform that (1) reduced local control, stressing that "teachers were State functionaries" and that local authorities had no rights over teachers, (2) ensured "private (Catholic) schools lost all subsidies," (3) removed from the Communes the choice of adopting a Catholic school to provide basic education, requiring them instead to build and maintain a state school, (4) stopped all ecclesiastical inspection of schools and ecclesiastical guidance in textbook selection, (5) dictated a program of studies for schools, and (6) "stated quite explicitly that in the future all teachers in government subsidized and controlled schools must be trained in State-controlled teacher-training establishments" (Mallison 1963, 232). The strong backlash against this law (dubbed *La Loi de malheur*, "the law calamitous"), led by Catholic supporters and clergy, led to a defeat of the Liberal party in the elections of 1884 (a defeat from which the party never recovered).

From time immemorial it has been recognized that the most important part of education is the set of beliefs, attitudes, dispositions, and values that young people acquire about themselves and their relationship to the natural, social, and political worlds in which they live. In formal schooling, instruction in skills and the inculcation of beliefs are inextricably mixed: there is no part of the curriculum in which what is being taught and how it is taught are not simultaneously conveying to students appropriate beliefs. While language acquisition is contractible, what languages are taught and in what language instruction is carried out convey important signals about beliefs—for example, children who are not taught in their mother tongue in school are sent a huge message about themselves and their language community. While reading is, on one level, a pure decoding skill, you cannot read without reading something that has meaning, and meaning is nearly always conveying beliefs, explicitly or implicitly. One cannot live in the postmodern world and be unaware that all social sciences are at their roots about beliefs. Those fields, such as mathematics and the physical sciences, that set themselves up as value neutral and claim not to inculcate beliefs are often the most hotly contested in respect to the beliefs they convey. A beliefs-neutral education is a self-negating position.

The historical rise of the modern school was therefore everywhere and always a contest for the control of socialization, with the fact that the inculcation of values was not third-party contractible always taken for granted. French Catholics knew that secular schools would undermine Catholicism, irrespective of any claims to neutrality, and French secularists knew priests who taught in secular schools could not be trusted.

The basic structures of the schooling systems were therefore laid down not by technical consideration of what would lead to the efficient production of skills or by any of the ideas of public economics about externalities and market failures. The differences across countries in their schooling systems are the result of struggles over who could control the socialization of youth and how. The centralization of France, the federalization of Germany, the localism of the United States, and "choice" in Holland were not the result of debates over the relative technical efficacy of these different systems but of the differences between the state and the population in ideas about legitimate socialization.

The Spread of Public Schooling

Inclusive and powerful systems of public schools did not exist anywhere in the world even two centuries ago . . . and a vigorous use of the historical imagination is needed to understand the transformation caused by the rise of nationalism. . . . The institutional mountain range that divides the older past from the present is nationalism and its individual peaks and great plateaus are the nation-states that use the school as an instrument of nationalism.

HARRY GEHMAN GOOD AND JAMES DAVID TELLER, *A HISTORY OF WESTERN EDUCATION*

The main intellectual puzzle of accounts that attempt to explain the rise of schooling is not explaining its rise in the historical developmental successes, such as France, Japan, and the United States. As we saw above, in such cases some simple combination of rising returns on formal schooling as part of an education, increasingly democratic political structures, and the demands of ideological control of socialization (either

Figure 5-1. Schooling increased massively in nearly all countries, including repressive, autocratic, and corrupt countries.

Percent of countries whose average years of
schooling increased by more than three, 1960–2010

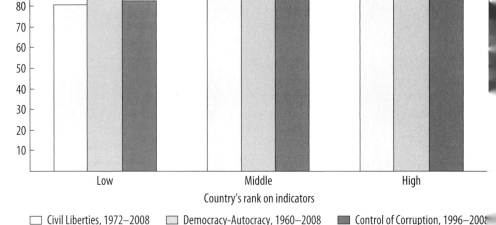

Country's rank on indicators

☐ Civil Liberties, 1972–2008   ☐ Democracy-Autocracy, 1960–2008   ■ Control of Corruption, 1996–200ε

Source: Author's calculations with Barro-Lee data on years of schooling, POLITY IV for Democracy-Autocracy, ICRG for Control of Corruption, and Freedom House for Civil Liberties (see Data Sources).

state-led, perhaps constrained by democracy, or driven by democracy) does the trick.

The hard thing is explaining the universality of the rise of schooling, in that enrollment is nearly universal in countries that are otherwise complete and abject failures economically, politically, or both (figure 5-1). The puzzle is not why the primary school gross enrollment rate (GER) in peaceful, equal, democratic, prosperous Costa Rica is 110 percent, the puzzle is why it is 113 percent in neighboring Guatemala, which has none of those traits.[4] The problem is not explaining a GER of 104 percent in Thailand but why it is 119 percent in neighboring Cambodia. In infamously corrupt Nigeria, the GER is 97 percent; in the borderline "failed state" of Pakistan the GER is 92 percent. The puzzle of schooling is that bad guys do it too.

4. All figures on gross enrollment rates are from the EFA monitoring report of 2010 (Education for All 2010).

To explain the common phenomenon across countries of the rise to (almost) universal schooling, mainly through publicly produced spider systems, we need not one but three different narratives, all of which lead to the same outcome (we'll come back to Occam and his razor), which can coexist in various mixes. The three accounts of the rise of modern schooling are:

—Demand, driven by a modernizing economy
—The pure drive for ideological control of socialization
—Isomorphic mimicry (Keeping up with the Joneses)

I take each of these in turn.

Demand, Driven by a Modernizing Economy

Primitive education was a process by which continuity was maintained between parents and children. . . . Modern education includes a heavy emphasis upon the function of education to create discontinuities—to turn the child of the peasant into a clerk, of the farmer into a lawyer, of the Italian immigrant into an American, of the illiterate into the literate.

MARGARET MEAD, "OUR EDUCATIONAL EMPHASIS IN PRIMITIVE PERSPECTIVE," 1943

The first narrative about the rise of schooling relates a fundamental shift in the economic activities that increased the private pecuniary returns to schooling. Early work on the economics of education emphasized that in a perfectly stagnant economy, there is no return on formal education (Schultz 1964). In the economy that characterized most of human history, in which daughters did what their mothers did and sons did what their fathers did, so that most of the population held the same occupation generation after generation, and in which technological progress was slow, so that the generations carried on doing the same tasks using roughly the same tools and techniques, education occurred mostly by apprenticeship and was conducted within the household or clan. It is only when technology creates relatively rapid change and the occupational shifts become massive that a monetary demand for anything like formal schooling emerges, because those with higher levels of education earn more money.

The increased economic returns on education have certainly been a major factor in the expansion of demand for schooling. However, private demand due to economic dynamism does not fully account for the universality of the expansion of schooling. Over the last fifty years schooling has risen massively, in both rapidly growing and economically stagnant

Figure 5-2. Countries in the lowest third of economic growth rates were most likely to double their years of schooling, 1960–2010.

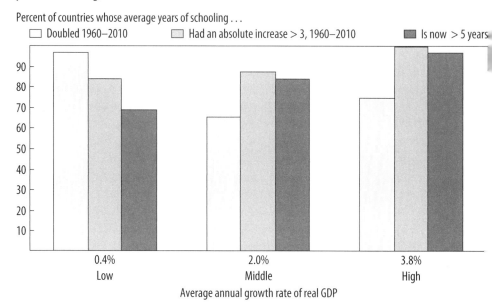

Percent of countries whose average years of schooling . . .

☐ Doubled 1960–2010   ▨ Had an absolute increase > 3, 1960–2010   ■ Is now > 5 years

Average annual growth rate of real GDP

Source: Author's calculations, based on data from Barro and Lee (2010) and Penn World tables.

economies. Figure 5-2 shows the differences in the growth rate of schooling across countries with low economic growth (less than 0.4 percent per annum), medium growth, and high growth. More than 95 percent of countries that had a low average annual growth rate of real GDP for the period 1960–2010 also saw the years of schooling of their population double. Of course, most of these countries started from a low base, but even in absolute terms, more than 80 percent of the low-growth countries saw their average years of schooling increase by more than three years.

In this narrative of the rise of schooling, governments play a responsive role. Parents demand more schooling and states, under the pressure of citizens, respond by supplying more of it. This explanation does not explain why governments are responsive by producing rather than financing schooling, but it can explain the rise of the demand for schooling.

Supply Driven, by a Need for Nation-State Control of Socialization

Let me stand a common observation on its head, to create a puzzle, which then points immediately to an answer. The common observation is that many communist states have achieved much higher levels of education than their per capita GDP would predict: places like Cuba are very educated for how poor they are. But stand that on its head. If education drives higher productivity, why is Cuba so poor with such high education? This creates a puzzle. If the expansion of schooling was not driven by a modernizing economy creating incentives for parents and children to become more educated, what accounts for the massive expansions of education, even in the face of economic stagnation, if not retrogression?[5]

This time it is an expansion in the demand for socialization, but with the causation flowing from demand by the nation-state for the socialization of the student. That is, instead of the student wanting skills and the state directly producing schooling to control the beliefs, in this case the state gets kids into school, even if not motivated by returns on skills, in order to create a set of beliefs.

Think of the "ideology"—a collection of beliefs—that most perfectly justifies a particular regime's control over the state. Now think of the "ideology" children would receive through their education and socialization if they had no formal schooling at all.

If the state's desired ideology and the traditional default ideology are close, that is, if a regime appeals to "traditional" values to legitimate its control of the state, then the regime's need to expand formal public schooling is low and its antipathy toward private schooling is low.

At the other extreme, imagine a regime that legitimates its control of the state on the basis of an ideology and that ideology is new, so that the folk socialization of a nonformal school-based education is unlikely to convey that ideology. In this case the gap between the "public school" socialization and either the "no school" socialization or the "private school" socialization is large and works to the disadvantage of the regime. In such a case we would expect regimes to both push to expand public schooling and exhibit antipathy toward private schooling (which would often, of course, exist as a recourse for parents who wanted to avoid the regime ideology).

There are four examples of predominantly ideological supply-driven situations (many of which blend): Marxist-Leninist/Maoist communist regimes, secular nationalist regimes in countries with Islamic populations, nation-creating states resisting regional or ethnic centrifugal forces, and regimes founded on personal ideologies.

5. This section is based primarily on a paper written jointly with Martina Viarengo (Pritchett and Viarengo 2008). It builds on earlier work by Lott (1999) and Kremer and Sarychev (1998).

The New Communist Man

That the Marxist-Leninist regimes used the expansion of educational systems as a means of ideological control is not disputed; in fact, it was an explicitly stated objective of those systems. In these cases one can see the tragic extreme of expanding schooling in the absence of any benign motivation on the part of the regime. According to official statistics, the number of children ages eight to fifteen in Ukraine almost doubled from 1928–29 to 1932–33, and enrollment reached 4.5 million. During 1932–33 there was also a combination of a purge of the Ukrainian elite with "nationalist" sympathies and a famine that cost somewhere between three and five million lives. Was Stalin of two minds about Ukraine, expanding schools for benign motives, yet killing, deporting, and confiscating food for malign motives? Of course not. The expansion of schooling, the purges, and the famine had the same objective—a suppression of Ukrainian nationalism and of opposition to Soviet (Stalin's) control.

China is sometimes used as a positive example of a "human development"–led strategy in which investments in human capital created the conditions for the economic take-off under Deng after 1978. In June 1966, schools in China were closed to allow students to take part in the Great Proletarian Cultural Revolution, and one of history's grandest experiments in education reform was fully launched. It was not until October 1967 that schools were encouraged to "prepare for the recruitment of new students," but the reopening of schools went slowly, and when schools were reopened it was not to return to studies. Rather, students were to return to schools to do a better job of "making revolution" and "resume the lesson of class struggle" and "smash the outmoded content and form of teaching" (Chen 1981, 91). In a country that had relied on examinations to choose civil servants for more than a thousand years, all examinations in schools were to be abolished. A return to academic subjects was impossible, if not downright dangerous, for teachers, so the reopened schools focused on ideology "adhering closely to quotations from Mao and songs such as 'East is Red' and 'The Great Helmsman' " (Chen 1981, 91) and devoted time to the "half study, half work" approach to schooling. Into this ideologically charged and chaotic system more and more students poured, with the result that "academic secondary" enrollments increased from 9.3 million students in 1956 to 58 million by the end of the Cultural Revolution in 1976 (Hannum 1999).

Statistical analysis confirms the two obvious points (Pritchett and Viarengo 2008). One-party states that adhered to communist ideologies had much less tolerance for private schooling: the share of secondary education in the private sector in these states in 1990 was essentially zero, compared to roughly 11 percent in multiparty democracies. But at the same time, these states had more total education (adjusted for level of income) than other countries.

Secularists with a Dominant Religion

I have found it impossible to come up with a generalized measure of the difference between a regime's desired ideology and the "no formal schooling" socialization children would receive, but religion provides clear examples of the differences this produces for state tolerance or encouragement of private providers.

In the Middle East, one can distinguish between secularist regimes and the generally more religiously conservative monarchies. Not surprisingly, the secularist regimes have five times lower secondary enrollment rates in private schools than the conservative monarchies (3 percent versus 15 percent).

This reflects similar struggles that happened in Europe and in Latin America, struggles that, as we have seen, have long-term consequences for the structure of schooling. If one compares the South American countries that had become secular versus those that declared Catholicism as their state religion in 1900, even one hundred years later one can see the persistent effect of the greater toleration of private (religious) schooling, with lower private school shares of secondary enrollment in 2000 in those countries that were "secular" in 1900. At the obvious extremes, Mexico, whose 1917 constitution explicitly forbade religious schools,[6] today has only 16 percent of secondary students in private schools, in contrast to the 56 percent in private schools in neighboring Guatemala.

Keeping the State Together, Even When It Is Not a Nation

In the postcolonial period, many countries struggled with the fact that their newly controlled states were not (yet) "nation-states"—that is, the territory controlled by the state encompassed more than one potential nation. What had been held together by colonial fiat had to be legitimized as a nation. In Benedict Anderson's (1983) classic phrase, the "imagined community" that made a nation had to be imagined and then encouraged in the imagination of others. Indonesia, for instance, is an archipelago of thousands of islands with hundreds of languages and (at

---

6. Article 3, section IV: "Religious corporations . . . shall not in any way participate in institutions giving elementary, secondary and normal education."

least) dozens of distinct cultures, to which two global religions, Islam and Christianity, arrived at roughly the same time, and hence each has strongholds. As one part of its effort to resist the centrifugal pressures, the government of Indonesia created a national language by imposing its use throughout the centrally controlled schooling system.

It's All about Me (and My Ideology)

In Tanzania in 1967, Julius Kambarage Nyerere, who served as the country's first president and had been an educator prior to entering politics, launched Education for Self Reliance, an ideological remaking of the schooling system. He feared that schooling was producing values that were not consistent with socialism or with the reality that most school-leavers were going to remain and work in agricultural areas. Primary education became the terminal degree for nearly everyone; access to secondary and higher education was incredibly rationed. The primary schooling curriculum was changed to promote more "cooperative" behavior. He also reoriented school studies to be less academic and more integrated with the life of the community. The education plan was an integral part of Nyerere's socialist vision of *ujama,* in the execution of which the rural population was resettled (voluntarily or otherwise) into organized settlements to better promote delivery of social services and more collective action.

The point of these individual stories about how the interplay of state and traditional ideologies interacted in the evolution of state engagement with schooling is that in nearly every historical narrative, there was some strong contest among alternative socializations of youth that became important in how the schooling system was shaped and what forces drove its expansion.

These first two forces are pretty much garden-variety demand and supply as the driving forces, though of course, the outcome is the match of supply and demand. In the first narrative the causal driver of change is the increase in demand for schooling because parents perceive their children need schooling because of the changing economy and dynamic life conditions. To this incipient demand governments respond with supply ("if there is to be schooling, we must do it") in order to control socialization. In the second narrative an autonomous shift in the nation-state and in how it is ruled can create a state that pushes supply, even ahead of parental demand, to create a venue for socialization. But in both cases the explanation of government production (or not) of schooling is the state's need for direct control of schooling because instruction in beliefs is not third-party contractible.

Isomorphic Mimicry

The pressures of survival in the natural world are so strong they produce all kinds of unnatural things. The example of the stripes of the scarlet king snake is not unique; the natural world is full of deceit. Predators like leopards have camouflage to look like their background to gain advantage on prey. Prey have camouflage to either hide or blend into the background to avoid predators. Mimicry of all kinds is common.

Among noneconomists who study education, the most widely accepted explanation for why bad countries do the good thing of expanding schooling is that nation-states are embedded in a world system. Isomorphism at the level of the nation-state leads even bad nation-states to want to signal that they are legitimate, full-fledged nation-state members of the world system (e.g., Boli, Ramirez, and Meyers 1985). Hence if nearly all other nation-states are expanding public schooling, usually with functional purposes and with functional schools, then many other nation-states will also expand public schooling, not because of any deep commitment to advancing the well-being of their people but because it is what all other nation-states are doing.

As we saw in the previous chapter, this is potentially a powerful explanation as to why many governments adopted and ran school systems, with no particularly benign motive.

Just So Stories That Just Ain't So

It ain't what you don't know that gets you into trouble. It's what you know for sure that just ain't so.

MARK TWAIN

A man was sailing in a hot air balloon but hit a fog so dense he lost his bearings, could not see the ground, and became hopelessly lost. In a brief moment of clearing he saw another man walking along a road. "Where am I?" he shouted down. "You are up in a balloon," came the reply. "You must be an economist," said the man in the balloon. "Exactly correct, but how did you know?" From the balloon: "Because your answer was precisely correct and yet completely unhelpful."

The noneconomist reader may want to move on as I take up some intramural issues with my disciplinary tribe. Economists have done policy discussions of education a disservice in three distinct ways, each perpetuated by different ideological strands within the profession.

Normative as Positive

One of the most powerful ideas in economics, going back to Adam Smith's invisible hand of the market and progressively subjected to mathematical formalization, is that, under suitable conditions, the equilibrium of a market in which each individual pursues his or her own well-being will result in socially desirable outcomes. Deviations from these strict conditions are common. Economists call them "market failures." There is an area of economics, sometimes called "welfare" economics or "public economics," that asks whether, in the face of market failures, it would be possible for someone, say, a "social planner," to design and implement a policy that would lead to an outcome that would be preferred by *everyone*. With no restrictions on the instruments available to a social planner, the answer is nearly always yes, the optimal outcome can be reached even with market failures. Classic examples encountered in economics courses are negative externalities in which the smoke from my factory goes into the air and harms others, a harm that I as a factory owner do not "internalize" in my profit-maximizing calculations. But a "social planner" could impose a tax on the production of smoke that, combined with lump sum transfers, could make everyone, including me, the factory owner, better off. So far, so good, and many deep and important insights have come from pursuing this logic.

The problem arises when normative stories become "just so" stories that pretend to be causal accounts of the world, in which the *normative* analysis of what could, if it were to happen, improve well-being becomes a *positive* "explanation" of what actually happens. So if we happen to observe that factory smoke is taxed in a situation in which taxing factory smoke would be normatively optimal, one could jump to the conclusion that smoke is taxed *because* that taxation is optimal.

Nah, I can hear you saying, not really, no one would really make that mistake; you are attacking a straw man. You imagine that no one actually confuses normative, the hypothetical construct of a benevolent social-welfare-maximizing planner, with a real-world description of what the governments of Hastings Banda and Soeharto and Stroessner actually did. Yes, actually, economists do this all the time, particularly with schooling. The World Bank's website on education, meant to "educate" people about the economics of education, in 2000 claimed:

> Governments around the world recognize the importance of education for economic and social development and invest large shares of their budgets to education. The reasons for state intervention in the

financing of education can be summarized as: High returns, Equity, Externalities, Information asymmetries, Market failure.

Here I note that concepts like "market failures" are given as *reasons* for state intervention, a positive account of why governments "invest large shares of their budgets to education." As I have shown elsewhere, none of these normative reasons actually works as a positive account of what governments actually do, but that is probably either obvious or just not that interesting to the noneconomist reader, and not really the point.

The major problem is that there are three ways in which normative as positive, or NAP, accounting goes beyond a mere waste of time for a smallish (a few hundred, perhaps a thousand) number of academics to potentially do intellectual harm in the real world.

First, a narrative in which things are the way they are because that is the optimal choice of an agent who is striving to improve social well-being means that things can only get better in two ways: through an expansion of the resources available or through "technological progress." This suggests that the two ways to improve the performance of education systems are advocacy (to get the optimizing agent more resources) and research (to create new knowledge for the optimizing agent to use). There is no question that this narrative might have some elements of truth in some places and at some times, but as a general view about the means of improving performance of schooling systems it has absolutely nothing going for it. Besides being suspiciously self-serving about justifying the important role of researchers, this view risks creating complacency, suggesting things are basically right and just need tinkering with.[7]

Second, and much worse, many of the NAP explanations rationalize government actions in schooling on the premise that governments (the "social planner") care more about the education of children than the parents do because of the "positive externalities" to schooling. While NAP proponents do not mean it to, this creates an intellectual environment that justifies overriding parents' needs, demands, and desires in favor of the supposedly more socially attuned objectives of the government. This is not just false as a descriptive model but positively pernicious. (Elsewhere I have argued—see Pritchett 2002 and Pritchett and Viarengo 2008—that there is no feature of real-world schooling systems in developing countries that NAP accurately explains.) These ideas create

---

7. As we saw in chapter 3, much of the research done under the rubric of NAP examining the educational production function (the school and classroom correlates of student learning) makes rearranging the deck chairs on the *Titanic* look like rational prioritization.

intellectual legitimacy for taking control out of parents' hands—
something states often want for reasons less than benign. Third, an NAP
accounting can easily be stood on its head: one can take a simple empirical observation and then invent the "positive" explanation for it, and
really ask whether the proposed explanation fits. We can take as an
example the question of this chapter of why schooling systems tend to be
so big. Economics has an easy answer: economies of scale. That is, costs
are lower in larger systems. If one has to produce an explanation of positive realities that are also normatively attractive, then one gets into doing
detective work backward. That is, since we know schooling systems for
basic schooling are huge (at the level of nation-state or province) and
economies of scale are the positive explanation of hugeness, then even if
we don't see them, we know there must be economies of scale.

The key test of whether economies of scale can explain the size of
public systems is whether the private sector does the same activity at
similar scale. For instance, the state-run post office is a modern marvel of
centralization, and when the private sector delivers mail (or packages) it
often does so through huge centralized organizations as well. While the
U.S. Postal Service has 785,000 employees, United Parcel Service has
425,000 employees and FedEx has 240,000. The centralized organization is amenable to the activity of delivering post and packages, as there
are economies of coordination, and delivering the mail can be carried
out with just an address: a single piece of hard, easily encoded,
third-party-verifiable information about the intended recipient. Everything but the address (name, location) can be invisible to the delivering:
whether the address is a huge office building, a tiny box, a mansion, a
hovel; whether the addressee is tall or short, nice or mean, rich or poor,
or for that matter even a person and not a church or a corporation. The
ease with which all of the relevant information can be transmitted, along
with economies of scale in coordination, leads postal delivery services to
be huge organizations, as large size is productively efficient and organizationally viable—whether public or private.

In contrast, nearly all organizations providing services, especially professional services, are extremely small organizations. The largest law
firms in the United States have fewer than four thousand lawyers (the
largest in all of Latin America has 444). Most dentists have traditionally
worked in practices of one or two dentists. A survey of architects in the
United States showed that three quarters worked in practices with five or
fewer partners. In occupations or sectors (and even product lines within
sectors) in which the quality of the service provided requires detailed

adaptation to a specific case, and in which the quality of the service provided is based on information that is complex, difficult to encode, and hard for a third party to verify, then managing organizations with large numbers of employees becomes very difficult. Hence, unless some other positive economies of scale are sufficiently powerful to offset this observation, professional services firms tend to be small, with relationships handled without complex and rigid rules or organizational policies (including human resource policies), with performance assessed directly, and with high-powered incentives easier to create (such as small business owners).

The question is, is schooling more like delivering the mail or more like practicing dentistry? It is pretty obvious that when the private sector provides quality education, there are few, if any, economies of scale, and organizational expansion is very, very, hard. Harvard University, four hundred years into its existence, still has only about six thousand undergraduate students. There is enormous evidence that, in the activity of imparting instruction, economies of scale are just not achievable, which is obvious as mom-and-pop, one-school firms easily compete head-to-head with large schooling systems.

Vouchers: Settling for Pyrrhic over Victory

No one susceptible to economic reasoning can read the clarion call for vouchers in Milton Friedman's classic *Capitalism and Freedom* and not be persuaded. Persuaded, that is, that *if* it were the case that the *objective* of state engagement in schooling was the promotion of contractible skills, *then* the use of "money follows the student" schemes—or, more crudely, vouchers—would be a more effective policy than governments directly producing schooling. Over the years objections have been raised to arguments for vouchers—that they would lead to segregation, that they would perpetuate inequality. But as Caroline Hoxby's (2001) paper shows, with even more technical sophistication than Friedman, "Anything Q can do P can do better." That is, any goal that government supply can accomplish by increasing the quantities (Q) of schooling available (or targeting that Q to regions or races) could be accomplished more effectively by a suitably designed price (P) scheme. But that "anything" that P can do must be third-party contractible, otherwise the P incentive schemes can be undermined.

The problem with arguments for vouchers is that, just as Samuel Goldwyn explained the fate of his intended blockbuster, "They stayed away in droves." Modern schooling systems have been around for at least a hundred years. There are now almost two hundred countries. With all those chances for countries to adopt a voucher system (as opposed to portable scholarships as a minor frill in a fundamentally spider system), there have been precious few successes. Holland has a "money follows the student" system with parental choice, but for reasons detailed above that owe nothing to Professor Friedman or a belief in free markets. Besides moves in that direction by a few ex-communist countries immediately following the transition, such as the Czech Republic, Chile in 1981 is the only definitive adopter of a voucher-like system.[8]

Every time a voucher scheme has been put before the voters in the United States, it has been defeated. In this regard, Utah is particularly remarkable. Utah is one of America's consistently most conservative states (Obama got only a third of the state's general election vote in 2008, for instance). For this and other reasons Utah was believed by voucher advocates to be a state potentially receptive to the voucher program (Schaeffer 2007). However, when Utah voters had to decide whether to adopt the country's first statewide school voucher program, which would have been open to anyone, an overwhelming majority of Utah's voters, 62 percent, rejected it. The proposed law lost in every county. A "conservative" political agenda that cannot win in Utah cannot win.

Good Stories, Overextended

The last danger of economic thinking is that good stories of specific cases, particularly when they can be fleshed out with mathematics and provided some empirical support, too quickly become the accepted explanation and are too easily extended in terms of both the range of cases they are held to explain and the range of phenomena they are held to encompass. Some excellent works on the rise of education address the positive political economy in an interesting and theoretically plausible way (not, that is, the simplistic NAP accounting). The economic historian Peter Lindert's *Growing Public* (2004) is an excellent account of the historical rise in social spending in OECD countries. Daron Acemoglu and

---

8. Even in the case of Chile, a country where Chicago School economists had great influence over policy, it is obvious that the real reason behind the switch was not the control of socialization, but this time in reverse. Chile's teachers' unions were at the time dominated by hard-line, left-wing ideologists. It is plausible that Pinochet anticipated, correctly, that nearly all the move out of public schools would be into Catholic-operated schools, with an ideological orientation typically much more sympathetic to his views (and much less sympathetic to Marxism). By privatizing the school system he effectively moved a quarter of all children outside the reach of the public sector teachers' unions.

James Robinson (2000) have an intriguing model explaining the rise of schooling in the West as a bargaining game between "elites" and "the masses." Claudia Goldin and Lawrence Katz (2008) have written a monumental empirical account of the rise of schooling in the United States. Theorists such as Dennis Epple and Ricard Romano (1996) have constructed voting models that can generate a positive political economy of public production. None of these scholars would claim or have claimed that their work generalizes to explain the rise or features of schooling systems more broadly. Yet exactly such a casual overgeneralization from the history of the UK or the United States to completely different settings happens all too often.

The Beatles. Espionage and double agents. Church organists. Referenda in Utah. Fun stuff, you might say, but what does it have to do with reforming primary education in India or Brazil or Tanzania or Afghanistan?

There is a Russian fable about a bird that left too late on her southward migration and got caught in a snowstorm, could not fly, and was freezing to death. Along came a sympathetic cow, who said, "There is not much I can do for you, but my poop is warm and if you were inside my fresh pile for a minute you could warm up enough to fly on." So they tried that, and it worked. The bird warmed up, started stretching her wings. Just as she was about to fly a wolf came along, snatched her out of the pile, wiped her off, and gulped her down. The moral of the story is that not everyone who puts you in a steaming pile is your enemy, and not everyone who takes you out of one is your friend.

Just because schooling is a great thing for a child, perhaps even a fundamental human right, does not mean that those who engage in it do so for entirely benign motivations or in the right way.

The expansion to universal coverage has been universally successful because it has met a universal range of needs of states—and of the political regimes that control them.

The systems are big, but the part of education for which big is better is the control of socialization. The size of schooling systems has historically been determined by the size of the need for control of socialization.

Schooling is publicly *produced* rather than publicly *supported* or *financed* because the inculcation of belief is not third-party contractible and because public control of socialization requires some direct control of producers.

You cannot search if you are convinced you have already found what you need. Nothing about the current schooling systems in developing countries was designed or adopted for the purpose of reaching learning goals. It would be extremely unlikely that a hippopotamus, an animal whose evolutionary design was premised on living in large bodies of water, just so happened to be the perfect animal to cross the desert in a caravan. The spider systems we have today were designed in the nineteenth century and adapted and adopted in the twentieth century to meet a certain set of demands: to prepare workers for a transition out of agriculture, to build nations to support states, and to legitimate the regimes that controlled those states. It would be extraordinary indeed if those spiders just so happened to be systems designed for the learning and educational challenges the youth of the twenty-first century will face.

CHAPTER **6**

The Rebirth of Education as Starfish Ecosystems of Educators

Our lives have been transformed by two different logics that have brought starkly different outcomes: Moore's law and Baumol's cost disease.

We are today awash in computing power, electronic memory, and communication bandwidth. The typical American teenager plays games with more computing power than NASA used to send a man to the moon—and back (which was the impressive part). Cell phones have penetrated the planet; at their peak expansion more cell lines were added each month in India than the total number of landlines available in 1994. The bandwidth to share text, images, and video is nothing short of astounding.

In 1965, Gordon Moore noticed that the number of transistors that could fit on an integrated circuit chip had doubled every two years since 1958, and he thought the trend might continue, at least for a decade. Dubbed Moore's law, the contention that integrated circuit capacity—and other measures of computing power—would double every two years has proved uncannily accurate up to today. As a result, computing power has become essentially free: the Yale University economist William Nordhaus (2007) calculates that compared to manual computing—the only possibility in, say, 1850—our computing power is several trillionfold higher, and that since 1950 the economic cost of computing has fallen by a factor of a billion. The spectacular software and Internet applications used every day by hundreds of millions of people around the world—Google, Wikipedia, Facebook, Skype, not to mention the ubiquitous cell phone—are built on the hardware foundations of Moore's law.

In 1966, William J. Baumol and William G. Bowen, writing about the performing arts, noted exactly the opposite phenomenon. They pointed out that it takes the same time to perform a Mozart symphony today as it did in Mozart's time. Therefore, the cost of a live performance of a Mozart symphony must increase as the price of labor increases; there *cannot* be gains in labor productivity. This relationship, namely, that there are labor-productivity-resistant services whose cost must increase with the cost of labor, has been labeled Baumol's cost disease.

As we have seen in earlier chapters, basic education has not experienced productivity increases that would accord with Moore's law. On the contrary, in many countries the performance of learning has been even worse than that predicted for Baumol's disease as costs per student have risen even as measures of student learning have fallen.

While Moore's law and Baumol's disease have some underlying technological foundations, both are the result of the organization of human systems. Moore's law, which began as a crude heuristic based on the past, became a goal for the future for the people and the firms in the domain: they had the performance pressure of making Moore's law take effect, again and again, and they succeeded in doing so. In contrast, some sectors have allowed Baumol's cost disease to become an excuse, and organizations construct the camouflage of isomorphic mimicry to insulate value-subtracting and rent-extracting organizations against performance pressures, thus creating a self-fulfilling prophecy of stagnation and decline. The rebirth of education will require schooling systems to be freed from their Taylorist roots as instruments of uniform implementation of a top-down program and transformed into systems that free, foster, and scale innovations and dynamism.

Spiders are neither better nor worse than starfish; they are each the result of natural evolution and have claimed niches in an ecosystem. The key question is what mode of system organization is best adapted to a particular challenge. The schooling challenges of past decades, particularly the logistics of physical expansion, are adequately handled by spider systems. However, the challenges of the future, of using schools to create viable opportunities for the children of the twenty-first century by promoting learning, can best be met by starfish systems. Perhaps paradoxically, this is especially true in developing-country contexts, where people see the need for "order" but the spider systems are at their weakest (Pritchett 2013).

But just being a starfish ecosystem is not enough. There are six traits of an effective starfish ecosystem needed for quality education:

— *Open:* How is the entry and exit of providers of schooling structured?

— *Locally operated:* Do those who manage schools and teach in schools (and the local coalitions of parents and citizens they are accountable to) have autonomy over how their school is operated?

— *Performance pressured:* Are there clear, measured, achievable outcome metrics against which the performance of schools can be assessed?

— *Professionally networked:* Do teachers feel a common professional ethos and linkages among themselves as professional educators?

— *Technically supported:* Are the schools, principals, and teachers given access to the technical support they need to expand their own capacities?

— *Flexibly financed:* Can resources flow naturally (without top-down decisionmaking) into those schools and activities within schools that have proved to be effective?

These six elements do not dictate the exact design of a system. It would, of course, be contradictory to decry spider systems and then insist on a single model or instantiation of a starfish system. But the pieces of a starfish ecosystem do have to be coherent. There are hundreds of types of automobiles in the world, from Mini Coopers to Formula One racers to luxury sedans. Each of those vehicles works. Each has interrelated functional systems of engines to generate power, transmissions to take that power to the wheels, brakes to stop the car, and steering mechanisms to guide the car. But ramping up these subsystems one at a time doesn't necessarily produce a better car—strapping a massive engine into a Mini Cooper with the same transmission and brakes makes it a death trap, not a hot rod.

I am not going to tell you how to design the best car, or the best engine, or the best brakes. I realize that many of those reading this book will be disappointed, having hoped for a blueprint, a ready-made model for success. I probably could provide such a model, but I won't, for four reasons. First, as the Zen teaching goes, "If you should meet Buddha on the road, kill him" (a statement that, in keeping with the Zen koan tradition, I cannot explain). Second, the implementation of starfish principles must be contextual. I have worked on education issues in India, Argentina, Paraguay, Indonesia, and Egypt (among other countries), and, while I might be able to provide for each a starfish system approach conforming to the six desirable traits listed above, in each case the exact formula would be very different, depending on existing political, social, and educational contexts. Third, the book is already long. In a book like this I can only provide a vision of what a system of education could be, not a buildable blueprint. But blueprints of successful systems can and are being built on the foundations I describe. Fourth, if you don't design it, it isn't yours, as you cannot juggle without the struggle (Pritchett 2013).

Success at Scale Requires Systems for Scaling Success

One charge that could rightly be leveled at this book so far is that the general tenor is pessimistic: chapter 1 says learning levels are low; chapter 2 tells us more years of schooling won't solve the learning problem; chapter 3 argues just more inputs alone will provide a little help, not a lot; chapter 4 suggests more of the same can actually block better learning; chapter 5 argues that the systems we have were built for ideological socialization in the nineteenth (and twentieth) centuries, and not for developing student capabilities to meet twenty-first-century needs. And now I want to talk about creating a positive dynamic of progress?

But success is out there. There are many actors out there in many guises—in the private sector, among NGOs, and inside government systems—doing fantastic things even in difficult country contexts such as Pakistan and Nigeria and Nepal. The problem is that failure is out there too, and we haven't figured out how to consistently build education ecosystems whose natural operation would promote the good and weed out the bad. Lots of people have figured out how to build good, even great, schools—which is terrific—but what I want to imagine is an ecosystem of schooling from which better and better schools are the natural outcome.

Success Is Already Available, in Lots of Contexts

The cause for optimism is that, even in countries with poor average results, and even in the most difficult situations, such as isolated or rural environments, there are schools that succeed in promoting high levels of learning. This is true among community and NGO efforts, with budget-level private schools, and in the government sector.

Community and NGO Schools

Concern over the quality of government schools has produced activists and NGOs that either run their own schools or intervene in various ways to increase learning in government schools. Worldwide, a number of individuals and movements have started and operate schools. The Fe y Alegria movement, which was started by the Jesuits in Venezuela in 1955 to promote comprehensive education and social change, has grown to have more than a million students reached with one type of activity or another. Recently, Bunker Roy and his "barefoot" approach in Rajasthan India have received wide attention. Both these efforts are the continuation of a long heritage of similar approaches.

Many NGOs have been engaged with academics in doing rigorous evaluations of the learning impact of their interventions and so have hard evidence of the massive gains available. For instance, the Indian NGO Pratham did remedial education in classrooms in two cities in India by pulling out the students who were behind to work with tutors for half of the school day. Studies showed that the learning of students who began in the bottom third improved by .43 standard deviations (Banerjee, Cole, et al. 2010). In a different setting, village volunteer tutors were trained for a mere four days, after which they were able to help children develop the fundamental skills required for them to succeed in school and raised the proportion of children who could read by 23 percent (Banerjee, Banerji, et al. 2010). A month-long summer camp that targeted low-performing children in Bihar, India, raised over half of these children one level in reading (out of five levels) at the end of a month—equivalent to the gain of a year of schooling (Banerjee and Walton 2011). These tactics have since been scaled up by the government to an entire district, with promising results (as of early 2013).

Communities themselves, even without the intervention of NGOs, can often improve schools when given the chance. An evaluation of the effect of turning schools over to community-based management in Nepal found significant decreases in school attrition rates (especially among disadvantaged groups), improvements in school processes (such as whether principals warned teachers about nonperformance, and improved outcomes on science learning assessments) (Chaudhury and Parajuli 2010).

But my point is not to single out specific NGOs or their ideology, or specific interventions; nor do I propose community-based management as the best approach and one that should be replicated. The point is, there is a continuous stream of available innovations out there, literally thousands of local examples of success, spanning every region and country, but many scale too slowly to have an impact on national learning outcomes. Even as dozens of fantastic actors and innovations on the education scene in India are improving outcomes locally, the national learning outcome continues to stagnate, or worse, as the latest ASER results suggest flattening learning profiles (ASER 2013).

Private Sector: Budget-Level Private Schools

One of the ways in which parents have coped with failing and unresponsive public school systems has been to move into private schools. Whereas formerly only the elite may have gone to private schools, there has been a massive proliferation of private schools, especially in Asia and Africa. These budget-level private schools are producing better learning outcomes, often substantially better, than publicly controlled schools—even for the same students—and often at much lower cost.

Tooley and Dixon (2005) compared private schools and government schools in four urban areas, three in Africa and one in India, on learning outcomes in math and language. In some of the locales the learning outcomes in mathematics were higher in the private schools by almost an entire student standard deviation. These differences are shown in figure 6-1, where I also include other tested subjects, such as religious and moral education in Ga, Ghana, and social studies in Lagos, Nigeria, to show that these gains owe not simply to private schools concentrating exclusively on math, as the learning gaps are just as large. One of the most important features of this study is that it included not just the prestigious and exclusive private schools but also schools that operate completely outside the current educational systems as unrecognized or unregistered schools. Even in these schools, which do not attract wealthy or elite students, the students are outperforming those in government schools.

Of course, these findings don't prove that private schooling is the *cause* of the superior performance. The hardest thing about deciding whether private schools are performing better is not knowing whether students in private schools are performing better—they almost always are—but whether the improved student performance is because of a selection effect, so that children who would otherwise have performed better anyway are in private schools, or because private schools provide more learning for the same students.

Figure 6-1. Even unregistered, low-cost private schools have students outperforming those in government schools.

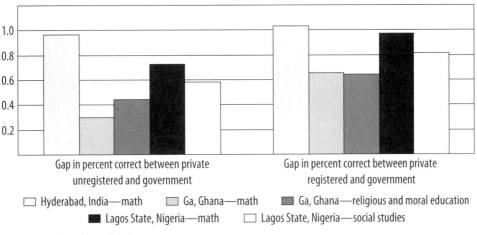

Effect size (student standard deviations)

Gap in percent correct between private unregistered and government

Gap in percent correct between private registered and government

☐ Hyderabad, India—math   ▨ Ga, Ghana—math   ▨ Ga, Ghana—religious and moral education

■ Lagos State, Nigeria—math   ☐ Lagos State, Nigeria—social studies

Source: Tooley and Dixon (2005).

As discussed in chapter 4, the LEAPS study in Pakistan shows that children in private schools are between 0.7 and 1.2 student standard deviations (depending on which subject) ahead of students in private schools, even for the same underlying quality of student (statistically speaking).

This isn't to say that across the board, private schooling is better than that available in government-run schools; in general, the evidence that private schools outperform government schools in well-functioning systems of education is weak. In the United States, where there has been the opportunity to do the most rigorous experimental studies, most researchers agree that the private sector edge in learning is nothing like a full effect size, almost certainly not even a tenth of an effect size, and some legitimately dispute whether the private sector causal impact is even positive. Even in India the estimates of the gains from private schooling range from zero in some states to almost a full student standard deviation in others (Desai et al. 2008). In Uttar Pradesh, given what we have seen in previous chapters about its weaknesses, the typical student has learning higher by 0.69 of an effect size by being in a private school.

Government Schools

Thus, the learning increments from private schooling noted above do not speak against the capability of governments to produce educational success; indeed, governments can and do produce massive gains when the conditions are right. For instance, one set of efforts has focused on getting children reading fluently in early grades. An increasing body of evidence from interventions that follow the "five T's" (time on task, teaching teachers, texts, tongue of instruction, and testing) supports the concept that early intervention can produce massive results. In the Early Grade Reading Assessment Plus (EGRA+) in Liberia, a rigorous evaluation showed effect sizes in oral reading and reading comprehension of 0.8 (Korda and Piper 2011). Similar experiences include Breakthrough to Literacy in Zambia (USAID 2011), the Malandi District Experiment in Kenya (Crouch and Korda 2009), Systematic Method for Reading Success (SRMS) (South Africa) (Piper 2009), and Read-Learn-Lead (RLL) in Mali (Gove and Cvelich 2011).[1]

Broader than just the success of specific interventions inside government schools is the observation that even in low-performing government systems one finds excellent schools—but also, even nearby and even operating under apparently exactly the same conditions, terrible schools. The LEAPS study in Pakistan found that in English performance, the best government school scored 845, only slightly behind the best private school, which tested at 850. However, the worst government school averaged only 84, or tenfold lower. The problem is not that government schools cannot succeed, for in nearly all developing countries some of the very best schools are government schools. The problem is, as the LEAPS study authors emphasize, "when government schools fail, they fail completely" (Andrabi et al. 2007, 31).

The upside of the high-performing government schools is that they prove it is possible. The question is how to bring the lower-performing government schools up to the standard of the high-performing government schools. And the answer isn't inputs. In Pritchett and Viarengo (2009) we used the PISA data to calculate the difference in the average scores of students in different schools, differences evident even when statistically the schools had the same students and the same inputs. We found that even when there is the "illusion of equality," namely, that all public schools have the same processes and procedures and inputs, there are massive differences in what students know. For instance, in Mexico the student standard deviation on the PISA assessment was 79 points. The standard deviation across government schools, even adjusting for the

---

1. I thank Luis Crouch for these references, and for his guidance on EGRA and remediation.

Figure 6-2. **Both government and private sectors have top-performing schools in Mexico on the PISA assessment, but essentially** *all* **of the weakest-performing schools—those more than 100 points below the average—are government schools.**

Kernel density

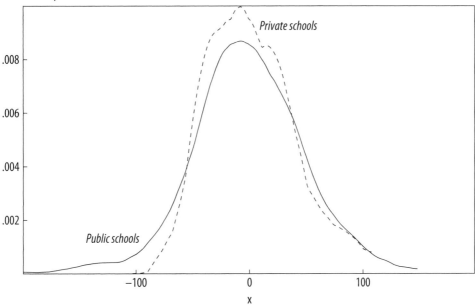

Source: Pritchett and Viarengo (2009).

background characteristics of students and for measured inputs, was 30 points. So if the weak schools (one school standard deviation down) could reach the same level of performance of the strong schools (one standard deviation up), the average student scores could increase by 60 points—which is a substantial part of the gap between the United States and Mexico. As figure 6-2 shows, the difference between government and private school quality in Mexico is not at the top, it is at the bottom, with very weak schools in adjusted (for students and inputs) learning.

Unleashing the Power of Loosely Coupled Systems for Education

Why don't all these great ideas about how to do education scale better?

The problem in education doesn't seem to be a need for better mousetraps but that the available mousetraps are not being sprung.

There is a joke that economists tell that is worth telling because it is telling. An economist is walking down the sidewalk toward his friend. He walks right by a hundred-dollar bill lying on the ground. His friend is stunned. "I thought economists valued money." "Oh, it cannot have been a hundred-dollar bill. Had it been a real hundred-dollar bill, the free market would have picked it up already."

Advocates in education, on the other hand, seem to have no end of (metaphorical) hundred-dollar bills—great ideas and interventions that, if only they were to be adopted, would lead to large improvements in quality of learning at low cost. As obtuse as it may seem, one does have to stop and ask, "If your idea is so great, why isn't it already the existing practice?"

In 1997 two guys thought they had a better idea for searching the Internet. In 2011 some 4.7 billion searches were done using their search engine every day. Larry Page and Sergey Brin no longer spend time convincing people Google has better search algorithms. People tried it, liked it, adopted it, and it scaled (and wow, did it scale!).

In 2004 a college sophomore thought he had a cool idea for how people could interact over the Internet. By 2012 there were a billion people using Facebook. People tried it, liked it, adopted it, and it scaled (and wow, did it scale!).

But spider systems can block great ideas from scaling. The most dramatic shift from spider systems to starfish systems in my lifetime has been in telephone service. With the old wire-based technology, telephone services were a "public monopoly" and hence were either taken over completely by government firms or strongly regulated. In places with reasonable governments, this did not work too badly, and access to telephones expanded and things worked OK. In India in 1998, more than a hundred years after telephone service had become widespread, there were only 14.9 million landlines in India. The regulators had a stranglehold on expansion of service, and getting a telephone was a Herculean feat (of patience, political connections, and/or bribery).

With the advent of cellular technology, telephone service switched from being something a spider could dominate to a starfish system where people could just do it. In 2010 there were more people getting a cell phone, and hence access to a vital service—15 million in a *month*—than got a landline in the first fifty years of Indian independence. This break from a top-down spider system has been replicated around the world. African countries with governments incapable of managing anything have had massive expansions of cell phone coverage. You can get a working cell phone in South Sudan (I have) or Somalia (I hear).

How does system design promote appropriate scaling up? A system design answers the questions of *who* does *what* and *why*.

Suppose a girl shows up at the door of a school today, ready, anxious, and able to learn. What must happen for this girl to have a successful schooling experience that will produce an education that prepares her to meet the challenges she will face in her adulthood (which will last almost until the twenty-second century)?

There must be a place to learn, and that place can be more or less conducive to learning. There must be learning materials of various kinds, from desks to chalk to textbooks to laboratory equipment. There must be a curriculum: people have to know what the learning objectives for this girl are, what is it that she should learn. There must be teachers who have command over the material to be taught and possess some pedagogical knowledge about how to teach someone, and these teachers must be motivated to teach. There has to be some way of assessing the girl's progress and using that feedback to dynamically shape her learning experience.

Even at this incredibly schematic level of description this is already a lot of things to do, involving in one way or another many different people with quite different skill sets. Some people have to know how to build buildings, some people have to know how to make books, some people have to know how to measure learning, some people have to know how to teach, some people have to know how to teach other people to teach.

How things are going to get done involves some specification of *who* is going to do *what* and *why*. Table 6-1 illustrates for India the various functions and activities that go into a school system. Whether the system entails allocation across levels of government in a scheme of fiscal federalism (as in the table) or whether allocation occurs between the public and private sectors, there is some implicit or explicit allocation of responsibilities. Who is going to set standards? Who is going to build buildings? Who is going to order the chalk? Who is going to assign teachers to schools and classrooms? Who is going to assess the performance of schools?

How, who, what, and why can be answered in very different ways. Table 6-2 illustrates (again) the fundamental distinction—that can be made in many ways—between systems. One dichotomy that does not appear on the list of spider system versus starfish system distinctions in table 6-2 is "private versus public" sectors or "market versus government." The debates over public versus private schooling are so loud and so vociferous, so full of sound and fury, it is easy to miss that they signify (almost) nothing. The business historian Alfred Chandler has shown that the rise of the modern spider bureaucratic organization in America was

Table 6-1. A system is defined in part by the allocation of responsibilities across actors.

		Responsibility owner					Village		Service provider (school)
Function	Activity	Central	State	District	Block	Gram Panchayat	User groups		
Standards	Curriculum design Learning achievement standards								
Planning	Plans for physical expansion Plans for quality improvement								
Asset creation	Social capital Physical capital								
Operation: non-teacher	*Beneficiary selection:* Choice of students for targeting programs Enrollment *Recurrent:* Textbook choice or purchase Learning materials *Maintenance:* Maintenance of school buildings and facilities Monitoring of school processes								
Operation: teacher	Hiring Assignment Training Salary Supervision Dismissal								
Monitoring and evaluation	Test of learning achievement								

Source: Adapted from Pritchett and Pande (2006).

Table 6-2. A fundamental divide exists in system approaches.

A _Teleological agents_	B _Emergent orders_	_Representative authors and their discipline or domain_
Spiders	Starfish	Ori Brafman and Rod Beckstrom, organization
Tightly coupled	Loosely coupled	Larry Constantine, computer science (and Karl Weick, organizations)
High modernism	Metis	James Scott, politics
Planners	Searchers	William Easterly, economic development
Hierarchy	Polyarchy	Elinor Ostrom, politics
Managerialism	Owner operation	Alfred Chandler, economic history
Legal/rational	Charismatic/value	Max Weber, sociology

driven by the private sector. As he shows in *The Visible Hand* (1977) and *Scale and Scope* (1990), many of the features of modern spider organizations originated as responses to the potential (but not yet realized) economies of scale and the need for tighter organization in what were then privately owned industries, such as the railroads, steel, and oil. Well into the twentieth century, governments in America were much more like starfish—localized, less formalized, more "bottom up"—while private businesses were leading the charge in massive-scale organizations that relied on top-down control of a bureaucracy.

The dominant way of organizing basic education has been to fill in the functions chart of table 6-1 entirely with the direct employees of a single ministry. In this case, the system of public support for education is exclusively a spider system, and there is little or no support of any kind flowing from the spider organization to other schools in the system. These spider systems of schooling can be national or federalized (as in India), but nevertheless remain very large. Typical school systems in large countries employ tens of thousands of teachers, with centralized responsibility for hiring and allocating these teachers. The legacy systems of basic schooling in most developing countries around the world look very similar because they are almost exclusively large government-owned spiders, both as organizations and as systems.

The choice between the spider and the starfish mode of organization is not a decision that should be made about "education" or "primary education"—rather, it depends on what is being done. Some activities are perfectly suited to a spider mode of organization, so that whether those activities are conducted by the state or by private actors, similar organizations emerge. For instance, activities that require a great deal of coordination among actors for success will be organized by spiders. The high cost of laying railroad tracks, combined with the very high cost of making sure two trains on the same track at the same time headed in opposite directions are operating safely, means coordination is essential. This has led railroad organizations to have massive scale, in both market and socialist systems. In contrast, moving things by truck sacrifices the economies of scale achievable with railroads for the gains of not needing central coordination: millions of trucks can be on the highway without any one agent being the central dispatcher.

But the spider versus starfish distinction in *systems* is even more complex, as often the entire chain of production requires multiple activities, some of which have larger economies of scale, scope, or coordination while others are best done locally. This can lead to different organizations making different choices. Some organizations might increase to the efficient scale of the activity in the production chain that requires the largest size, at the risk of losing effectiveness in the activities best done at a smaller scale, but decreasing the costs of coordination across organizational boundaries. But when a system is open, other organizations may remain small and deal at arm's length with other, larger spider organizations doing the activities with economies of scale.

This is the case with schooling. The scale at which standards should be set doesn't correspond at all to the scale at which teachers should be hired. These activities can be decoupled and hence carried out by completely different actors.

Learning about Schooling from Instruction

We all know how to do many things we did not learn by formal schooling. Most people have mastered at least some skills or capabilities that take years to acquire proficiency in: playing a musical instrument, participating in a sport, speaking a foreign language, knowing a religious text well. Most of these skills are acquired with instruction outside formal school settings. Moreover, key parts of education and socialization happen in voluntary associations, religion being the most obvious example. In voluntary associations, specialized knowledge and requisite beliefs are passed from one generation to another, sometimes by way of formal schooling, but often in instructional settings not affiliated with schools.

While basic schooling has some unique features, it also has much in common with other forms of instruction. Schooling is just one format in an extended, coordinated sequence of instructional episodes. Before turning to an analysis of basic education according to starfish principles, it is worth starting with the variety of nonschooling instructional experiences.

Piano lessons have a completely open structure. Suppose you want to learn to play the piano. There is a huge array of options. You can take private lessons from an independent private teacher who provides at-home lessons. You can arrange to take lessons at a local music school. You can take group lessons. You can buy a book and teach yourself. You can take an online course on the Internet. You could just buy a piano and tinkle around. Piano learning definitely has the completely open structure of a starfish (table 6-3).

The pressure on the system is for each of the possible providers of piano instruction to attract students. But how do you know if you are receiving good instruction? You can find out about piano teachers by word of mouth among your social network, or by trial and error, or through online discussions and reviews. I hated taking piano lessons, but my parents insisted I should learn at least enough piano to be able to play the hymns in church. I hated lessons with each so I switched instructors, four times. As it turns out, I just hated piano lessons.

Piano teaching is loosely networked. There is little or no public sector support for piano lessons of any type. There are few spider organizations in the actual giving of piano lessons, but there are several interesting features. First, the production of books from which to learn piano is, as a result of market forces, much more concentrated than the giving of lessons. Second, there are particular schools of piano pedagogy, such as Suzuki, that have features of a spider system.

The result is that piano lessons are widely available, but they are heterogeneous in quality (large numbers of children begin and drop out without learning much), and the different modes of instruction are strongly stratified on class and status.

Piano lessons are just one example of a completely open-structured, weakly performance-pressured, weakly networked, publicly unsupported, starfish system of instruction. A similar analysis would apply to learning to play other musical instruments and engaging in other cultural activities, such as dance or singing. Huge numbers of children participate in sports, with a mix of learning on their own, participation in instruction through organized leagues, and private instruction. This mixed mode also applies to instruction for adults, an example being learning a foreign language, which may involve a mix of tutors, taking classes offered by a range of providers, self-instruction with tapes, or Internet-based learning.

Table 6-3. Different types of instruction are available in the United States as they range across the spider-starfish continuum.

	Piano lessons	Sports	College test prep (e.g., for SAT)	Christian religious instruction (e.g., Sunday school)
Open?	Yes	Yes	Yes	Yes (across denominations as individuals can move, new denominations can enter)
Locally operated?	Yes	Yes	Mixed	Yes
Performance pressured?	Yes—informally, with thick accountability	Yes—competition reveals level (if not value added)	Yes—highly pressured on a single demonstrable outcome	Yes—by multiple actors (parents, children, religious organization) and goals
Professionally networked?	Modestly (no organizational hierarchy)	Modestly (no organizational hierarchy)	No	Mixed—some spiders, but mostly strong networking within denominations
Technically supported?	No (at discretion of instructor)	Mixed (through sport-specific associations)	All firm-level training	Mixed—with training often provided centrally
Flexibly financed?	No subsidies	No subsidies	No subsidies	Cross-subsidy to training of youth within the denomination
Result	Multiple modes of instruction (including self-instruction), heterogeneous quality, mixed results (high dropout rate), access stratified based on ability to pay		Spider organizations (e.g., Kaplan) dominate, with many smaller competitors	Mixed modes used by various denominations from complete starfish to somewhat spider

Interestingly, the public sector is often indirectly involved in markets for instruction, through licensing requirements, but does not actually produce any instruction. For example, (some) people in the United States wanting to get a driver's license not only have to pass a state test but also must demonstrate before taking the test that they have completed a mandated course of instruction. The actual instruction, however, is done through a starfish system of large numbers of small, independent driving schools.

Vocational licensing often has the same structure, with public sector requirements for both passing an examination and completing a given number of hours of instruction or training. Again, the state imposes the requirement and controls who receives accreditation to provide training, but it does not produce the training. This leaves a large body of small, independent training providers who are pressured to attract students.

The exception to the very decentralized, starfish nature of instruction in the United States might be test preparation. Test prep firms like Kaplan may capture a significant fraction of the market for paid test preparation. But in some ways, this is the exception that proves the rule. By creating a very narrow set of performance expectations, the tests (such as the SAT) themselves narrow the variability in demand from test takers: people who attend test prep classes want better test scores, full stop.

In *systems* of instruction, predominantly spider systems or even systems dominated by a few large spider organizations are extremely rare. Organizing the process of teaching and learning as a spider—a large hierarchical organization with multiple units—is an anomaly in the world of instructional services.

Adopting a starfish system approach doesn't mean making basic education look more like piano lessons, it means making basic education more like an open, locally controlled, performance-pressured, professionally networked, inclusively supported starfish system. These approaches can be a *means* to producing a dynamic system of education that can provide universally the quality of educational outcomes youth need for the twenty-first century. But they do not create a single blueprint. As the next section shows, starfish systems come in many designs.

Three Examples of Starfish Systems for Success

Three different types of successful starfish systems suggest different ways in which success can be achieved. The higher education system of the United States plus the UK (and the "Anglo" world) has achieved top status worldwide in providing quality learning. The International Baccalaureate program, run by an organization of the same name in Switzerland, successfully prepares a mix of international students for advanced studies through distance learning and evaluation in both private and government-operated schools. And the country of Brazil has improved its standings in basic education metrics through devolving control to local agents and instituting a practice of federal monies following students. These three examples underscore the many forms consistent with a starfish mode of organization and the different paths to success that can be operationalized.

Higher Education

The United States plus the UK and the EU-27 (the EU minus the UK) are of similar size in population (with the EU's population slightly larger), have a similar magnitude of total economic output (with the EU's slightly smaller), have similar types of governments and capabilities, and have similar levels of completed schooling. But these two demographic areas are poles apart when it comes to the quality of higher education. The Annual Ranking of World Universities (ARWU), published by the Center for World-Class Universities and the Institute of Higher Education of Shanghai Jiao Tang University, China, ranks the world's top universities mainly on their research output and quality, as well as on how many alumni win prestigious academic awards, a ranking that leans toward schools that emphasize the natural sciences. As table 6-4 shows, the United States and the UK together have sixty-five of the world's top one hundred universities. Continental Europe manages only twenty-three of the top one hundred. The United States and the UK together have 2.8 times as many universities in the top one hundred as Europe does. Even if one moves to the top two hundred universities, the United States and the UK together still have twice as many as the EU. (Since any league table of universities inevitably inspires controversy, I used three other rankings, one from the UK, one from Russia, and one just using Web presence, to be sure this basic conclusion was robust. It is.)

While many focus on the top of the rankings, the top ten or twenty, what is really striking about U.S. and UK higher education is the depth of the bench. The "middle tier" universities in the United States would be superstars in any other country. And vice versa, the next-to-the-top universities in most countries in continental Europe would be hard-pressed to be middle-of-the-pack American universities. An example is France, a country with more than 60 million people, a glorious history, and a long tradition of academic excellence but lacking the equivalent of a Harvard or an Oxbridge, as its best universities rank with Carnegie Mellon (United States) or Bristol (UK). Even more striking is the paucity of quality universities: the third-best university in France by the ARWU rankings would be the forty-fourth best in the United States, tied with the University

Table 6-4. The quality of universities in the United States and the United Kingdom dominates that of continental European institutions, with the U.S. and the U.K. having more than half of the top 100 universities in the world.

Ranking method	Number in U.S./U.K.	Number in continental Europe	Ratio of U.S./U.K. to European institutions
In the global top 100			
ARWU	65	23	2.8
THE-QS	49	20	2.5
Global universities	60	17	3.5
Webometrics	76	10	7.6
In the global top 200			
ARWU	106	57	1.9
THE-QS	82	52	1.6
Global universities	87	60	1.5
Webometrics	116	48	2.4

Sources: Author's calculations, based on data from the ARWU 2009 survey, the THE-QS 2009 ranking, and the Webometrics 2009 ratings.

of Rochester. In the THE-QS ratings, the fourth-best university in France would be the forty-third best in the United States, just ahead of the University of Virginia or Ohio State University. And the French are among the better of Western Europe. Neither Italy nor Spain has a single university in the ARWU top one hundred, which puts their best on a lower ranking than the U.S. universities rounding out the top one hundred, such as Indiana University, Bloomington, and Arizona State University. In the THE-QS top two hundred the top Italian university has a global rank of 174th, and the top Spanish university is rated 171st. Again, it doesn't surprise anyone that many of the world's very best universities are in the United States, but the depth of the bench—Texas A&M, which is ranked the third best university *in Texas*, is ranked higher than the *best* university in Spain or Italy—is probably a shock to most.

It is easy to rule out some possible explanations of this amazing depth in quality of the United States and the UK (given their conjoint population size). First, this is not the result of "first mover" advantages, as Harvard was barely a glorified high school when Heidelberg was hundreds of years old—not to mention parvenus that emerged from agricultural colleges like Texas A&M and Ohio State University. Second, it is not the result of "agglomeration economies," which theoretically would allow bigger populations to support more quality universities, as the UK has roughly the same population as France or Italy.

What we know for sure is that the success of Anglo universities is not the result of spider-like top-down control. There is no "spider" inside the U.S. success: there is neither strong centralized decisionmaking with strong direction over the system nor any single organization dominating the overall system.

My argument is that the Anglo world—the United States and the UK—has produced superior results in higher education because it combines the six traits into a successful starfish system: open, locally operated, performance pressured, professionally networked, technically supported, and flexibly financed. Empirical research has shown that university research output in the United States and Europe is higher when institutions are more autonomous and there is more competition for research funds (Aghion et al. 2009).

International Baccalaureate

The International Baccalaureate (IB) is an educational organization based in Switzerland and begun in 1968 with the goal of supporting the growth of, and providing a common structure for, students preparing for higher education in international schools around the world.[2] The IB has experienced significant growth since that time and is now associated with more than three thousand schools in nearly 140 countries that currently offer its programs to more than 850,000 students. The initial focus of the IB was on a two-year Diploma Program for students ages sixteen to nineteen. Since 1994 the IB has introduced the Middle Years Program and Primary Years Program, which provides structure, assessment tools, networking, and support for their programs' students as young as age three. With its early work done predominantly in private international schools, the IB has now expanded its reach to a broader range of institutions. Over half the schools now authorized to offer one or more of the three IB programs are government-operated schools.

The schools associated with and approved by the IB organization to offer the IB show diversity in the size, structure, philosophy, and many other important educational elements. The IB does have requirements for admission of schools into participation in the program but they are based on the

---

2. This section draws on materials prepared by Danny Smith.

implementation of a certain set of educational objectives and standards for learning and assessment and little else. A school hoping to implement one or all of the three IB programs goes through an evaluation process that includes facilities and faculty, but the IB does not make significant requirements beyond this. Schools are free to define their missions and communities in many other ways, allowing the IB program to fit well into large schools, small schools, public schools, private schools, parochial schools, charter schools, and single-sex schools. Some schools elect to provide the IB program for students of all ages, while others implement only one or two of the three programs. A broad educational mission allows the IB flexibility to work within a very expansive group of educational environments and philosophies that are completely autonomous in operation.[3]

What the IB program does is create clear, concrete, measurable standards in each academic domain (including art and music) and provide objective external assessment of the extent to which students have met those objectives. Students' work is submitted to the IB program, which provides independent evaluators to assess student work against the curricular objectives that were set. These are not standardized exams but rather involve portfolios of work that are assessed, and students must meet thresholds of quality to receive the IB degree.

While providing significant guidance and support for objective evaluation, the IB does not tell teachers and schools exactly how every element of assessment should take place. Particularly in the Primary Years Program and the Middle Years Program there are very few standardized tests created, graded, or even evaluated significantly outside the individual school's community. However, the IB provides significant support regarding the curricular objectives, proper assessment tools, and best methods for determining various grade levels and subjects. Additionally, the IB program makes available training and support to schools and teachers, and instruction in how to meet those standards.[4]

3. The IB does require that certain staffing roles be filled. A coordinator is required for the Diploma Program and its accompanying Community, Actions, and Service requirement. Likewise, the school should designate a coordinator responsible for evaluation, professional development, assessment, and other activities The IB does not specify exactly who should fill these roles for each school and provides significant freedom to individual schools to meet these needs. At larger schools there may be administrators taking on IB roles and objectives as their full-time duties, while smaller schools may have an IB coordinator who is also teaching classes or fulfilling a variety of other duties not associated with the program.

4. In the interests of full disclosure, my wife participates in IB-sponsored training through teaching the "Theory of Knowledge" component of the IB program.

Recent Progress in Brazil

In 2000, Brazil participated for the first time in the PISA exercise and recorded the lowest scores among all countries on mathematics.[5] By 2009, though it still lagged, Brazil had gained 52 points in mathematics and had the third largest gain of any country over the 2000–2009 period. Brazil has set a goal of being at OECD levels of learning quality by 2021. While it is obviously impossible to parse out the many changes that led to this progress, we can point to four things have happened.

First, Brazil set about to measure learning and progress in learning. The country initiated a sample-based biannual assessment in mathematics and Portuguese in grades four, eight, and eleven in 1995 so that learning progress could be tracked. In 2005 it moved to a census-based assessment in grades four and eight. This expansion to census (versus sample) testing means that nearly every single education establishment knows how its students are performing in learning. Moreover, realizing that schools could game learning tests by changing enrollment (say, by holding low-performing children back in grade three so they do not take the grade four examination), the Brazilian policymakers developed an index of progress, the IDEB (Índice de Desenvolvimento da Educação Básica), that combines information on school progression. Now every school, every municipality, and every state knows its IDEB score and how it is changing over time. This provides a performance metric against which many different initiatives and efforts can be judged.

Second, there was a massive reform of the financing of education between the federal government and states and municipalities that accomplished three things. (1) It established minimum levels of spending. (2) It made "money follow the student" so that municipalities, rather than seeing increasing enrollment as a cost burden, saw they could expand education and get more resources for doing so. (3) The funding was flexible within categories (for example, of teacher and non-teacher inputs). This caused a massive rise in the proportion of students enrolled in municipal versus state-run schools.

Third, traditionally, the federal government had played little or no role in education, with states taking the lead. The federal government ramped up its support in core areas while not taking on the actual running of any

---

5. This section draws on Bruns, Evans, and Luque (2012).

schools. The federal government created the legal framework, established the curriculum, focused on measurement, provided technical support in the form of textbooks and teacher training, and targeted support to low-performing municipalities.

Fourth, the Brazilian government addressed problems of income inequality and poverty by creating transfers that supported poor households with school-aged children. By 2009 more than 17 million students were supported by cash transfers to their households based on their attending school.

Principles of Successful Starfish Systems

The essence of a starfish system of education is to move from a top-down, integrated system that controls all aspects of schooling to a system that is only loosely coupled so that small units—schools and small groups of schools—have greater autonomy. But, as experience with decentralization and with market systems has shown, merely having autonomy does not ensure positive results. The *ecosystem* determines outcomes. Each of the six traits is reviewed to see how it fits into the overall system design.

Open

How open is the system to novelty? How many new genetic variants are produced in each generation? How likely is it that any incumbent school will face a challenger?

In a pure spider system, new schools are created when and where the top agency decides schools are to be created. Each new school is essentially a clone of existing schools and is operated by the spider as an extension of the existing system. Entry of schools into the system, particularly schools that are part of the public ecosystem and receive public financing, adds no novelty to the system.

The essential characteristic of openness of a basic schooling ecosystem means that new schools can be *new*. New schools can bring in new ideas, new people, new pedagogical techniques, new modes of socialization. In other words, they introduce novelty into the system. However, a balance must be sought so that the system is open to novelty while those dimensions that support the purposes of publicly supported education are protected from excessive change.

To illustrate how different descriptive characteristics of starfish systems play out in determining outcomes, I will introduce very simple numerical simulations. These simulations are illustrative, not probative; they just demonstrate in a simple formal model how simple changes in system openness can lead to very different dynamics in overall system learning performance.

Imagine a checkerboard, on each square of which there is just one school (for simplicity; I'll relax this in a second). To initialize a scenario, we choose a "school" associated with a unique level of learning for each square as a random number from zero to one. Bad schools (with learning on this arbitrary metric of less than 0.33) are represented by black squares, mediocre schools (between 0.33 and 0.66) are gray, and the better schools (above 0.66) are white. All three of the leftmost graphs show the same base case, with an equal mixture of bad, medium, and good schools randomly distributed over the grid.

What is the dynamic of this grid? Our first thought experiment is that in each year, each checkerboard either faces an entrant or not with the *same* probability (that is, entry does not depend on the quality of the existing school). If a school does face an entrant, the entrant chooses a random draw from the same underlying distribution of quality as existing schools. That is, we are not assuming that "entrants" are *on average* better than incumbents for any reason.

The key feature of this simulation is that if the entrant is better than the incumbent, then the entrant replaces the incumbent in that period. The process is then repeated, and in the next period the same thing happens: entrants might come, and if they are better they replace the existing school. I run this simulation forward for ten years.

Figure 6-3 shows the results of this simulation to underscore the central role of openness of a system in improving learning results. In the top row of graphs the probability of entry is 5 percent per year, that is, only one in twenty incumbent schools will face a challenger. When the ecosystem is this closed, the graph changes very slowly, and even after ten years the ecosystem still has many bad schools. This illustrates the consequences of no organizational learning (no incumbents are getting any better) combined with a closed system. This simulation is actually favorable to spider systems, and, as we have seen, many spider systems have essentially zero entry probability (bad schools are not replaced) and little organizational learning.

In the middle row of graphs, all that changes in the simulation is that the chance any given school will face a challenger rises from 5 percent each year to 25 percent each year. Now one sees dramatic changes. The

Figure 6-3. Open entry accelerates the diffusion of innovations and improvements in school quality.

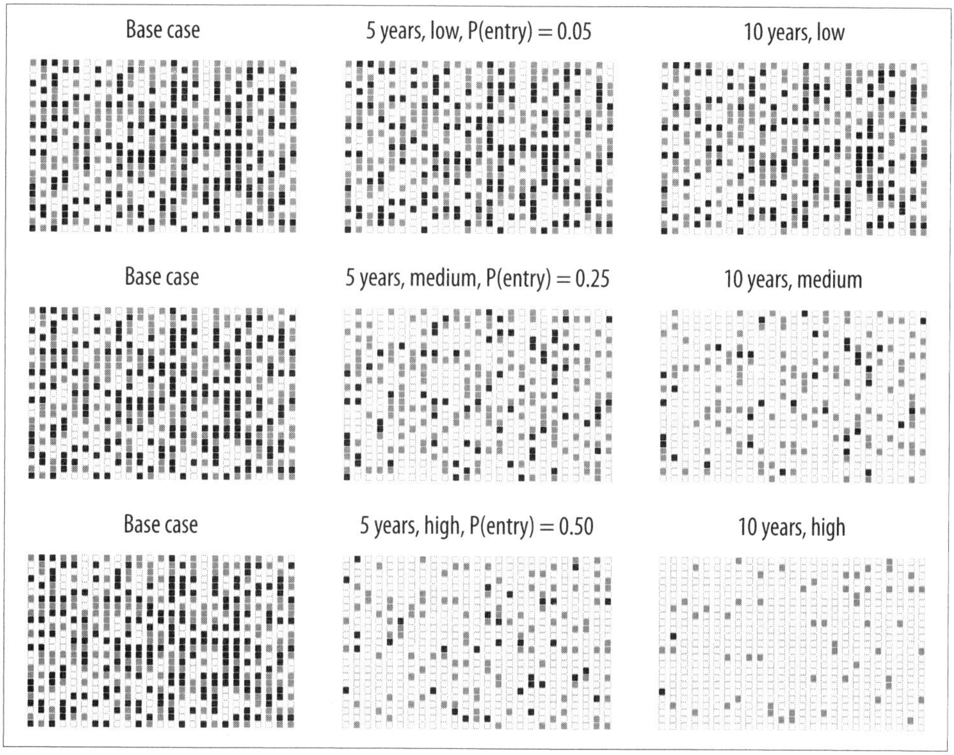

Note: All assuming zero retention of low-quality schools.

worst schools are much rarer, and even the mediocre schools are visually much less of the population.

When entry reaches 50 percent per year (which is admittedly very high), then in ten years' time, bad schools are practically gone, and even very few of the mediocre schools survive the pressure of a constant stream of new entrants.

This simulation is powerful when we think of all the ways we biased against improvement in average learning outcomes through limiting the entry of new schools. After all, in this scenario no school ever improves. In this simple simulation school quality is like eye color; schools are born with it. We also biased against the power of entry because new entrants are not purposive—they don't go after bad schools, they are random. We also biased against entry because we didn't assume that the *population* of new entrants would be any better than the initial population—I am not building in that, say, "charter" or "private" schools are *on average* better than public schools, for instance. Nevertheless, just replacing worse schools with better schools cumulatively transformed the entire educational landscape.

The amazing power of starfish systems emerges from the fact that the overall system performance can improve even without any existing organizational structure improving. If one started with a set of schools, then even if no school were able to "learn" how to improve its overall educational performance, the overall system performance could improve over time.

Moreover, this doesn't even require that the new entrants be somehow equipped with new technical knowledge or a formula. In all of the simulations the new entrants took a random draw from exactly the same distribution of productivity of the existing schools—there was no "technological progress" that only the new entrants could take advantage of. They were just like the old guys.

What makes the power of evolution or emergent order or creative destruction work is just that the more productive are more likely to survive and to thrive (that is, take on larger shares of the task). Trial and error alone can lead the overall sector to progress, even with no technological change and even if every school, once launched, congealed and could not improve.

This power of ecological learning is important because, as we saw in chapter 4, organizational learning is often very difficult. After all, successful organizations are often successful because they hit on a formula that matches a particular context and then just perfect themselves at the formula they have and build that formula into the very fabric of the organization. If that formula ceases to work with the context, it is often next to impossible to change the organization's culture—and new organizations come along that embed the new formula into their new culture, and thrive (Barnett 2008).

As I argued in chapter 5, since schooling is not third-party contractible and the socialization of beliefs is an integral and legitimate part of socialization, it has become, in many societies, including societies that are generally free and liberal, politically unacceptable to have completely open entry into basic schooling. It is simply unacceptable to have schools premised on white supremacist ideology in the United States or radical Islam in Pakistan or ethnic separation in many countries. Therefore, the entry process for schools cannot be an open market like the entry process for restaurants or the manufacture of shoes or instruction in piano.[6] Schooling *is* different, and the purely open market is not appropriate as the ecosystem for schools.

On the other hand, the overwhelming tendency is to overcontrol the entry of schools such that the possibility of innovation is precluded, and especially the disruptive innovation that is needed to accelerate progress in learning. That is, when spider systems open up incrementally, the political economy often insists that the new alternatives look exactly like the spider schools in every respect. In particular, rules of entry often perpetuate precisely the kind of input orientation (rather than performance orientation, with openness about how that is done) that stifles the spider system in the first place. For instance, India's recent Right of Children to Free and Compulsory Education Act, better known as the Right to Education Act, passed in 2009, while laudable in many respects, acknowledges that the private sector has expanded and essentially become a parallel system to the existing public system as people coped with the dysfunctional public schools. However, the act defines "quality" as inputs and attempts to impose purely input-driven standards on the private schools, even though there is no evidence in the Indian context that input standards produce learning.

While tight regulation of entry based on inputs seems attractive as it "protects" parents and children from "risky" or fly-by-night schools, this is the most dangerous form of the regulation of entry, for two reasons. First, input regulations are almost inevitably controlled by incumbents, and incumbents, whether in the private or the public sector, have every incentive to use entry regulation to thwart entrants. It is a myth that private sector firms favor competition. In a capitalist system one of the first things private sector firms do whenever they can is use regulation to prevent new entrants, to protect their position.

Second, input regulation almost inevitably means input isomorphism. If there is a conventional wisdom about what good schools look like, then this orthodoxy, even if it lacks any grounding in empirical evidence,

---

6. While I am deliberately avoiding too much discussion of the American schooling system, readers will recognize this as the essential element of the charter school movement in the United States. Charter schools' entry needs to be regulated to avoid financing of schools that violate the current interpretation of the U.S. Constitution that disallows financing religious schools and to avoid fly-by-night private charters, but at the same time, limiting charters to too few entrants or over-regulating charter school entry defeats the system impacts and keeps them merely marginal.

can block entrants. Input-based orthodoxy is particularly pernicious as it blocks disruptive innovations.

As just one of hundreds of possible examples of innovation that are out there, take the LEAPS Science and Math schools in South Africa. They are based on a particular philosophy of education that involves linkages with the community, tutoring, high expectations of students, and a particular set of core values. But they are also cognizant that to be scalable, the model needs to address the problem that excellent teachers can be expensive and are a key input, and look for ways to maximize the impact of the teachers they have through the innovative use of computers and peer-to-peer instruction. If this model had to wait for the approval of bureaucratic committees, the desire for assured input quality might easily have missed the point of the quality the LEAPS model provides.

Locally Operated—While Embedded

Schools need to be autonomous, but autonomous while embedded in an ecosystem that promotes and supports high performance, which are the aspects of the ecosystem that underlie the next four principles. There is ample evidence that reforms like "markets" or "vouchers" or "decentralization" *can* work to provide an environment for improvement. But whether *can* work translates into *does* work depends on the details. As we saw above, when spider systems are dysfunctional or even value subtracting, then just freeing schools from the burden of the tight coupling into the web of a dead spider can lead to large gains in performance. But the experience with Chile shows that moving to markets alone does not, in and of itself, provide a sufficient dynamic for sustained performance.

The key is to pull apart all of the many functions and activities and allocate those across the system such that the local component of the system provides a constant stream of innovation and new ideas and can use the local nature of the operation of the system for thick accountability (more below), while the national level provides a framework for standards and monitoring and evaluation of performance and the intermediate levels provide support to the local levels. As table 6-5 shows at a schematic level of functions only, not specific activities, the result is neither pure spider nor pure starfish (nor pure in-between) but a hybrid.

By "local" I mean "local" in the sense of your local barber or hairdresser, your local grocer, your local congregation—*local* as a geographic and social space that forms some type of community. Table 6-6, with its delineation of tiers of government, allows a definition of what is local. Discussions of decentralization that begin from fiscal decentralization

Table 6-5. The key is uncoupling the system and allowing each tier of government (and nongovernment and market) to do what it does best.

"Pure" alternatives of spiders or starfish with tight coupling at central or at school level . . .

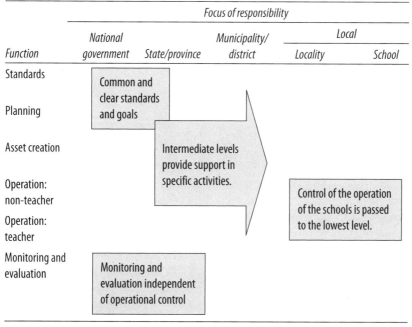

. . . while "pull-apart" systems have local operation embedded in the structure and measurement of performance and support.

Table 6-6. Appropriate allocation of activities will provide a high-quality teaching force.

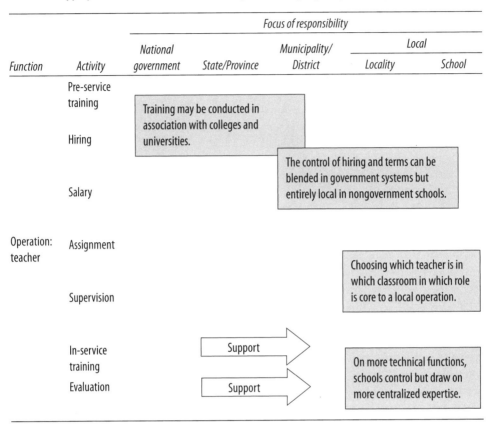

Function	Activity	National government	State/Province	Municipality/ District	Local — Locality	Local — School
	Pre-service training	Training may be conducted in association with colleges and universities.				
	Hiring			The control of hiring and terms can be blended in government systems but entirely local in nongovernment schools.		
	Salary					
Operation: teacher	Assignment				Choosing which teacher is in which classroom in which role is core to a local operation.	
	Supervision					
	In-service training	Support →			On more technical functions, schools control but draw on more centralized expertise.	
	Evaluation	Support →				

across tiers of government rather than from underlying functions can lead to confusion. In most countries of the world a "decentralization" that is a "federalization" of moving responsibility from the national government to states and provinces often just shifts a spider system into a modestly smaller jurisdiction, with no real change. Similarly, the intermediate tier between the "state" and the school—in India this would be a district, or in an urban environment a municipality—often is too large to realize any gain from being local but too small to be responsible for setting curricular standards or handling monitoring and evaluation.

Table 6-6 also makes it clear that there are three distinct functions: setting up the game, providing training and coaching, and the actual playing itself. In an analogy to sport, there is the league or association, which sets the rules and provides the officials and referees that enforce the rules and declare the official times and scores; there are the trainers and coaches, who help athletes do their best; and there are the actual athletes. In using a sports analogy I am not saying there are "winners" and "losers." Many individual sports with widespread participation, like running or swimming or tennis or bicycling, encourage each individual to do his or her best—within a structure. In the schematic there is a support role, like that of a coach or trainer, which is a role that intermediate tiers of government can provide.

Table 6-6 also makes the most controversial point in the whole book (which so far has been pretty free from controversy—and irony): for local operation to mean anything significant, it must mean that the local level has responsibility for teachers. An enormous amount of the discussion of greater school autonomy or empowerment has dealt only with the operational aspects of the school that don't involve teachers, such as procuring chalk, sweeping the grounds, and fixing the windows. This is not trivial. When spider systems turn dysfunctional but keep responsibility for everything centralized, even the simplest functions are done badly. The movements to push control of operational expenditures to the school level with transparency as to the flows do lead to significant one-off gains. However, if schools are not allowed to choose which teachers will teach, then local operational control is just rhetoric.

Since teachers are the essential component of education, it is worth elaborating on how an embedded starfish system of local operation would work, as this illustrates the mix of local control and technical support. Of course, this description is still schematic and not at the level of granularity and detail—which will depend on context—that an actual plan would be, but it illustrates the major points.[7]

Obviously, each school would not create its own pre-service training curriculum. Such training would continue to be done at a higher level and provided by a mix of institutions, from dedicated teachers' colleges to more general colleges and universities.

The key to local control is *assignment*. One major difficulty with spider systems is that they conflate the *hiring* process with assignment. In the interests of "quality control," many systems establish mechanisms for hiring the "best" teachers according to narrow, "thin" criteria, such as

---

7. For a more detailed discussion in the context of India, see Murgai and Pritchett (2006).

scores on a test. Once hired, these teachers are then assigned to schools based on some bureaucratic system such as a points system of preference (often one in which seniority has the most weight). These systems mean that local principals or local school boards or committees have little or no control over who is teaching in their school. A school cannot create a vision and a mission and a sense of being a unique and special place when it cannot control who teaches in the school and in what capacity or classroom.

The assignment function can be either entirely coincident with the hiring function (as in NGO or private schools) or these functions can be distinct. That is, a level above the locality can create the cadre of potential teachers, those who are authorized to be assigned by a local school, while the local schools choose which of those potential teachers are assigned. This approach can create some productive tension between professional and local accountability (discussed below).

In-service training is an example of a mix of local control and support. Each school cannot possibly be expected to create the necessary training for each of its teachers (from potentially pre-K to advanced levels) in each domain (math, science, music, art, social studies, etc.). By the same token, however, top-down control over in-service training can lead to training that is disconnected from the real needs of schools and teachers. With local control, schools can define their training needs and then seek out the training they need from an array of options offered by different producers of teacher training. The budget for this training can be controlled separately from the routine financing of the school so that schools are given adequate incentive to invest in their teachers.

This is not intended to be a detailed blueprint but rather a schematic that illustrates once again the need to pull apart tightly coupled systems, but pull them into pieces that are connected in sensible ways. Local control of the operation of schools does not mean every school for itself; it means allowing maximal local control over those decisions for which local control is most beneficial while embedding each school in an ecosystem of standards and evaluation and providing support.

Performance Pressured

Built into the previous traits of *open* and *locally operated* systems is the idea that the system can be *performance pressured*. Natural evolution describes a pressured system. In evolution, the performance pressure is reproductive ability. Organisms with higher reproductive performance grow in number; those that adapt poorly or not at all to changing ecosystems decline.

Pressure for performance in starfish systems does not lead to everything being the same. The performance-pressured system for animals has produced millions of species, which run the gamut from single-celled bacteria to whales and elephants. The order that includes the insect beetles contains almost half a million distinct species. The surviving species share nothing in common: not size, color, shape, diet, mode of reproduction, or survival strategy. The only thing they share is that they survive the pressure of limited resources and have found some niche in their ecosystem.

The same is true of functionality. Lots of animals swim: salmon swim, dolphins swim, otters swim, ducks swim, penguins swim, jellyfish swim. They all do so in ways that are consistent with the underlying facts about water but have ended up with very different ways of propelling themselves through water. There is no one best way to swim. All that is needed is genetic variation plus performance pressure in the form of higher survival value for better swimmers, and swimming performance "naturally" improves, not because some central agent decided on the best way to swim based on what looks the best but because of performance.

Researchers in Pakistan ran an experiment of choosing some villages in which every child was tested in grade three, and "report cards" for both public and private schools were provided to parents (Andrabi, Das, and Khwaja 2009). This was a massive infusion of information into the system—but without changing anything else. The researchers found four effects, all of which are revealing about the channels whereby information changes the behavior of actors in the system.

First, many of the private schools that were "bad" on the initial report card improved substantially—by, on average, 0.34 effect sizes. One response to performance pressure is to improve.

Second, many private schools that were revealed to be bad just closed. The bad schools in report-card villages were much more likely to close (twelve percentage points) than were either good schools or schools in villages with no report cards.

Third, good private schools that stayed open did not improve by much, though they did lower fees.

Fourth, there was some modest improvement in government schools, but no closures. The learning gains in bad government schools were only at a 0.078 effect size—4.5 times smaller than the learning gains in bad private schools. Clearly, the government schools were less responsive in every way to information provision than were private schools.[8]

We can simulate the impact of performance pressure using the same evolution of the checkerboard of schools as was used earlier. This time, rather than varying the probability of a new entrant, I vary how easily these new entrants can attract students if they are better. In the earlier example we assumed that the higher learning school attracted all students. In this simulation we vary the incumbent advantage by changing what fraction of students stay in the incumbent school.

The first panel of figure 6-4 shows the evolution of the system when incumbents retain 90 percent of students no matter the performance of the new entrant. In this case, even with lots of new entrants, the average quality of the system stays low over extended periods—ten years on, most students who started out in bad schools are still in bad schools.

The second and third panels show the dynamics as more and more students move to the better school. If the more productive entrants get half the students, the dynamics already improve, with many fewer students in bad or mediocre schools. Of course, if the dynamics reach the level where most students (90 percent) switch to the higher-quality entrant, then the results are better still (approaching those of figure 6-3, where it was assumed 100 percent of the students moved).

Saying a system should be "performance pressured" is meaningful, as it rules out many existing systems that have no learning performance pressure at all, but it doesn't imply there is one single best measure of performance or that "performance" should be reduced to a few or "basic" criteria. Schooling systems are everywhere and always complex and intrinsically political and social arrangements about how children are raised. While this book is very strong on promoting learning, the idea that school performance can be reduced to outcomes on a few standardized tests in a few domains (such as math and reading) is beyond absurd. Citizens as parents care about how their children are treated, they care about the values schools instill, they care about equality of opportunity, they care about lots of different capabilities. And citizens disagree about all these things. Some want schools to teach more basic skills, some want schools to teach students more creativity, some want students socialized

<hr/>

8. The differential responsiveness of public sector schools to external performance pressures likely accounts for the mixed findings, even within the same country, for information campaigns, with some studies showing an impact of information campaigns alone (Pandey, Goyal, and Sundararaman 2009) and others showing no impact (Banerjee, Cole, et al. 2010).

Figure 6-4. When the incumbent is not pressured (schools retain students even when of lower quality), the dynamics of improvement are slowed.

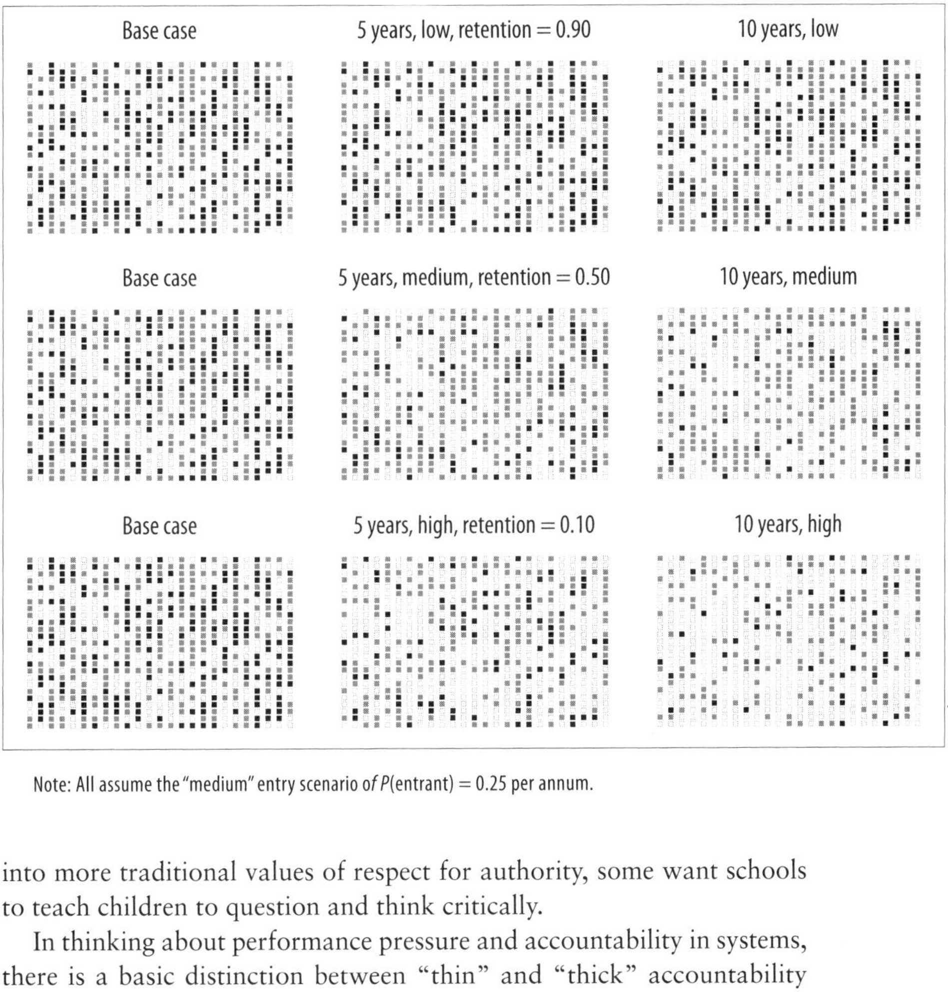

Note: All assume the "medium" entry scenario of P(entrant) = 0.25 per annum.

into more traditional values of respect for authority, some want schools to teach children to question and think critically.

In thinking about performance pressure and accountability in systems, there is a basic distinction between "thin" and "thick" accountability (Pritchett, Samji, and Hammer 2013). Thin accountability is a mode of accountability appropriate to a purely logistical task, such as delivering the mail. Everything about a package that is relevant to the post office can be reduced to a few simple bits of information—the address and the mode of delivery. Each agent of a postal service can be held accountable for following the appropriate action, which can be specified by a very narrow set of rules.

But the delivery of most services is much more complex than delivering the mail and is implementation-intensive in that success requires the agents to carry out actions that are based on subtle, often difficult to observe and impossible to make "objective" aspects of the situation. An example here is marriage and matchmaking. Coupling people cannot be reduced to logistics because each person is unique.

The mix of accountability based on information about objective measures of learning performance and based on parental (and student) choice isn't a trade-off relative to current situations—the volume can be turned way up on both. Lots and lots more information about learning performance made publicly available and transparent creates performance pressure. That said, this information should not to be used to manage a school organization as if it were a post office based on this thin information. Rather, the combination of local operation and increased parental choice among alternatives leads to a thicker form of accountability.

Performance pressure has to be built into the ecosystems of basic schooling, taking into account what we have seen through experience.

Choice Needs Information

In a pure choice mode, where money follows the student, performance pressure would come from schools trying to attract and keep students. This may or may not create pressure for better academic performance. If parents have little or no information about a school's performance, particularly how much value added it offers, then choice systems can lead to parents choosing schools based on reputations and social signals about the student body. This runs the risk of competing on ducks. Literally. Since parents are looking for a school where their child will be happy, one strategy is to make the exterior of the building look attractive by painting brightly colored yellow ducks on the exterior. Without any information available on actual student learning, a performance pressure becomes ducks.

High Stakes for the Student Can Improve Performance—but Not Schools

A reasonable person might wonder why, in a book that opens with poor learning performance in some developing countries but high measured performance in East Asian countries, the simple solution isn't for more countries to adopt the "East Asian" model of schooling. This is because there are two key features to the East Asian success in producing high test scores: capable bureaucratic spider systems and high stakes for the student testing. A country cannot simply choose to have an East Asian (Japanese, Korean, Singaporean) quality of administration. It comes from a history—and with a price.

The second feature is high stakes for the student testing. In nearly all high-performing East Asian countries there is a long history (in the case of China, literally thousands of years) of using examinations to determine life chances. Many of these countries promoted widespread basic education but also rationed entrance into university—and especially the top universities, from which the elite was drawn—based on an exam. There is no question that high stakes for the student examinations that are life-determining induces effort—indeed, amazing effort—in improving the scores on those examinations. To the extent that other assessments like PISA or TIMSS are correlated with that skill set, this will show up as impressive average scores.

However, high test performance in high-stakes-for-students systems says little or nothing about the quality of schools, in three respects. First, nearly all examination takers supplement their public schooling with tutoring, and hence their scores reflect the combination of schools and tutoring; it could well be that the school learning is perfectly ordinary. Second, high-stakes examinations induce students to learn what is on the exam—independently of whether that constitutes a complete, or even relevant, education. The examination for choosing national (imperial) civil servants emphasized the ability to write beautifully structured essays on Confucian principles into the twentieth century, which directed enormous intellectual effort into producing better Confucian essays, for good or ill. Third, the outcome needs to be judged on a "per effort" basis: simply making students work harder to overcome mediocre schools and instruction might work, but does not mean on a "per effort" basis this is fair to students.

Parental Choice with High Academic Performance Information and Salience

One key to a performance-pressured system is the creation of standard examinations that are low stakes for students but whose results are published and disseminated at every possible level—school, locality, municipality, state, nation. The constant flow of information about performance increases the salience of academic performance in parental choices.

I am *not* saying that information about student learning performance should be mechanically used in a way that is high stakes for the school. While I have been consistently avoiding detailed discussion of the U.S. experience with the No Child Left Behind Act because I do not want to get distracted into the hotly charged particulars, let me just state that what I am saying is the opposite of the way in which NCLB was implemented and used. That is, I am proposing that *information* about performance at the school level be widely disseminated so that it is *one element* of the choices parents and students make in their exercise of thick accountability. I am against using any single concise set of thin accountability metrics by a top-down authority to manage schools.

I am also aware of all of the complexities of making available average performance on assessments or examinations at the school level. Empirical studies have shown again and again the overwhelming importance of student background as a correlate of performance on formal examinations. Hence, school averages mainly reveal the socioeconomic background of the students in the school. They actually say very little about the quality of the instructional experiences in the school. If schools are recruiting new students based on their published average scores, this can lead them to game the system in various ways, both through explicit cheating, which can be controlled, and through attempting to select the best students into their schools.

There are more sophisticated ways of processing the assessment information that statistically adjust the raw data to estimate the school's "value added," or what the school does with the students it has. The publication of such assessments alongside the raw data could be very helpful to parents, but the publication of both is likely still merited to let people process as they will.

The important thing is not to let the best be the enemy of the good when the good could be the enemy of the awful. That is, the attention to testing in the United States as a result of NCLB has produced an impressively sophisticated debate with appropriate cautions about the risks of high-stakes testing (again, performance pressure *is not* high-stakes testing), the bias of teacher attention, cheating, selection, and so on. But this book is about countries that are now massively (100 to 200 IASSD points) behind the United States. This suggests that all is not well, and that publicizing learning performance will not drag many fantastic teachers away from the loving instilling of creativity and critical thinking into rote learning. Acting as if the lessons from NCLB are relevant to Uttar Pradesh or Kenya or even Mexico is letting academics search with a microscope where the data happen to be, under a street light, even though we know the keys to the car are not there.

People in all countries care about their children and are making decisions about schooling now based on whatever information they have, which is imperfect at best. It is not as if not publishing information relieves parents from the responsibility of doing the best for their child so they don't have to make choices. But they do have to choose, and adding information will make for better choices.

Professionally Networked

A starfish system is characterized by looser, less hierarchical connections among its constituent elements than a spider system, but a starfish is an organism that does have connections. Even if schools are treated as individually autonomous units of a system of schooling, they are still potentially connected, particularly through the voluntary association of the people in the schools, both administrators and teachers. They can learn from one another through observation and communication. The number and type of communications between units are other important characteristics of a system. So far in this chapter the emphasis has been entirely on ecological learning, on how open and performance-pressured systems can improve even without organizational learning. But organizational learning accelerates progress, too.

Figure 6-5 illustrates the power of connections by taking the same basic setup used earlier: a grid of individual schools. This time, however, in each period of the simulation, before a school faces a potential entrant the school looks at a fixed number of other schools. The school observes which of these is the best and then learns from that school, which is crudely modeled as moving 10 percent of the distance from its own current quality to that of the best school it observed. In this simulation I vary the number of connections. If there are no network connections, each school is an island, and the system behaves as in the previous simulations, depending exclusively on entry and performance pressure for improvement.

What is strikingly evident from figure 6-5 is how much connections *can* matter. With no connections (and low entry and low pressure), the top row shows almost complete stagnation (the patterns are almost exactly the same over the ten-year simulation). However, even if each school is connected to only five other schools through observation, and even if they move only 10 percent of the distance, the effect is powerful: in the middle row all the bad schools (with scores less than 0.33) disappear in just ten years. With strong connections (the bottom row of figure 6-5), nearly all bad and mediocre schools disappear in just ten years through a little bit of learning each year. When schools and teachers are linked, even modestly, then performance percolates through the system.

The notion of a professional network is central to ideas of how new ideas and new "achievable practice" are achieved. The spider model of learning is that the "brains" of thinkers examine evidence and decide

Figure 6-5. In a simulation in which schools improve by emulating the schools they are connected to, the pace of improvement depends on the number of connections.

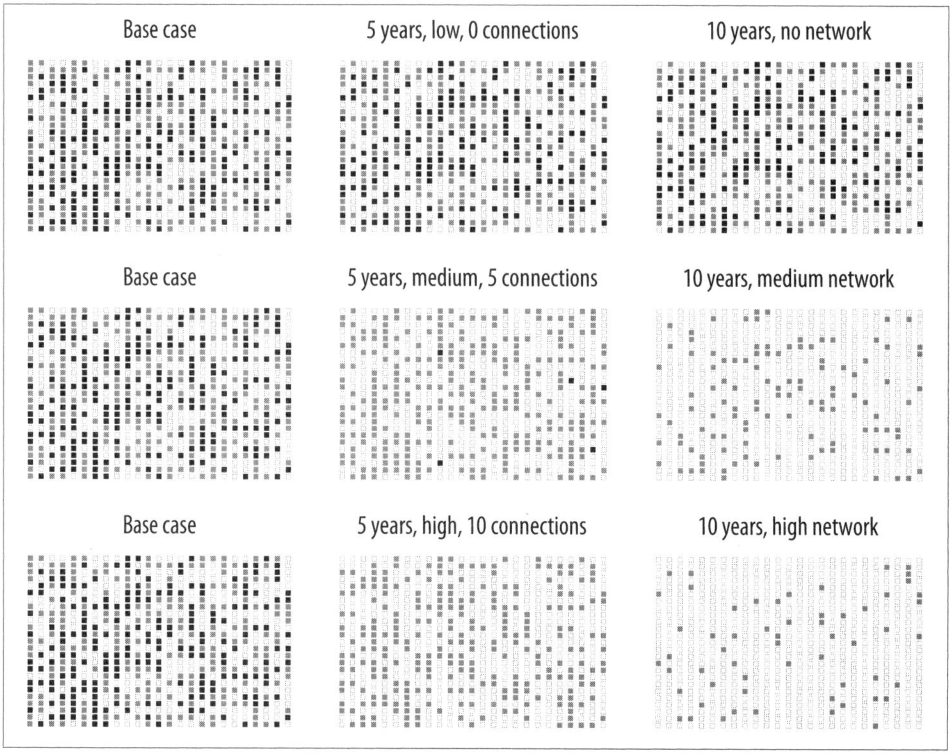

Note: All simulations done at low entry (P(Entry) = 0.05) and low performance pressure (retention = 0.90).

what is best, and then diffuse these ideas through top-down training that changes the behaviors of the teachers, who adopt the new ideas because they are told to. In the starfish model of the diffusion of better teaching and learning practices, individual teachers take on new practices because they believe these new practices are better. While not too much should be read into words, in English the word for professional firms *is* "practices"—doctors, dentists, lawyers, architects have *practices*.

Based on the experience with using networks of superintendents in the United States, a group of scholars (City et al. 2009) has extended the notion of professional practice in education to "instructional rounds" to get all parts of the system working together. They note that autonomy in the classroom can lead to isolation in the classroom, and that teachers often don't know how to improve while those attempting to "train" them don't know either—or know what is really going on in the classroom. They emphasize the improvement of practices, defined as "protocols and processes for observing, analyzing, discussing and understanding instruction that can be used to improve student learning at scale." The introduction to their book, based on years of working with four networks in different parts of the United States, gives a summary of the lessons learned (City et al. 2009, xi):

— Teaching matters most.
— An effective theory of action connects the central office and the classroom.
— Systemic improvement is not linear.
— Districts need to continuously measure progress.
— Solutions must be adapted to local contexts.
— Modeling alone is not sufficient; accountability counts.
— Communities of practice accelerate learning.
— External assistance is helpful.

They note that networks can be a powerful force, but can also be neutral or negative, as well as positive. The assumption that schools look at their network and emulate the best is only an assumption. A different assumption would be that schools looked at the schools they were connected to and improved only if they were the worst, while "slacking off" if they were the best—so that their comparisons with other schools bred complacency. In this case there would actually be a negative tendency toward mediocrity, with a muddle in the middle.

Professional, Not Hierarchical, Networks

Professional associations that create common professional identities and aspirations can be a powerful force for improvement. Perhaps the single worst consequence of organizing schools around a single spider governmental ministry of education has been the tendency to then organize teachers as if they were workers rather than professionals.

All professionals have organizations. Doctors are organized into professional associations. Lawyers are organized into professional associations. Architects are organized into professional associations. Economists have a professional association. These organizations carry our similar functions: promoting the interests of their members, providing for credentials and certification, providing for professional discipline of misconduct (through disbarment or revocation of licenses), and promoting learning among members to raise the quality of the service provided by the profession.

The example of American higher education is a case in point. Individual universities hire professionals from an array of different academic disciplines and the disciplines are organized into professional associations, which are often a primary locus of attention of individual professors, as much as or more so than their affiliation with the university itself.

This is to come back to teachers' unions, which are often made out to be the culprits that actively block education reform and progress. This view, however, doesn't see that teachers' unions and their behavior are symptoms, not the disease. The disease is spider systems of education, to which the rise of teachers' unions was seen as a necessary countervailing force. Taylorism begat Taylorism. Bureaucracy begat bureaucracy. Spider organization of schools begat spider organizations of teachers. The end of spider systems of organization as the dominant mode of organizing schools will naturally lead to a rise in the role of professional associations among teachers as professional associations that promote better teaching—and better conditions for teachers.

Technically Supported

My colleague Luis Crouch has a wonderfully pointed analogy for the need to create appropriate incentives and accountability while providing support. Suppose you kidnapped a dozen nuclear physicists and locked them in a building with the right materials and gave them the strong incentive that if in a year they had not built a workable nuclear weapon, they would be killed. There is some chance that at the end of the year, you would have a nuclear bomb. Suppose, alternatively, you kidnapped by mistake a dozen economists and locked them in the same building with the right materials, but without access to books or the Internet, and gave them the same ultimatum. At the end of the year you would have a dozen dead economists.

Autonomy and performance pressure need to be combined with support to educators so that they can learn to do better. We have seen that training detached from clear goals and performance pressures doesn't lead to success: all of the existing systems with low (and declining) learning have massive programs of pre-service and in-service training of teachers and educators. But, by the same token, pressure alone without support can produce frustration, as often those involved just don't know how to do better.

I visited government schools in India that were participating in a program run by the Azim Premji Foundation, an innovative NGO, that aimed to improve schools by providing feedback to teachers and principals about what their children did and did not know. The assessment was very sophisticated in using clusters of questions to identify areas of conceptual learning—for instance, not just whether students could do multiplication problems but whether they understood conceptually that multiplication is repeated addition, and whether they understood the concept of place so they could do carry in multiple-digit multiplication proper. I visited with one headmaster and asked about the study. She pulled it out from the bottom shelf of a locked cabinet where it had been stored since she had read it. As we went over the results, we saw they were disastrous: in some instances forty-eight of fifty children in a class had not mastered simple, grade-appropriate concepts. I asked her how she and her teachers had responded to the study; how had they changed their instructional practices? She shrugged and said, "We need to teach more."

Training to Support Starfish Systems

Spider systems of schooling often have spider systems of training people to work in spider systems. That is, and not surprisingly, pre-service and in-service training replicate the top-down, input-oriented, one-size-fits-all character of the schooling system itself. If students are to be treated like cogs in a machine, it is not surprising that teachers are initiated into the culture by being treated that way themselves.

Once schools are autonomous and performance pressured, they can identify and seek the training and skill sets they need. For this to happen, the same principles have to apply to training as to basic education. That is, schools and teachers must be able to identify the goals they have and what they need to do to meet those goals, and financing must be flexible so that they can go out and get those skills from an array of providers.

This is a role that levels of government and administration higher than the school can play—not by giving them a monopoly as the producers of such training but by providing the technical expertise to enable a mix of own-produced and certification of providers of training. Districts, municipalities, and associations of schools can collaborate to support schools, not by dictating what they need but by providing an array of options.

Research into "What Works" That Actually Works to Change Practices

The second area where technical support is important is the application of existing known methods of rigorous experimentation to testing out new ideas. In the field of development economics there has been an explosion in the use of randomization and other rigorous methods to explore the impact of various projects and programs. Throughout this book I have been able to draw on experimental evaluations that just did not exist a decade ago.

This research function is another area where higher levels can take primary responsibility. Not each school is going to maintain the capability to be rigorous experiments. The overall system of monitoring needed to create performance pressure itself creates ample scope for tracking progress and using the data to identify promising approaches. Rigorous evaluation of approaches as they scale is needed to prevent isomorphic mimicry and to forestall "best practice" fads from becoming ingrained before they are proven.

However, the traditional approach of monitoring and evaluation needs to be supplemented in starfish systems with real-time *experiential learning* to create a learning plan of monitoring, experiential learning, and evaluation (Pritchett, Samji, and Hammer 2013). Experiential learning is just the extension of the ideas of the use of rigorous techniques for identifying causal impact by incorporation of within school and within project treatments into real time management.

Experiential learning is a necessary addition to the ongoing expansion of the traditional approach of evaluation, for two reasons. First, there are just too many ideas to be tried out in too many circumstances for a small, slow, and expensive set of rigorous experiments to be a useful approach. Since solutions will be contextual, the external validity of individual experiments is limited. Systemic success is bound to be interactive, so "one-at-a-time" evaluations cannot reveal universal truths. That is, performance pressure works less well without local autonomy than with it, and similarly, local autonomy works better with performance pressure than without it. Both may work better with openness than without it. As John Roberts (2004) emphasizes in the context of the modern firm, "one-at-a-time" experiments may well leave massive gains from simultaneous changes undiscovered.

Suppose you put your toast in the toaster and push the lever down, but the toast doesn't pop up brown. It could be the setting was too low, or the heating elements are broken, or the toaster wasn't plugged in, or a fuse blew, or power is out in the neighborhood. Suppose with the toaster unplugged we do the rigorous experiment of putting toast in at five different settings. The finding will be that toaster setting does not affect the brownness of the toast, a finding that would be completely scientific and completely accurate—and also completely idiotic.

Second, experiential learning brings experimentation within the organization so that, with support, those who are to implement are also engaged in the learning. This embeddedness increases the likelihood that the results produced are believed and implemented, and that the findings can be replicated when scaled over a larger arena. There is actually no evidence that randomized evidence leads to adoption and replication. In fact, as discussed in chapter 4, rigorous experimental evidence exists that rigorous experimental evidence doesn't lead to the impacts it predicts: the Kenyan Ministry of Education implementing an intervention "proved" to work found it didn't work.

Learning that affects behavior at scale is a social process that uses rigorous techniques, but as one element of an overall dynamic strategy of organizations. Fraker and Shah (2011), for instance, offer an analysis of which research ideas should be pursued in education in Hyderabad to provide a learning strategy that leads to cumulative gains.

Flexibly Financed

The model for restaurants, as one example of a localized nontradable service, is a relevant example of a structured, pressured starfish system. People choose whether to "home-produce" their meals (with a huge array of choices of "in-home" value added, from cooking using raw ingredients to buying prepared meals that need only to be heated) or eat out.[9] When they eat out, they can select from a huge array of choices, from high-end restaurants to family-style diners to fast-food restaurants. Even in the budget or fast-food segment of the market there are choices to be made between franchises and locally owned and operated restaurants and between competing franchises. About the only structure to this starfish system, besides the constraints that affect all businesses of registration and land-use planning (which affects the location of the business), is the hygiene regulations to protect the public from food-borne illnesses. Within this system individual restaurants come and go: the same location may host different chains in a few years' span, local mom-and-pop diners hold their own (or fail to do so) against franchises, and whole new cuisines rise and fall. While this diversity results in enormous heterogeneity in the quality of food consumed, both across individuals, based on their tastes, and across people and households, based on their ability to pay, no one worries particularly about either the heterogeneity of the dining experience or the particular dimension of income inequality that is manifested in the choices made.

---

9. Fast-food marketers focus on "share of stomach" to emphasize that the main choices are not necessarily between franchises but between home production and other.

Schools, however, are not restaurants. As education, the preparation of children for their adulthood, necessarily goes deeply to core social values, no one can be indifferent to inequality in education. In schooling-based education systems, this means it cannot be a matter of indifference that children from poorer households or whose parents have less educational preparation receive lower-quality educations.

Support can flow from the public sector directly or indirectly to parents and students to make the choices they find best. The structure of this support will determine how the overall starfish system will operate. There are other ways of supporting parent and student choice, such as subsidizing transport.

Support and pressure are tightly linked. If schools respond to financial support (and this is true of nonprofit schools as well, as they too need resources), then how the support flows will determine what pressures they feel. If the support flows as grants from the state, then the school will aim to please those who make the grants; if support follows enrollment, the school will target enrollment; if it follows some metrics of performance, the pressure shifts to those metrics.

Flows of public sector support through starfish systems can address the problems of inequality. But as with the other characteristics of a starfish system, it depends on how support is structured: Does it flow to all students? Only to targeted students (and if so, how are they targeted)? Can schools that receive student support from the state "top up" their fees with other charges to parents?

Some forms of support may also be provided directly to schools. For instance, farming is an activity that is usually organized with many small autonomous farmers. Extension services provide support to producers to adapt and adopt new innovations. In a starfish system support could be provided directly to schools of various types to help them innovate, learn from other schools, receive training, and so forth. Such support could include support made available to teachers for training, skill upgrading, external supervision, peer monitoring, and the like. These types of activities are organized within spider systems, but they can also be provided in a starfish system, with the difference that support is more flexible and hence more complex to administer.

Flexible Financing Fit to Functions

Everything that is done has to be paid for. Financing needs to be flexible if it is to allocate funds across the agents involved according to their functions. There are system functions such as meeting standards, monitoring and evaluation, and regulation that need to be financed. Some training functions need to be financed. The bureaucratic advantage of spider systems is that all of these functions are brought into a more or less organizationally unified budget of a single ministry or department and then allocated across uses. In a starfish system, the overall flow of funds is matched to the needs for specific functions.

Such matching of funds to needs is necessarily complex, for two reasons. First, the allocation of overhead costs is always problematic and can lead to the false appearance of cost savings. The per student cost of a mom-and-pop, stand-alone private school will be lower than the average per student cost in a government school, a figure that includes the administrative overheads of managing the system. But the unwarranted assumption that giving every child a voucher that would cover the per student cost of a private school would generate savings ignores the fact that if the system is to be more than a pure unregulated market, there must be some central functions.

Second, in a loosely coupled system the allocation of budget matters for real outcomes. For instance, suppose the budget for in-service training goes to a municipality-wide organization that is given responsibility for providing in-service training to all schools (of whatever type) in the municipality. If this budget is not based on performance, then the training organization can be unresponsive to schools' needs, and hence ineffective. On the other hand, if schools are mandated to spend on in-service training (say, 1 percent of the teaching payroll) but without stipulation as how is the funds are to be spent, then schools could easily be ineffective themselves and waste the money on ineffective training (but which benefits them). These are tensions. But many other professional systems, such as medicine and law, have dealt with the issues of keeping professional staff up-to-date and improving practice through a mix of financing modes of training and the provision of training. Voluntary associations often bear the costs of quality or certification or testing—or can be made to pay for it.

The Varieties of Starfish Experience: Common Principles, Lots of Implementations

The traits and principles of starfish systems discussed above are not a blueprint, or even a plan. Rather, they are useful for guiding the questions that should be asked and answered about an overall system of basic education:

— Is the system too closed or too open to new entrants? Is there
   space in the system for novelty to be introduced, both within

existing schools and as space for new schools that embody new ideas to enter? Are existing political interests using isomorphic mimicry to protect their space and block potentially disruptive innovations?

— Are schools (and organizations of schools) allowed sufficient operational autonomy to formulate and pursue a vision and a mission of success for that individual school?

— Is there adequate *performance pressure* in the system on the right objectives? Does the system allow persistent failure to succeed? Do schooling goals formulated merely as attendance and inputs masquerade as education? Does the system have clear, ambitious, but achievable goals for learning progress to guide student mastery of the capabilities students will need to perform in society as adults? Is there the right mix of "thin" and "thick" accountability? Are the stakes too high or too low for students? For schools? For the system itself?

— Are the actors in the system—teachers, headmasters or principals, administrators—professionally *networked* to provide distributed learning and ecological scaling of innovations? Do connections among actors facilitate both peer-to-peer and systemwide cooperative learning in relation to scalable instructional practices? Are teachers organized like professionals or like factory workers?

— Is the *technical support* for the system well designed in amount and pattern? Is support responsive to local demand around meeting performance pressures? Is the system of pre-service and in-service training mere credentialism and ticking boxes? Is rigorous evidence generated and used in the process of promoting learning?

— Are the flows of *funding* adequate and flexible enough to facilitate continuous improvement in schools and instructional practices? Is funding tied exclusively to inputs? Is the funding fungible across purposes (including between teaching expenditures and other instructional needs)? Can new entrants attract support? Does funding support parents and students and education or merely replicate existing political patterns of schooling?

No two countries, indeed, no two states or provinces, will answer these questions in the same way. There is no one right way to put all the pieces together to craft a system that works. One of the key lessons of history is that many countries have put together systems of schooling that were both consistent with the local sociopolitical context and led to high

Table 6-7. There are many ways to assemble starfish ecosystems of schooling.

		Starfish systems				
	Government-owned spiders	Locality-level decentralization	Charter schools (only public-sector entrants)	Community-controlled schools	Private (for- and not-for- profit entrants)	Pure markets for instruction (e.g., tutoring)
Open?	Closed	Entry only by localities	Entry by designated organizations	Entry only by locally organized groups	Open entry	Completely open entry
Locally operated?	No	Mixed	Yes	Yes	Yes	Yes
Performance pressured?	Mixed	Mixed	Mixed	Mixed	Yes	Depends on metric
Professionally networked?	Hierarchy	Regionally	Mixed	Mixed	Mixed	Weak
Technically supported?	Yes	Yes	Yes	Yes	Yes	No
Flexibly financed?	No flexibility	Mixed	Yes	Mixed	Yes	No financing

levels of learning. To take two examples illustrating different approaches, both successful, the Netherlands has a choice-based system, with religious and state providers competing on equal footing, while the United States has traditionally relied on local districts. Moreover, different types of accountability can be fruitful for different formats.

A performance-driven starfish system could be implemented in one of several fundamentally different ways (table 6-7):

— By developing *community-controlled schools,* in which groups of parents, affiliated with the most local level of government, are free to open their own schools (subject to some requirements) and attract students to the school.

— By allowing *private providers,* both for profit and nonprofit, to provide schooling, with some formula for how resources mobilized from the public sector might follow the student.

— By allocating control to very *small governmental jurisdictions,* which would not quite allow school-by-school autonomy but something very close to it (an approach not equivalent to the typical "decentralization").

— By using *charter schools*, where entry of a school to such a system is regulated but schools (still within the government sector) are allowed much greater autonomy.

To all advocates, I am sure this conclusion—that different approaches could be successful, depending on the root conditions—will be frustrating. I am not going to say that charter schools are the right answer. It depends on the context and the design. I am not going to say that private schools are the right answer. It depends on the context and the design. I am not going to say that local government control of school operation is the answer. It depends on the context and the design. Moreover, if a country has a strong and thriving spider system that is improving learning, then, with the right context and design, that system could work too.

I will say that labels are too crude to have a useful place in a discussion about evidence. Educators and development specialists constantly hear claims along the lines that "the evidence from X [Chile, Milwaukee, Kenya, Bihar] shows that system Y [charter, private, local government] doesn't work." This is like saying, "Tests of this particular medicine for allergies failed to show improvement, so this proves drugs don't work." I have adduced evidence from a number of sources and programs to illustrate principles that might work, not as requirements of any given path forward. The design of an ecosystem for high-performance learning in basic education will be contextual and complex, and we need to learn, experience by experience, about the principles underlying healthy school ecosystems.

The Rebirth of Education

The shell of an egg plays an important role in protecting the embryo while it matures. But eventually, for new life to emerge, the eggshell, useful as it was, must break.

The legacy systems of basic schooling have provided an adequate structure for an amazingly rapid expansion of the physical and human infrastructure needed to enable every child to attend school. This massive expansion of schooling is one of the pinnacle achievements of the twentieth century. Spider systems excel at logistics and at getting the right pieces into the right places.

However, these same structures of schooling have become ossified and now are often at cross-purposes with providing the education children now need. Most developing countries have schools that provide dramatically less learning than is possible, and the shell, rather than serving as a protective device for the system to grow, has become a defensive limitation that protects insiders from change—and squelches the changes many inside innovators want. Existing systems of schooling are locking countries into Baumol's cost disease of escalating costs with no gains in education, and are not creating systems of education whose progress adheres to Moore's law in learning itself.

Messy as it will be, the rigid shell of spider systems of schooling now must break to allow the rebirth of education.

References

Acemoglu, Daron, and James A. Robinson. 2000. "Why Did the West Extend the Franchise? Democracy Inequality and Growth in Historical Perspective." *Quarterly Journal of Economics* 115: 1167–99.

Aghion, Philippe, Mathias Dewatripont, Caroline Hoxby, Andreu Mas-Colell, and Andre Sapir. 2009. "The Governance and Performance of Research Universities: Evidence from Europe and the U.S." NBER Working Paper 14581. Cambridge, Mass.: National Bureau of Economic Research.

Anderson, Benedict. 1983. *Imagined Communities: Reflections on the Origin and Spread of Nationalism.* New York: Verso.

Andrabi, Tahir, Jishnu Das, and Asim Ijaz Khwaja. 2009. "Report Cards: The Impact of Providing School and Child Test-Scores on Educational Markets." BREAD Working Paper 226. Durham, N.C.: Duke University, Bureau for Research and Economic Analysis of Development.

Andrabi, Tahir, Jishnu Das, Asim I. Khwaja, and Tristan Zajonc. 2011. "Do Value-Added Estimates Add Value? Accounting for Learning Dynamics." *American Economic Journal: Applied Economics* 3 (3): 29–54.

Andrabi, Tahir, Jishnu Das, Asim Ijaz Khwaja, Tara Vishwanath, Tristan Zajonc, and the LEAPS Team. 2007. *Learning and Educational Achievements in Punjab Schools (LEAPS): Insights to Inform the Education Policy Debate.* Washington: World Bank.

Andrews, Matthew, Lant Pritchett, and Michael Woolcock. 2012. "Escaping Capability Traps through Problem-Driven Iterative Adaptation (PDIA)." Working Paper 299. Washington: Center for Global Development.

APRESt (see Data Sources).

ASER. 2006–2013. *Annual Status of Education Report,* various years (see Data Sources).

Atherton, Paul, and Geeta Kingdon 2010. "The Relative Effectiveness and Costs of Contract and Regular Teachers in India." CSAE Working Paper Series PS/2010-15. Centre for the Study of African Economies, Oxford University

Aturupane, Harsha, Paul Glewwe, and Suzanne Wisniewski. 2013. "The Impact of School Quality, Socio-Economic Factors and Child Health on Students' Academic Performance: Evidence from Sri Lankan Primary Schools." *Education Economics* 21 (1): 2–37.

Auguste, Byron, Paul Kihn, and Matt Miller. 2010. "Closing the Talent Gap: Attracting and Retaining Top-Third Graduates to Careers in Teaching. An International and Market Research–Based Perspective." Washington: National Association of Independent Schools.

Baird, Sarah, Craig MacIntosh, and Berk Ozler. 2010. "Cash or Condition? Evidence from a Cash Transfer Experiment." *Quarterly Journal of Economics* 126 (4): 1709–53.

Banerjee, Abhijit V., Esther Duflo, and Michael Walton. 2011. "Preliminary Report on the Impact Evaluation of Read India" (unpublished).

Banerjee, Abhijit, Shawn Cole, Esther Duflo, and Leigh Linden. 2010. "Remedying Education: Evidence from Two Randomized Experiments in India." *Quarterly Journal of Economics* 122 (3): 1235–64.

Banerjee, Abhijit V., Rukmini Banerji, Esther Duflo, Rachel Glennerster, and Stuti Khemani. 2010. "Pitfalls of Participatory Programs: Evidence from a Randomized Evaluation in Education in India." *American Economic Journal: Economic Policy* 2 (1): 1–30.

Banerji, Rukmini, and Michael Walton. 2011. "What Helps Children to Learn? Evaluation of Pratham's Read India Program in Bihar & Uttarakhand." Abdul Latif Jameel Poverty Action Lab.

Barnett, William P. 2008. *The Red Queen among Organizations: How Competitiveness Evolves.* Princeton University Press.

Barro, Robert, and Jong-Wha Lee. 2010. "A New Data Set of Educational Attainment in the World, 1950–2010." NBER Working Paper 15902. Cambridge, Mass.: National Bureau of Economic Research.

———. 2011. "A New Set of Educational Attainment in the World, 1950–2010." NBER Working Paper 15902. Cambridge, Mass.: National Bureau of Economic Research.

Baumol, William, and William Bowen. 1966. *The Performing Arts: The Economic Dilemma. A Study of Problems Common to Theater, Opera, Music and Dance.* New York: Twentieth Century Fund.

Behrman, Jere R., Piyali Sengupta, and Petra Todd. 2005. "Progressing Through PROGRESA: An Impact Assessment of School Subsidy Experiment in Rural Mexico." *Economic Development and Cultural Change* 54 (1): 237–75.

Bhattacharjea, Suman, Wilima Wadhwa, and Rukmini Banerji. 2011. *Inside Primary Schools: A Study of Teaching and Learning in Rural India*. ASER and Pratham Mumbai Educational Initiative.

Bold, Tessa, Mwangi Kimenyi, Germano Mwabu, and Justin Sandefur. 2011. "Does Abolishing School Fees Reduce School Quality? Evidence from Kenya." CSAE Working Paper WPS/2011-04. Centre for the Study of African Economies, Oxford University.

Bold, Tessa, Mwangi Kimenyi, Germano Mwabu, Alice Ng'ang'a, and Justin Sandefur. 2013. "Scaling Up What Works: Experimental Evidence on External Validity in Kenyan Education." Working Paper 321. Washington: Center for Global Development.

Boli, John, Francisco Ramirez, and John Meyer. 1985. "Explaining the Origins and Expansion of Mass Education." *Comparative Education Review* 29 (2): 145–70.

Brafman, Ori, and Rod Beckstrom. 2006. *The Starfish and the Spider: The Unstoppable Power of Leaderless Organizations*. New York: Penguin.

Bruner, Jerome S. 1996. *The Culture of Education*. Harvard University Press.

Bruns, Barbara, David Evans, and Javier Luque. 2012. *Achieving World Class Education in Brazil: The Next Agenda, Directions in Development: Human Development*. Washington: World Bank.

Carlile, Paul R., and Karim R. Lakhani. 2011. "Innovation and the Challenge of Novelty: The Novelty-Confirmation-Transformation Cycle in Software and Science." Harvard Business School Technology and Operations Management Unit Working Paper 11-096. Cambridge, Mass.: Harvard Business School.

Carpenter, Daniel. 2001. *The Forging of Bureaucratic Autonomy: Reputations, Networks, and Policy Innovation in Executive Agencies, 1862–1928*. Princeton University Press.

Chandler, Alfred, Jr. 1977. *The Visible Hand: The Managerial Revolution in American Business*. Belknap Press of Harvard University Press.

———. 1990. *Scale and Scope: The Dynamics of Industrial Capitalism*. Harvard University Press.

Chaudhury, Nazmul, and Dilip Parajuli. 2010. "Pilot Evaluation: Nepal Community School Support Project." PowerPoint presentation (http://siteresources.world bank.org/SOUTHASIAEXT/Resources/223546-1192413140459/4281804-1215548823865/NepalCSSP.pdf).

Chaudhury, Nazmul, Jeffery Hammer, Michael Kremer, Karthik Muralidharan, and F. Halsey Rogers. 2006. "Missing in Action: Teacher and Health Worker Absence in Developing Countries." *Journal of Economic Perspectives* 20 (1): 91–116.

Chen, Theodore His-sen. 1981. *Chinese Education since 1949: Academic and Revolutionary Models*. New York: Pergamon Press.

Christensen, Clayton. 1997. *The Innovator's Dilemma: The Revolutionary Book That Will Change the Way You Do Business*. Harvard Business School Press.

Christensen, Clayton, Jerome H. Grossman, and Jason Hwang. 2009. *The Innovator's Prescription: A Disruptive Solution for Health Care.* New York: McGraw-Hill.

Christensen, Clayton, Curtis W. Johnson, and Michael B. Horn. 2008. *Disrupting Class: How Disruptive Innovation Will Change the Way the World Learns.* New York: McGraw-Hill.

City, Elizabeth, Richard F. Elmore, Sarah E. Fiarman, and Lee Teitel. 2009. *Instructional Rounds in Education: A Network Approach to Improving Teaching and Learning.* Harvard Education Press.

Clemens, Michael. 2004. "The Long Walk to School: International Education Goals in Historical Perspective." Center for Global Development Working Paper 37. Washington: Center for Global Development.

Crouch, Luis, and F. Henry Healey. 1997. *Education Reform Support,* vol. 1: *Overview and Bibliography.* ABEL Technical Paper 1. Washington: USAID.

Crouch, Luis, and Melinda Korda. 2009. "Improvements in Reading Skills in Kenya: An Experiment in the Malindi District." Research Triangle Park, N.C.: RTI International.

Desai, Sonalde, Amaresh Dubey, Reeve Vanneman, and Rukmini Banerji. 2008. "Private Schooling in India: A New Educational Landscape." *India Policy Forum* 5 (1): 1–8.

DeStefano, Joseph, and Luis Crouch. 2006. *Education Reform Support Today.* USAID.

DiMaggio, Paul J., and Walter W. Powell. 1983. "The Iron Cage Revisited: Institutional Isomorphism and Collective Rationality in Organizational Fields." *American Sociological Review* 48 (2): 147–60.

Duflo, Esther, Pascaline Dupas, and Michael Kremer. 2012. "School Governance, Teacher Incentives and Pupil Teacher Ratios: Experimental Evidence from Kenyan Primary Schools." Working Paper No. 17939. Cambridge, Mass.: National Bureau of Economic Research.

Duflo, Esther, Rema Hanna, and Stephen Ryan. 2012. "Incentives Work: Getting Teachers to Come to School." *American Economic Review* 102 (4): 1241–78.

Easterly, William. 2006. "Planners vs. Searchers in Foreign Aid." Distinguished Speakers Program. Manila, Philippines: Asian Development Bank

Education for All. 2010. *Reaching the Marginalized. EFA Global Monitoring Report.* Paris: UNESCO and Oxford University Press.

Educational Initiatives. 2010. *Student Learning Study: Status of Student Learning across 18 States of India in Urban and Rural Schools.* Ahmedabad: Educational Initiatives, Pvt. Ltd.

Epple, Dennis, and Richard Romano. 1996. "Ends Against the Middle: Determining Public Service Provision When There Are Private Alternatives." *Journal of Public Economics* 62 (3): 297–325.

Filmer, Deon. 2000. "The Structure of Social Disadvantage in Education: Gender and Wealth." Policy Research Working Paper 2268. Washington: World Bank.

———. 2007. "If You Build It, Will They Come? School Availability and School Enrolment in 21 Poor Countries." *Journal of Development Studies* 43 (5): 901–28.

———. 2010 (see DHS in Data Sources).

Filmer, Deon, and Lant Pritchett. 1999a. "The Effects of Household Wealth on Educational Attainment: Evidence from 35 Countries." *Population and Development Review* 25 (1): 85–120.

———. 1999b. "What Education Production Functions Really Show: A Positive Theory of Education Expenditures." *Economics of Education Review* 18 (2): 223–39.

———. 2001. "Estimating Wealth Effects without Expenditure Data—or Tears: An Application to Educational Enrollments in States of India." *Demography* 38 (1): 115–32.

Filmer, Deon, Amer Hasan, and Lant Pritchett. 2006. "A Millennium Learning Goal: Measuring Real Progress in Education" Working Paper 97. Washington: Center for Global Development.

Fiszbein, Ariel, and Norbert R. Schady. 2009. *Conditional Cash Transfers*. Policy Research Report. Washington: World Bank.

Fraker, Andrew, and Neil Shah. 2011. *Learning to Learn: A New Approach to Education Policymaking in Hyderabad, India*. Cambridge, Mass.: Harvard Kennedy School.

Gardener, Howard. 1991. *The Unschooled Mind: How Children Think and How Schools Should Teach*. New York: Basic Books.

Glewwe, Paul W., and Ana Lúcia Kassouf. 2010. "What Is the Impact of the Bolsa Família Programme on Education?" One Pager 107. Brasília: International Policy Centre for Inclusive Growth.

Glewwe, Paul, Michael Kremer, and Sylvie Moulin. 2009. "Many Children Left Behind? Textbooks and Test Scores in Kenya." *American Economic Journal: Applied Economics* 1 (1): 112–35.

Glewwe, Paul W., Margaret Grosh, Hanan Jacoby, and Marlaine Lockheed. 1995. "An Eclectic Approach to Estimating the Determinants of Achievement in Jamaican Primary Education." *World Bank Economic Review* 9 (2): 231–58.

Glewwe, Paul W., Eric Hanushek, Sarah D. Humpage, and Renato Ravina. 2011. "School Resources and Educational Outcomes in Developing Countries: A Review of the Literature from 1990 to 2010." Working Paper 17554. Cambridge, Mass.: National Bureau of Economic Research.

Goldin, Claudia, and Lawrence F. Katz. 2008. *The Race between Education and Technology*. Harvard University Press.

Gonzales, Patrick, Juan Carlos Guzmán, Lisette Parelow, Erin Pahlke, Leslie Johcelyn, David Kastberg, and Treavor Williams. 2004. "Highlights from the Trends in International Mathematics and Science Study (TIMSS) 2003." NCES 2005-005. U.S. Department of Education, National Center for Education Statistics.

Good, Harry Gehman, and James David Teller. 1969. *A History of Western Education.* New York: Collier Macmillan.

Gove, Amber, and Peter Cvelich. 2011. "Early Reading: Igniting Education for All." A Report by the Early Grade Learning Community of Practice. Rev. ed. Research Triangle Park, N.C.: Research Triangle Institute.

Gundlach, Erich, Ludger Woessmann, and Jens Gmelin. 2001. "The Decline of Schooling Productivity in OECD Countries." *Economic Journal* 111 (471): 135–47.

Hannum, Emily. 1999. "Political Change and the Urban-Rural Gap in Basic Education in China 1949–1990." *Comparative Education Review* 43 (2): 193–211.

Hanushek, Eric A., and Ludger Woessmann. 2009. "Do Better Schools Lead to More Growth? Cognitive Skills, Economic Outcomes, and Causation." Working Paper 14633. Cambridge, Mass.: National Bureau of Economic Research.

Heston, Alan, Robert Summers, and Bettina Aten. "Penn World Table Version 6.1." Center for International Comparisons of Production, Income and Prices at the University of Pennsylvania, October 2002 (see Penn World Tables in Data Sources).

Holldobler, Bert, and E. O. Wilson. 1990. *The Ants.* Harvard University Press.

Hoxby, Caroline M. 2001. "All School Finance Equalizations Are Not Created Equal." *Quarterly Journal of Economics* 116 (4): 1189–231.

Katz, Donald R. 1987. *The Big Store: Inside the Crisis and Revolution at Sears.* New York: Viking.

Kelman, Steven. 2005. *Unleashing Change: A Study of Organizational Renewal in Government.* Brookings.

Korda, Medina, and Ben Piper 2011. *EGRA Plus: Liberia—Final Program Evaluation Report.* Research Triangle Park, N.C.: RTI International.

Koretz, Daniel. 2008. *Measuring Up: What Educational Testing Really Tells Us.* Harvard University Press.

Kremer, Michael, and Andrei Sarychev. 1998. "Why Do Governments Operate Schools." Unpublished.

Kremer, Michael, Karthik Muralidharan, Nazmul Chaudhury, Jeffrey Hammer, and F. Halsey Rogers. 2005. "Teacher Absence in India: A Snapshot." *Journal of the European Economic Association* 3 (2-3): 658–67.

LEAPS, various years (see LEAPS in Data Sources).

Leclercq, Francois. 2003. "Education Guarantee Scheme and Primary Schooling in Madhya Pradesh." *Economic and Political Weekly* 38 (19).

Levy, Dan, Matt Sloan, Leigh Linden, and Harounan Kazianga. 2009. "Impact Evaluation of Burkina Faso's BRIGHT Program." Final report prepared by Mathematica Policy Research Inc. Washington: Millennium Challenge Corporation.

Lewis, Bernard. 1961. *The Emergence of Modern Turkey.* Oxford University Press.

Lewis, Maureen, and Marlene Lockheed. 2007. *Inexcusable Absence: Why 60 Million Girls Still Aren't in School and What to Do about It*. Washington: Center for Global Development.

Lindert, Peter. 2004. *Growing Public*, vol. 1. *The Story: Social Spending and Economic Growth since the Eighteenth Century*. Cambridge University Press.

Lott, John. 1999. "Public Schooling, Indoctrination, and Totalitarianism." *Journal of Political Economy* 107 (6): S127–S157.

Mallison, Vernon. 1963. *Power and Politics in Belgian Education, 1815 to 1961*. London: Heinemann.

Mead, Margaret. 1943. "Our Educational Emphasis in Primitive Perspective." *American Journal of Sociology* 48 (6): 633–39.

Mintzberg, Henry. 1979. "The Structuring of Organizations: A Synthesis of the Research." Academy for Entrepreneurial Leadership Historical Research Reference in Entrepreneurship. University of Illinois at Urbana-Champaign.

Moore, Gordon. E. 1965. "Cramming More Components onto Integrated Circuits." *Electronics* 38 (8).

Moore, Mark. 1995. *Creating Public Value: Strategic Management in Government*. Harvard University Press.

Muralidharan, Karthik, and Venkatesh Sundararaman. 2010a. "Achieving Universal Quality Primary Education in India: Lessons from the Andhra Pradesh Randomized Evaluation Studies (APRESt)." Presentation to AP Directorate of Education. Additional annex slides delivered in personal communication to Lant Pritchett.

———. 2010b. "Contract Teachers: Experimental Evidence from India." Working paper (http://econ.ucsd.edu/~kamurali/papers/Working%20Papers/Contract%20Teachers%20(24%20May,%202010).pdf).

Murgai, Rinku, and Lant Pritchett. 2006. "Teacher Compensation: Can Decentralization to Local Bodies Take India from the Perfect Storm through Troubled Waters to Clear Sailing?" *India Policy Forum* 3 (1): 123–77.

Nordhaus, William. 2007. "Two Centuries of Progress in Computing Power." *Journal of Economic History* 67 (1): 128–59.

OECD, various years (see PISA in Data Sources).

Oster, Emily, and Rebecca L. Thornton. 2010. "Are 'Feminine Problems' Keeping Poor Girls out of School?" *New York Times Economix* (blog).

Ostrom, Elinor. 2008. "Polycentric Systems as One Approach for Solving Collective-Action Problems." Social Science Research Network.

Pandey, Priyanka, Sangeeta Goyal, and Venkatesh Sundararaman. 2009. "Community Participation in Public Schools: Impact of Information Campaigns in Three Indian States." *Education Economics* 17 (3): 355–75.

Passin, Herbert. 1965. *Society and Education in Japan*. New York: Teachers College Press.

Penn World Tables, various years (see Data Sources).

Peters, Thomas J., and Robert H. Waterman. 1982. *In Search of Excellence: Lessons from America's Best Run Companies*. New York: Warner Books.

Piper, Benjamin. 2009. "Integrated Education Program: Impact Study of SMRS Using Early Grade Reading Assessment in Three Provinces in South Africa." Research Triangle Park, N.C.: Research Triangle Institute.

PISA, various years (see Data Sources).

Powell, Walter W., and Paul J. Dimaggio. 1991. *The New Institutionalism in Organizational Analysis:* University of Chicago Press.

Pratham. 2012 (see Data Sources).

Pratham and ASER Center: New Dehli, India (see Data Sources).

Pritchett, Lant. 2002. "It Pays to Be Ignorant: A Simple Political Economy of Rigorous Program Evaluation." *Journal of Policy Reform* 5 (4): 251–69.

———. 2004. "Towards a New Consensus for Addressing the Global Challenge of the Lack of Education." In *Global Crises, Global Solutions,* ed. Bjorn Lomborg. Cambridge University Press.

———. 2013. "Folk and the Formula: Fact and Fiction in Development." WIDER Annual Lecture. Helsinki, Finland: United Nations University.

Pritchett, Lant, and Amanda Beatty. 2012. "The Negative Consequences of Overambitious Curricula in Developing Countries." Center for Global Development Working Paper 293. Washington: Center for Global Development. Reprinted as Harvard Kennedy School Faculty Research Working Paper Series RWP/12-035.

Pritchett, Lant, and Varad Pande. 2006. "Making Primary Education Work for India's Rural Poor: A Proposal for Effective Decentralization." *Social Development Papers: South Asia Series* 95 (June).

Pritchett, Lant, and Justin Sandefur. 2013. "Context Matters for Size: Why External Validity Claims and Development Practice Don't Mix." Washington: Center for Global Development, forthcoming.

Pritchett, Lant, and Martina Viarengo. 2008. "The State, Socialization and Private Schooling: When Will Governments Support Alternative Producers?" Cambridge, Mass., unpublished (available at www.hks.harvard.edu/fs/lpritch/Education - docs/ED - Gov action/Ideology and Private Schooling.pdf).

———. 2009. "The Illusion of Equality: The Educational Consequences of Blinding Weak States." Working Paper 178. Washington: Center for Global Development.

Pritchett, Lant, Salimah Samji, and Jeffrey Hammer. 2013. "It's All about MeE: Using Structured Experiential Learning ("e") to Crawl the Design Space." Harvard Kennedy School Faculty Research Working Paper Series (forthcoming).

Pritchett, Lant, Michael Woolcock, and Matt Andrews. 2012. "Looking Like a State: Techniques of Persistent Failure in State Capability for Implementation." UNU-WIDER Working Paper 63. Helsinki, Finland: World Institute for Development Economic Research.

Roberts, John. 2004. *The Modern Firm: Organizational Design for Performance and Success.* Oxford University Press.

SACMEQ, various years (see Data Sources).

Schaeffer, Adam B. 2007. "A Voucher Defeat in Utah." *Wall Street Journal,* November 8.

Schultz, Theodore. 1964. *Transforming Traditional Agriculture*. Yale University Press.

Scott, James. 1998. *Seeing Like a State: How Certain Schemes to Improve the Human Condition Have Failed*. Yale University Press.

Seabright, Paul. 2010. *The Company of Strangers: A Natural History of Economic Life*. Princeton University Press.

Smith, Adam. 1981 [1776]. *An Inquiry into the Nature and Causes of the Wealth of Nations*, vol 1., edited by R. H. Campbell and A. S. Skinner. Indianapolis: Liberty Fund.

Tanzania Ministry of Education and Vocational Training. 2012. Data downloaded in 2012 from www.necta.go.tz, available from book webpage.

TIMSS, various years (see Data Sources).

Tooley, James, and Pauline Dixon. 2005. *Private Education Is Good for the Poor: A Study of Private Schools Serving the Poor in Low-Income Countries*. Washington: Cato Institute.

Tyack, David. 1974. *The One Best System: A History of American Urban Education*: Harvard University Press.

United Nations Development Program (UNDP). 1998. *Public Report on Basic Education in India*. Geneva: UNDP in association with the Centre for Economic Development.

———. 2010. *The Real Wealth of Nations: Pathways to Human Development*. Human Development Report 2010. Geneva (http://hdr.undp.org/en/reports/global/hdr2010/).

USAID. 2011. *Improved Learning Outcomes in Donor-Financed Education Projects: RTI's Experience*. Washington.

Uwezo, various years (see Data Sources).

Warwick, Donald P., and Frederick Reimers. 1995. *Hope or Despair: Learning in Pakistan's Primary Schools*. Westport, Conn.: Praeger.

World Bank. 2004. *World Development Report 2004: Making Services Work for the Poor*. Oxford University Press for the World Bank.

———. 2007. *Toward High-Quality Education in Peru: Standards, Accountability, and Capacity Building*. Washington: World Bank.

Data Sources

Assessments of Learning

APRESt (Andhra Pradesh Randomized Evaluation Studies). These are a series of large-scale randomized evaluations carried out in the Indian state of Andhra Pradesh since 2004. Cumulatively over 150,000 students have been tested in primary grades (2 to 5) on literacy and numeracy skills using an assessment designed by Education Initiatives (see below). The main researchers have been Professor Karthik Muralidharan of University of California–San Diego and Venkatesh Sundararaman of the World Bank. The research has been supported by the Azim Premji Foundation and the government of Andhra Pradesh. Because the same questions are asked in multiple grades it is possible to trace out improvement in percent answered correctly across grades. Some of the tables and figures in chapter 1 are drawn from results provided directly to me by Professor Muralidharan.

ASER. The *Annual Status of Education Report* is an annual report originally produced by the Indian education nongovernmental organization Pratham (www.pratham.org); it is now facilitated by Pratham and produced by the ASER Centre (www.asercentre.org). The core of the ASER report is based on a large-scale survey (more than 500,000 children) that covers rural areas in (nearly) all districts of India. The survey does an in-home (not school-based) assessment of the reading and arithmetic competencies of all children in sampled villages ages 3 to 16. The assessment is done in the child's preferred language. The ASER has been produced each year from 2005 to 2012, with the fieldwork done September to December and results available by the following January (so the ASER published in 2006 refers to results from just a few months earlier in 2005).

The ASER instrument in 2008 also included items about practical skills, such as telling time and understanding money. Chapter 1 uses the raw data provided to me by the ASER Centre for analysis of learning profiles.

DHS (Demographic and Health Surveys). The Demographic and Health Surveys are a collection of comparable survey instruments and study methods carried out since 1984 as part of the USAID-funded Monitoring and Evaluation to Assess and Use Results Demographic and Health Surveys (MEASURE DHS) project. While the main focus of the surveys is family planning and child health, the survey instrument records the education attainment and enrollment of all children in the sampled households. This, combined with information about the household such as parental education, residence, and assets, allows the construction of enrollment profiles by age (and household or child characteristic) and attainment profiles of a cohort. Using these raw data (plus others), Deon Filmer, a researcher at the World Bank, documents and analyzes differences in educational attainment around the world as part of a project, Educational Attainment and Enrollment around the World (see Filmer, "Education Attainment and Enrollment around the World: An International Database," Washington: World Bank, 2010. http://econ.worldbank.org/projects/edattain). He provides data and graphs of enrollment and attainment profiles for a very large number of countries.

EI SLS (Education Initiatives Student Learning Study). The organization Education Initiatives (www.ei-india.com/) was founded in 2001 and specializes in the design and implementation of instruments for testing and assessing in schools. In 2009 (between January and September) with funding from Google.org, it carried out a large-scale assessment of children in grades 4, 6, and 8 testing more than 100,000 students in eighteen Indian states in both urban and rural areas. The instrument covered both language and math and tested both procedural learning and conceptual understanding in those domains.

LEAPS (Learning and Education Attainment in Punjab Schools). The LEAPS project (www.leapsproject.org/site/about/) is an effort by researchers from the World Bank, Pomona College, and Harvard University in collaboration with the government of Punjab launched in 2001. To measure learning outcomes, the LEAPS project administered detailed exams in English, math, and Urdu to students in grade 3 from 823 schools in 112 villages from 3 districts of Pakistan and then followed those same students until grade 6. By tracking the same children, the LEAPS data have learning profiles for the same students over time (in contrast to comparing results from the study of different students across grades at the same time or grades over time).

NAEP (National Assessment of Educational Progress). The NAEP (http://nces.ed.gov/nationsreportcard) is a nationally representative assessment of student skills in various subject matters and grades. Its long-term studies examine learning of students at ages 9, 13, and 17 periodically (every two to four years) in the subject areas of reading (since 1971), science (since 1969), and mathematics (since 1973). The commissioner of education statistics of the U.S. Department of Education is responsible for carrying out the NAEP.

Penn World Tables. The Penn World Tables (Alan Heston, Robert Summers, and Bettina Aten, *Penn World Table Version 6.1,* Center for International Comparisons of Production, Income and Prices, University of Pennsylvania, October 2002) provide time series national accounts data for a set of 189 countries, in common prices, so that real comparisons can be made both between countries and over time.

PISA (Program in Student Assessment). The OECD (Organization for Economic Cooperation and Development) launched the Program in Student Assessment (www.oecd.org/pisa/) in 1997. The PISA assesses the capabilities of 15-year-olds enrolled in school in participating countries through testing of a representative random sample. The PISA has been conducted in rounds every three years since 2000 with a different focus area of assessment in each round. In 2006 the focus area was mathematics and in 2009 reading. There was an extra round of assessments called the 2009+ that included more traditionally developing areas, including two states of India (Himachal Pradesh and Tamil Nadu).

SACMEQ (Southern and Eastern Africa Consortium for Measuring Educational Quality). The SACMEQ is a consortium of education ministries from fifteen southern and eastern African countries (www.sacmeq.org/). It assesses a nationally and regionally representative random sample of students in grade 6 in the domains of reading and mathematics. There have been three rounds: 1995, 2000, and 2007.

TIMSS (Trends in International Mathematics and Science Study) is an internationally comparable assessment of grade 8 students' mastery of mathematics and science (http://timssandpirls.bc.edu/). TIMSS is a product of the International Association for the Evaluation of Educational Achievement (IEA). It has been carried out in participating countries every four years since 1995, and the latest data used for this book were the results from the 2007 round (the 2011 round became available in December 2012). The participating countries include both developed and developing countries and regions.

UWEZO (meaning "capability" in Kiswahili). This is an adaptation of the ASER model for testing and assessing all children aged 6 to 16 in the basics of literacy and numeracy in three east African countries (Tanzania, Uganda, and Kenya). It was carried out by the organization TAWEZA for the first time in 2009 (published in 2010), and the assessment has been done annually.

Rankings of Universities

Chapter 6 compares the position in the global rankings of American and British universities versus those in Europe. Given that any ranking of the "quality" of universities is necessarily controversial, I used four different sources of rankings to ensure the robustness of the particular finding of the dominance of U.S./U.K. (and more broadly "Anglo") universities. This use of many different rankings was not to endorse any particular ranking or even set of rankings but rather precisely so as to not endorse any particular method(s) as superior. The key fact—the dominance of U.S./U.K. universities—emerges in all of the rankings (and in rankings such as those from Leiden, which are based purely on publications in the sciences [www.leidenranking.com/ranking]).

Annual Ranking of World Universities. "The Academic Ranking of World Universities (ARWU)" was first published in June 2003 by the Center for World-Class Universities and the Institute of Higher Education of Shanghai Jiao Tong University, China, and then updated on an annual basis. ARWU uses six objective indicators to rank world universities, including the number of alumni and staff who win Nobel Prizes and Fields Medals, number of highly cited researchers selected by Thomson Scientific, number of articles published in the journals *Nature* and *Science,* number of articles indexed in Science Citation Index—Expanded and Social Sciences Citation Index, and per capita performance with respect to the size of an institution. More than 1,000 universities are actually ranked by ARWU every year and the best 500 are published on the web (www.arwu.org/aboutARWU.jsp).

THE-QS World University Rankings (www.topuniversities.com/university-rankings/world-university-rankings/2009). The *Times Higher Education Supplement* and QA in 2009 ranked universities based on a composite of surveys (40 percent to academic reputation and 10 percent to employer reputation), faculty citations (20 percent), faculty-student ratios (20 percent), and 5 percent each to percent of faculty and students who are international.

Global University Rankings-Reitor. This is a ranking by Russian researchers to rate universities in a way that they felt was fairer to Russian (and former Soviet) institutions of higher education. It was carried out in 2008 and published in February 2009 and is not periodic.

Webometrics. "The Ranking Web," or Webometrics, is the largest academic ranking of higher education institutions. Since 2004 and every six months, an independent, objective, free, open scientific exercise is performed by the Cybermetrics Lab (Spanish National Research Council, CSIC) for providing reliable, multidimensional, updated, and useful information about the performance of universities from all over the world based on their web presence and impact (www.webometrics.info/en/Methodology).

Index

Scott, James, 6

Searchers vs. planners, 6, 10

Secondary schooling: dropout rate in move to, 59–60; dropout rate of girls in, 84; grades covered by, 66; universal, 52, 57, 58

Secularist regimes with dominant religion, 183

Seeing Like a State: How Certain Schemes to Improve the Human Condition Have Failed (Scott), 6

Self-organizing systems, 6

Serbia, PISA reading test scores in, 46

Seychelles: expanded schooling in, 76; learning pace in, 94

Shah, Neil, 237

Singapore, level of learning in, 45

Skills vs. beliefs, 167

Smith, Adam, 141, 186

SMRS (Systematic Method for Reading Success, South Africa), 200

Socialization process: control by nation-states of, 165, 173, 180–85; direct control vs. third-party control of, 165, 166–71

Socioeconomic conditions: and grade attainment profiles, 55, 56; and physical abuse in India, 128–29; and school performance, 230

South Africa: dropouts in, 80, 81; early intervention for reading in, 200; expanded schooling in, 75, 76; LEAPS Science and Math schools in, 220; learning pace in, 94; level of learning in, 45, 46

Southern and Eastern Africa Consortium for Monitoring Educational Quality (SACMEQ), 74–76, 92–94, 255

South Korea: level of learning in, 46; PISA reading test scores in, 46; spending and learning outcomes in, 111

Spain: spending and learning outcomes in, 111; universities in, 211

Spending and learning outcomes, 107–13

Spider schooling systems, 164–92; blocking of great ideas from scaling by, 202; camouflage of, 120–63; demand-driven by modernizing economy, 179–80; disruptive innovation in, 154–63; inculcation of beliefs by, 165, 166–71; input expansion by, 89–119; isomorphic mimicry by, 165, 185; metaphor for, 5–6; normative as positive in, 186–90; obsolescence of, 11–12; overgeneralization in, 190–91; questions about, 165; rise of, 7–9, 171–77; spread of, 177–85; starfish systems vs., 6, 9, 203–06; supply-driven by need for nation-state control of socialization, 180–85; vouchers in, 189–90; weaknesses of, 5–6, 242–43

Sri Lanka, learning achievement in, 103, 104–05

The Starfish and the Spider: The Unstoppable Power of Leaderless Organizations (Brafman & Beckstrom), 5

Starfish ecosystems of educators, 193–243; in Brazil, 214–15; budget-level private schools as, 198–99; community and NGO schools as, 197–98; currently successful, 196–201; design principles of, 10–11; examples of, 209–15; flexible financing of, 195, 237–39, 240; freedom and choice in, 12; government schools as, 199–201; in higher education, 210–12; International Baccalaureate as, 212–13; learning from instruction for, 206–09; local operation of, 195, 220–24, 240; metaphor for, 5–6;

The Center for Global Development

The Center for Global Development works to reduce global poverty and inequality through rigorous research and active engagement with the policy community to make the world a more prosperous, just, and safe place for us all. The policies and practices of the rich and the powerful—in rich nations, as well as in the emerging powers, international institutions, and global corporations—have significant impacts on the world's poor people. We aim to improve these policies and practices through research and policy engagement to expand opportunities, reduce inequalities, and improve lives everywhere. By pairing research with action, CGD goes beyond contributing to knowledge about development. We conceive of and advocate for practical policy innovations in areas such as trade, aid, health, education, climate change, labor mobility, private investment, access to finance, and global governance to foster shared prosperity in an increasingly interdependent world.